THE FOURTH GRAMMATICAL TREATISE

THE FOURTH GRAMMATICAL TREATISE

EDITED BY

MARGARET CLUNIES ROSS
AND
JONAS WELLENDORF

VIKING SOCIETY FOR NORTHERN RESEARCH
UNIVESITY COLLEGE LONDON
2014

© Margaret Clunies Ross and Jonas Wellendorf 2014

ISBN:
978 0 903521 90 1

Printed by Short Run Press Limited, Exeter

CONTENTS

PREFACE AND ACKNOWLEDGEMENTS	vii
GENERAL ABBREVIATIONS	ix
INTRODUCTION	xi
1. Date, provenance and nature of *FoGT*	xi
2. *FoGT* within the traditions of grammar and rhetoric	xiv
a. *FoGT* within the Icelandic tradition of grammatical learning	xiv
b. *FoGT* and the Latin tradition	xix
3. The makeup of *FoGT*	xxxvii
4. Knowledge of *D* and *G* in Iceland and Norway	xl
5. The nature and origin of the poetic examples in *FoGT*	xlv
a. Named poets and poems	xlv
b. The anonymous stanzas	xlix
c. Dominant themes of the anonymous stanzas and their prose exegesis	liii
6. The present edition: guiding principles	lvii
a. Normalisation of the Icelandic text	lvii
b. Reproduction of the text and the translation	lix
c. Commentary	lxii
7. Previous editions of *FoGT*	lxii
TEXT AND TRANSLATION	1
COMMENTARY	50
DOCTRINALE (ll. 2560–2639): TEXT AND TRANSLATION	145
TECHNICAL TERMS USED IN *FoGT*	152
BIBLIOGRAPHY	157
INDEX	173

PREFACE AND ACKNOWLEDGEMENTS

The present edition is the result of a happy collaboration between two scholars with particular interests in a common text, the so-called *Fourth Grammatical Treatise* (*FoGT*), the understanding of which requires expertise in the medieval Latin grammatical and rhetorical tradition that made it possible for an unknown fourteenth-century Icelander to compose the work and, in addition, knowledge of the vernacular tradition of skaldic poetry, with which he illustrated it. Jonas Wellendorf has been responsible for placing *FoGT* in its Latin context, editing and translating the prose text and providing commentary on it, while Margaret Clunies Ross has edited, translated and provided commentary on the poetic examples. The Introduction is the work of both editors.

Up to now, *FoGT* has been a somewhat neglected late medieval Icelandic text, especially by comparison with other vernacular treatises on poetry, such as the *Edda* of Snorri Sturluson and *The Third Grammatical Treatise* (*TGT*) by Snorri's nephew Óláfr hvítaskáld 'White poet' Þórðarson. The editors hope that demonstrating *FoGT*'s relationship to earlier Icelandic treatises, especially to *TGT*, and clarifying its relationship to its sources, as well as setting out the relationship between the prose text and the poetic examples, will make its merits as a product of fourteenth-century Icelandic scholarship easier to understand and appreciate.

Late in the process of preparing the edition, Jonas Wellendorf received Cyril de Pins's unpublished doctoral thesis '*Hending ok kenning*: Les théories linguistiques dans l'Islande médiévale (XIIe–XIVe s.): Lecture du Codex Wormianus' (Université Paris 7-Diderot, Dec 2013). No attempt has here been made to incorporate the findings of this work, which includes a treatment of *FoGT* on pp. 546–609, but it should be mentioned that the thesis, in discussing *FoGT*, draws on a set of glosses on *Doctrinale* by a Petrus Croccus. These glosses occasionally illuminate the prose text of *FoGT* in a different way from those the present edition has drawn on.

Margaret Clunies Ross would like to place on record her gratitude to the Centre for Medieval Studies at the University of Bergen, and to Professor Else Mundal in particular, for providing her with facilities and accommodation in August 2011, which allowed her to work with Jonas Wellendorf there, and to Jonas for delaying taking up an appointment in the Department of Scandinavian at the University of California, Berkeley.

Jonas Wellendorf would like to thank the Centre for Medieval Studies at the University of Bergen for generous support of a conference on vernacular *grammatica* in the summer of 2011 and the Committee of Research at The University of California, Berkeley for a research-enabling grant that allowed him to study Codex Wormianus at the Arnamagnæan Manuscript Collection in Copenhagen. He would also like to thank Frank Bezner (UC Berkeley), Haukur Þorgeirsson (Stofnun Árna Magnússonar í íslenskum fræðum) and Stefan Hagel (Austrian Academy of Sciences).

We are grateful to Alison Finlay, Carl Phelpstead and Anthony Faulkes for their careful attention to our manuscript. Any remaining errors are our own responsibility.

Margaret Clunies Ross and Jonas Wellendorf
Sydney and Berkeley, November 2014

GENERAL ABBREVIATIONS

This list excludes common abbreviations, such as e.g., cf. and etc., as well as those of the names of the Books of the Bible. Abbreviated titles of frequently cited works (like *SnE*, *TGT*) and information about editions of these and other abbreviated bibliographical references (like *AÍ*, *SkP*, *SnE* 1998) are listed alphabetically in the Bibliography at the end of the edition. Abbreviated references to Old Norse poetry edited in *SkP* are to *SkP* sigla, which abbreviate the name of the poet (or state Anon, if anonymous), and name of poem, and give stanza and line number followed by relevant volume number in superscript roman, e.g. Arn *Þorfdr* 17,4^{II} = Arnórr jarlaskáld Þórðarson, *Þorfinnsdrápa*, stanza 17, line 4, Volume II. *SkP* sigla may be found on the skaldic poetry editing project website at abdn.ac.uk/skaldic/db.php

4°	quarto (refers to size of manuscript leaves)
acc.	accusative
add.	added (by editors)
adj.	adjective
c.	*circa*, about
CE	Common Era
d.	died
dat.	dative
e-m	*einhverjum*
e-s	*einhvers*
e-t	*eithvert*
e-u	*einhverju*
f.	folio (page)
fem.	feminine
fl.	*floruit*, flourished, period of someone's active life
fol	folio (refers to size of manuscript leaves)
gen.	genitive
Gr.	Greek
hap. leg.	*hapax legomenon* (pl. *legomena*), unique word(s)
indic.	indicative
l.	line
Lat.	Latin
lit.	literally
ll.	lines

loc. cit.	*loco citato*, (in) the place cited
masc.	masculine
ms.	manuscript
mss	manuscripts
n.	note
neut.	neuter
nn.	notes
no.	number
nom.	nominative
nos	numbers
pres.	present
pret.	preterite
ptc.	participle
pp.	pages
q. v.	*quod vide*, which see
r	recto
r.	reigned
sg.	singular
st.	stanza
sth.	something
sts	stanzas
subj.	subjunctive
s. v.	*sub verbo*, under the word
v	verso
x	designates paper manuscripts (in shelf marks)
†	textual material that is impossibly corrupt or cannot be made sense of
[. . .]	indicates damaged or illegible text

INTRODUCTION

1. Date, provenance and nature of *FoGT*

The Fourth Grammatical Treatise (*FoGT*) is extant only in the Codex Wormianus, AM 242 fol (W) of c. 1350 (*ONP* Indices, 438), where it is found on pages 111–19 of the manuscript's seventh gathering, immediately following the end of *The Third Grammatical Treatise* (*TGT*).[1] It has neither prologue nor epilogue and one is left with the impression that it comes to an end without having been brought to a conclusion. Its text is very sparsely annotated, though some parts have been underlined, and its influence in the medieval period and beyond is uncertain. However, it was definitely known to and used by Magnús Ólafsson in the early seventeenth century. He reproduces five stanzas and some passages of prose commentary originating from the treatise in his *Edda* of 1609.[2] Johansson (1997) has made a close codicological and paleographical analysis of the manuscript and its components, and his views about the place of *FoGT* in the make-up of the manuscript are on pages 56–59 and 207–08 of his monograph. He argues that the compilation, of which *FoGT* is a part, is unlikely to have been written for the first time in W, suggesting that W was a copy of an earlier compilation, and that the scribe of W and the redactor of the manuscript were two different men. If this was so, *FoGT* must have been quite a recent work at the time of its copying into W.

The hand of the scribe of W has been identified in several other manuscripts, all probably associated with the northern Icelandic Benedictine monastery of Þingeyrar in the middle part of the fourteenth century (Jakob Benediktsson 1980, 9–12). Johansson describes these manuscripts (1997, 66–80) and lists them all at the conclusion of his study (1997, 224). Þingeyrar in Húnavatnssýsla, established in 1133, was a centre of literary activity and manuscript production in the fourteenth century, some of it destined for the export trade to Norway (Stefán Karlsson 1979). It has been considered for some time that W was probably a product of the Þingeyrar scriptorium (cf. *SnE* 1924, i–ii; Nordal 1931, 17–18) and that some of its contents,

---

[1] In accordance with current scholarly practice, reference is given to page numbers rather than folio numbers of W throughout this edition.
[2] These stanzas are *FoGT* 7, 9, 27, 44 and 56. See further *LaufE* 1979, 160–61, 179, 250–52 and notes, 363–64. Stanzas 7, 9, 27 and 56 are also in Resen's *Edda Islandorum* of 1665 (*RE* 1665, Gg 1v, Hh 2r, Ii 3v and Kk 1v).

including *FoGT* and the *ókend heiti* section added to W on pages 167–69, show a connection with other texts with a probable northern focus, like *Heiðarvíga saga* (Nordal 1931, 17; ÍF 3, cxxxiv–cxliv; *LaufE* 1979, 58; Nordal 2001, 88).

W contains versions of all four parts of the *Edda* of Snorri Sturluson (*Snorra Edda*), although *Háttatal* is separated from the other three parts by all four major Icelandic grammatical treatises (see Section 2 a below), which are present in this manuscript together with a unique Prologue to them and various other texts (for a list, see Table 1 in Johansson 1997, 29). Both the character of the *Snorra Edda* text in W, being more expansive and learned in places than its other medieval exemplars, and the completeness of W's record of Icelandic grammatical literature indicate that this manuscript was the product of a scholarly environment in which both foreign and indigenous grammatical learning was cultivated. W presents the collected Icelandic medieval grammatical literature as a package introduced by a Prologue that many consider the work of the author of *FoGT*, who may also have been the compiler of W (Sverrir Tómasson 1993). Clearly whoever determined the contents of W was particularly interested in both the practice of Icelandic poetry and its analysis in the context of *grammatica*.

The author of *FoGT* is unknown. However, beginning with Sveinbjörn Egilsson (*SnE* 1848–87, II 190–91 n. 1; cf. *FoGT* 1884, lxxvii–lxxx), the suggestion has been made that the author of *FoGT* and the redactor of W may have been Bergr Sokkason, who became a monk in the Þingeyrar monastery in 1316 or 1317 (Sverrir Tómasson 1982, 26, 162). He also studied at the only other Benedictine monastery in Iceland, Munkaþverá, and was appointed abbot there in 1325. The date of Bergr's death is not known for certain (Foote 1959, 24–25 and notes 57–59). Bergr is known to have composed a *Nikulás saga erkibiskups* and a number of other works (Sverrir Tómasson 1982). *FoGT* cites three *helmingar* from a poem about St Nicholas (sts 6, 24 and 25), thus showing a parallel interest in this popular saint. There are several other possible authors of *FoGT*, however, also associated with Þingeyrar, including Árni Lárentíusson, born c. 1304, and entered as a monk at Þingeyrar in 1316–17 (ÍF 17, 332–33), and Abbot Arngrímr Brandsson, the probable author of *Thómas saga erkibiskups* II, *Guðmundar saga biskups D* and *Clárus saga* and a prolific composer of religious poetry, who was active at Þingeyrar from the 1340s.

Introduction xiii

The date of composition of *FoGT* cannot be later than the date of W, determined by most scholars on palaeographical grounds to be c. 1350. The *terminus post quem* may be provided by st. 10, which refers to a fire probably at Skálholt cathedral in 1309 during the reign of a King Hákon, probably Hákon V háleggr 'Long-leg' Magnússon, who died in 1319. Based on this evidence, a date of composition somewhere between 1320 and 1340 seems most likely, not much earlier than the probable date of the compilation of W.

In its present form, *FoGT* refers to *The Third Grammatical Treatise* (*TGT*) (c. 1250) of Óláfr hvítaskáld 'White Poet' Þórðarson (chs 9, 11 and 12). This, and the way in which the two treatises appear one after another in W, indicate that *FoGT* was conceived as a continuation, and possibly even an update of the earlier work. A three-line initial marks the beginning of *TGT* in W (at p. 94), while two-line initials are used to indicate chapter divisions in this work. The beginning of *FoGT* has been marked only with a two-line initial. This might be interpreted as a sign that the scribe or compiler of W did not consider *FoGT* an entity of its own, independent of *TGT*. When Rasmus Rask published his edition of *Snorra Edda* and the related grammatical treatises in 1818 he too presented *TGT* and *FoGT* as a single work (*SnE* 1818). The author of *FoGT*, on the other hand, clearly distinguishes himself from Óláfr Þórðarson, the author of *TGT*, and his references to the latter take the form *Óláfr segir* 'Óláfr says' (chs 9 and 11).[3] Both *FoGT* and the second part of *TGT* (the so-called *Málskrúðsfræði* 'Knowledge of the Ornaments of Diction') deal with rhetorical figures, but the two texts only overlap in a few instances. *FoGT* st. 1 can be seen as a corrected version of the same stanza in *TGT* that is presented in a garbled form in W (*TGT* 1884, 17 ll. 19–20). Another stanza found in both treatises is *FoGT* st. 32 (*TGT* 184, 77). *TGT* presents the stanza as an example of the incorrect use of the plural (*soloecismus um talnaskipti*) while *FoGT* explains the use of plural as the figure *lepos*, a polite way of addressing a man of high standing. One can see this example as an attempt to correct the teaching of *TGT*. A third instance of overlap between the two texts is more difficult to explain (see Section 4 below).

The composition of *FoGT* is not likely to have been motivated solely by its author's desire to complete or correct *TGT*. *FoGT* is a rather different work from *TGT* in several respects, to be discussed

---

[3] A third reference to *TGT* (in ch. 12) is formulated in a more general way.

below. These differences include the exemplification of rhetorical figures through the use of a much higher percentage of anonymous stanzas, many probably of the author's own invention, than is found in *TGT*, the strongly religious character of many of the poetic examples, and the presence of several lengthy excursuses to the prose text in which the author expounds the meaning of his poetic examples in terms of Christian allegory or moralisation. These excursuses go well beyond the level of explanation that would be required solely to account for the rhetorical figures that occasioned the composition of the stanzas themselves. To the extent that much of the poetry in *FoGT* has a strongly religious dimension, the author of the treatise may have seen himself as consciously expanding the scope of poetic commentary on Icelandic Christian verse beyond what was hinted at in the very last part of *TGT*, which for the most part keeps to secular examples. A further difference between *TGT* and *FoGT* can be detected through an analysis of the subject matter of the exemplificatory stanzas, which pursue several distinct themes throughout the treatise. These are discussed in Section 5 c below. In this respect and in its moralising excursuses, *FoGT* is comparable with European prescriptive treatises on poetics from the thirteenth century, like Geoffrey of Vinsauf's *Poetria nova*, which the author may possibly have known.

2. *FoGT* within the traditions of grammar and rhetoric

a. *FoGT* within the Icelandic tradition of grammatical learning

FoGT is chronologically the latest of a number of Old Icelandic vernacular texts that were to a greater or lesser extent the products of medieval grammatical learning. The tradition of composing them continued beyond the Middle Ages in Iceland in works such as Magnús Ólafsson's *Laufás Edda* (1609), some of whose contents indicate that more grammatical material existed in medieval Iceland than has survived today, some of it probably from lost parts of W (*LaufE* 1979, 156–79). The extant vernacular grammatical texts from medieval Iceland can be divided into three groups. The first group is largely concerned with phonology and orthography, and includes the *First Grammatical Treatise*, the *Second Grammatical Treatise* and the first part of *TGT*, the so-called *Málfræðinnar grundvöllr* 'The Foundation of Grammar' (*TGT* 1884, 33–59; Wills 2001). Of these the earliest and probably the most original is the *First Grammatical Treatise*, which Hreinn Benediktsson (1972, 23–25) dates between

1125 and 1175 (cf. Haugen 1972, 4). The dating of the so-called *Second Grammatical Treatise* is uncertain, though its most recent editor, Fabrizio Raschellà (1982, 126–32), places it in the period c. 1270–1300. *Málfrœðinnar grundvǫllr* (c. 1250) is based largely on the first two books of Priscian's *Institutiones grammaticae* (see Section 2 b below). Its principal subject is the nature of sound, including particularly the human voice, and various ways in which sound can be analysed and written down. It includes a discussion of the Latin and the runic alphabets and their application to the writing of Old Norse.

The second group of texts, of which there are only two medieval members, is principally concerned with metrics, though their authors' concerns extend beyond metrics proper to stylistic and rhetorical aspects of the Icelandic verse-forms they exemplify in their treatises. In both cases, the authors of these metrical texts were themselves practising poets, and that is an important connection in a medieval Icelandic context, where poetic theory and poetic practice were always closely related. The earliest of the two metrical works is the poem *Háttalykill* 'Key to Verse-forms', its title probably a calque on the Latin term *clavis metrica*, composed by the Orcadian jarl Rǫgnvaldr Kali Kolsson and the Icelander Hallr Þórarinsson in Orkney, probably in the mid-twelfth century. Rǫgnvaldr's death in 1158 or 1159 provides a *terminus ante quem* for this work, which is attributed to the two skalds in *Orkneyinga saga* (ÍF 34, 185), although the only known manuscripts of it both date from c. 1665 (Jón Helgason and Holtsmark 1941, 7–21; Gade forthcoming). The poem consists of forty-one pairs of stanzas, each pair illustrating a particular verse-form, and each pair having as subject a legendary hero or historical Scandinavian king. There is no analytical commentary in prose attached to this metrical key, as there is for its successor, although many of the verse-forms are named.

The second metrical treatise is the *Háttatal* 'List of Verse-forms' section (*SnE* 2007) of *Snorra Edda* (c. 1225), a work in four parts on various aspects of the poetic arts which, in all its dimensions, escapes precise classification as a grammatical treatise, though it is certainly informed by grammatical learning.[4] While the *Skáldskaparmál*

---

[4] The first and second parts of the *Edda*, the Prologue and *Gylfaginning* 'The deluding of Gylfi' (*SnE* 2005), present Snorri's digest of Old Norse pre-Christian myth and a key to its interpretation, topics that were important for poets to know because they were integral to the system of kennings and *heiti* that is fundamental to the skaldic art. Whether Snorri's grammatical learning

'Language of Poetry' section of the work (*SnE* 1998) deals with the diction of Icelandic skaldic poetry, *Háttatal* describes different verse-forms, all of which are exemplified in 102 stanzas of an encomium Snorri composed in praise of the young king of Norway, Hákon Hákonarson, and his co-regent, Jarl Skúli Bárðarson, probably shortly after Snorri's first visit to Norway in 1218–20. The prose passages of *Háttatal* in which the various verse-forms are defined exerted a clear influence on the authors of both *TGT* and *FoGT*, especially those passages in which Snorri gives the indigenous names of some of the verse-forms and describes their stylistic effects. Thus *Háttatal* cannot be classified purely as a metrical treatise, as some of its concerns overlap with and influence works of the third group of grammatical treatises, discussed below. As far as the native *termini technici* of skaldic poetry are concerned, Snorri appears to have been the first person to commit them to writing in a semi-systematic way, and his successors followed him in this, sometimes repeating his terminology, though not always using it to refer to the same poetic device, at other times using different terms altogether.

The third group of grammatical treatises comprises those concerned with poetic diction and the figures of rhetoric. Some members, principally the second part of *TGT*, *Málskrúðsfrœði* 'Knowledge of the Ornaments of Diction', and *FoGT*, are clearly dependent on Latin models for their basic content and structure and offer Icelandic versions of well-known schoolroom texts with poetic illustrations of the various figures either taken from the compositions of named skaldic poets, mostly Icelanders, or from anonymous vernacular sources. The other members, principally the *Skáldskaparmál* section of *Snorra Edda*, and the fragmentary treatise known as *Litla Skálda* (*SnE* 1931, 255–59), are not so clearly dependent on specific Latin models. They list a series of important referents for the chief ornaments of skaldic diction, *kenningar* and *heiti*,[5] and specify how these referents should

---

included some direct knowledge of Latin *grammatica* is hard to gauge, though it seems probable (Clunies Ross 1987, especially chapters 2 and 4; Marold 2012). Faulkes, however, maintains that Snorri knew no Latin (2008, 311 and elsewhere).

[5] The native term *kenning*, when applied to poetry, means a periphrastic description of an unnamed referent, usually comprising two nouns or a compound noun that can be disaggregated into two parts, like Arn Þorfdr 17,8^{II} *limdolgr* 'foe of branches' [FIRE]. A *heiti* is a name or appellation that is often but not always found exclusively in poetry, like *bál* 'pyre, beacon', *logi*

be described in terms of periphrases formed on conventional vernacular rhetorical models, whose names may possibly be indebted to Latin terms (cf. Halldór Halldórsson 1975; Malm 2009), but whose essential qualities are likely to be of native origin.

These models include terms for pre-Christian supernatural beings, later extended to embrace the Christian belief system, men, women, ships, battle, arms and armour, gold and other man-made ornaments, and aspects of the natural world, like various animals, the sun and moon, trees, the sea and rivers. In *Skáldskaparmál* the prescribed periphrases are introduced using the question and answer format familiar from medieval Latin schoolroom texts. For example, Snorri lists the recommended periphrases for the concept 'fire' in this way:

> Hvernig skal kenna eld? Svá at kalla hann bróður vinds ok Ægis, bana ok grand viðar ok húsa, Hálfs bani, sól húsanna. (*SnE* 1998, I 39)
>
> How shall fire be described? Thus, by calling it brother of the wind and of Ægir, killer and damager of wood and buildings, killer of Hálfr, sun of the houses.

Both here and in many other such lists in *Skáldskaparmál* we find a combination of periphrases alluding to figures of Norse myth or legend, like Ægir, a supernatural being of the sea, or Hálfr, a legendary king who was burnt to death in a hall fire, with references to phenomena known from early Scandinavian social life, like the destructive effect of fire on trees and buildings. In many instances in *Skáldskaparmál*, the prescribed lists are illustrated with quotations of a *helmingr* or a stanza, sometimes with a number of stanzas, from named or sometimes anonymous vernacular poets. These lists with their examples are never compared directly to Latin figures or approximated to the Latin poetic examples found in Latin treatises, though it is possible that knowledge of the format of Latin schoolroom treatises may have served as the inspiration for Snorri's arrangement of his material.

The authors of *TGT* and *FoGT* depart radically from Snorri's practice of listing types of *kenningar* and *heiti*, although they do illustrate the Latin figures they present with Old Norse examples. Their aim was to follow their Latin sources in presenting and describing Latin rhetorical figures in Icelandic prose, and then to illustrate them with

'flame' or *eisa* 'embers', beside the more common noun *eldr* 'fire'. *Heiti* provide a store of alliterative variation for both base-words and determinants of kennings, but may also occur as simplices in poetry.

Icelandic examples, thus demonstrating a belief in the common origin of the Norse and classical languages and poetic arts that is clearly articulated in the introduction to *TGT*'s *Málskrúðsfræði*:

Í þessi bók má gǫrla skilja, at ǫll er ein listin, skáldskapr sá, er Rómverskir spekingar námu í Aðenisborg á Grikklandi ok sneru síðan í latínumál, ok sá ljóðaháttr eða skáldskapr, er Óðinn ok aðrir Asíamenn fluttu norðr hingat í norðrhálfu heimsins, ok kenndu mǫnnum á sína tungu þesskonar list, svá sem þeir hǫfðu skipat ok numit í sjálfu Asíalandi, þar sem mest var fegrð[6] ok ríkdómr ok fróðleikr veraldarinnar (normalised from *TGT* 1884, 60).

In this book it may be clearly understood that the art of poetry which the Roman sages learnt in Athens in Greece and then transferred into the Latin language is the same art as the verse-form of songs or poetry which Óðinn and other men of Asia brought hither northwards into the northern hemisphere; and they taught men this type of art in their own language, just as they had organised and learnt it in Asia itself, where beauty and power and knowledge were the greatest in the world (Clunies Ross, trans., 2005, 190).

Sometimes the authors of both treatises admit that certain Latin figures are not commonly found in Norse poetry,[7] but for the most part they try to offer vernacular examples that they present as illustrating the figures described in their sources. The outcome of this process is that they frequently present examples of Norse poetics that are of minor importance to vernacular poetry rather than of central significance to it. In terms of producing equivalences in Icelandic poetry to the Latin examples from the treatises, the author of *FoGT* is amazingly skilful, as will be examined in detail in Section 5 below, but the examples he presents are probably his own compositions invented for the purpose rather than examples taken from existing poems in the vernacular repertoire. This phenomenon is less true of *TGT*, where only 31% of the verse examples are anonymous, by contrast with just over 76% of the illustrations in *FoGT* (cf. Clunies Ross forthcoming). Thus *TGT* and, to a greater extent *FoGT*, mediate between Latin and Norse traditions; they follow their Latin sources in their choice and sequence of the figures described, but they illustrate their treatises

---

[6] W's reading *fegrð* has here been preferred to A's *frǫgð* (cf. *SnE* 2005, 4).
[7] For example, the author of *FoGT* admits that he cannot find the kind of *exflexigesis* (Latin *efflexegesis*) that foreshadows future events in Old Norse poetry: *en eigi finn eg það í norrænu skáldskap* 'but I do not find this in Norse poetry' (ch. 10).

with vernacular examples, many probably invented by themselves to demonstrate the repertoire of native poetry. In this process, somewhat paradoxically, they depart to a certain extent from the actualities of vernacular Norse poetic composition.

b. *FoGT* and the Latin tradition

The 27 chapters of *FoGT* define and illustrate 34 rhetorical devices which are primarily designated with denominations of Greek origin. Throughout *FoGT* refers to these devices with the term *fígúra*. *Fígúra* is a loan word from Latin where the word *figura* 'shape, form, (grammatical or rhetorical) figure' was used as a technical term from the time of Quintilian (c. 100 CE) onwards. In Latin, *figura* was used alongside the synonymous *schema* that had been borrowed from the Greek σχῆμα 'form, shape, (rhetorical or grammatical) figure'. This second term is used a few times in *TGT* (1884, 75, 91, 101). Elsewhere *TGT* uses *fígúra* in the same way as *FoGT*. In the following, the rhetorical devices will be referred to as figures in accordance with *FoGT* and *TGT*.

The definitions of the figures in *FoGT*, their designations and the order in which they are presented depend on Latin models. Most important is the *Doctrinale* (*D*) by Alexander de Villa-Dei, but some material has also been derived from Eberhard of Béthune's *Graecismus* (*G*). In general the doctrine of *FoGT* coincides nicely with the Latin tradition, and some of the verses with which the treatise illustrates the various figures are clearly patterned on examples given in *D*, *G* or in the commentary tradition to these two texts (*Dg* and *Gg*—the *g* is for 'gloss'). The importance of *D*, *Dg*, *G* and *Gg* for the understanding of *FoGT* was discovered and thoroughly documented by Björn Magnússon Ólsen in his edition of the text (*FoGT* 1884, lxxii–lxxiii *et passim*).

FoGT and *Málskrúðsfræði* (the part of *TGT* which is dependent on Donatus's *Barbarismus*) both deal with figures, but the two texts differ from one another in that most of the examples of *FoGT* were apparently devised by the author of the treatise himself with the particular purpose of being included in the treatise. The author of *Málskrúðsfræði*, on the other hand, primarily sought out his examples in the existing corpus of skaldic poetry. This difference between the two treatises can be accounted for by viewing *Málskrúðsfræði* as a grammatical treatise and *FoGT* as a treatise that is primarily rhetorical in nature.

The two disciplines, *grammatica* and *rhetorica*, have a long and complicated history of rivalry (see Copeland 1991, 11–21), and both disciplines at various points laid claim to the doctrine and lore of figures. In antiquity the double aim of *grammatica* was correct language usage and the understanding of the works of the poets—in Quintilian's formulation *recte loquendi scientia et poetarum enarratio* (Quintilian I, 4.2). The first goal was to be achieved with the help of the second, so that mastery of the rules of language came through the study of the classics. In many ways *grammatica* was a descriptive and a hermeneutic discipline. The language of the classics often deviated from that which was considered normal usage, and the grammarian would explain these perceived deviations as figures applied for one reason or the other by the authors of the classics. *Rhetorica* was also occupied with the figures, but from a different perspective. The aim of this discipline was not correct use of language but persuasive use of language; this meant that *rhetorica* was less concerned with the structure of the utterance than with its function and effect. The rhetorical tradition emphasised practice and therefore tended to the prescriptive or preceptive rather than the descriptive.

Neither the Latin tradition behind *Málskrúðsfræði* nor the text itself contains practical advice on the use of the figures. As grammatical texts they describe, define, exemplify and explain the figures already found in existing texts, but they give no guidance on how to use them. *FoGT* is somewhat different in this respect and often provides advice on the use of particular figures (see chapters 9, 12, 13 and others). Even when no explicit advice on the use of a particular figure is given the general tendency of the treatise can be said to be preceptive. In the prologue to the four grammatical treatises in W, one can detect a similar preceptive mode when the text states that *nú skal lýsa ... hversu kveða skal* (Ólsen, ed., 1884, 153) 'Now it will be explained how one shall compose [poetry]'.

The differences between the grammatical and rhetorical traditions concerning the figures will be made clear by the following brief outline of the Latin tradition behind *Málskrúðsfræði* and *FoGT*. At the outset it should be mentioned that the title *Málskrúðsfræði*, rendered above as 'Knowledge of the Ornaments of Diction', could also be translated simply as 'Rhetoric'. This title was first introduced in the edition of Sveinbjörn Egilsson (*SnE* 1848, 181) and has no medieval authority.

The history of the doctrine of the figures remains to be written but it seems clear that, at least from the time of Donatus (c. 350 CE) onwards, it occupied the middle ground between grammar and rhetoric in the West.

Traditionally the figures were divided into two main groups: figures of diction and figures of thought. A figure of diction is a figure that depends on the choice and/or arrangement of words in an utterance. One example of this is the figure *epimone* in *FoGT* (ch. 23) which is brought about by the repetition of a given word at specific points in the utterance. Conversely, a figure of thought is independent of the words with which it is expressed. An example from *FoGT* is *prosopopoeia* (ch. 5), which is defined as *ísetning nýrrar persónu* 'the insertion of a new person [in a text]', e.g. by the personification of abstract concepts or if a speaker addresses inanimate entities. *FoGT*'s second example of *prosopopoeia* (st. 15) shows that it is possible to combine the two kinds of figures in a single utterance. In this stanza *Ölmusugjöfin* 'the alms-giving' is personified (i.e. 'Alms-giving'), hence it must be classified as a figure of thought. The personified Alms-giving, however, expresses itself with the help of a figure of diction in that all lines of the second *helmingr* of this stanza begin with the same word and are structured in the same way (a subject ('I') is followed by a two-syllable verb in the present tense and a one-syllable object).

Neither *Málskrúðsfræði* nor *FoGT* mention this two-fold division of the figures into figures of thought and figures of diction, but in one instance *TGT* does refer to the figures of diction:

> Scemalexeos heyrir svá til soloecismum sem metaplasmus barbarismum í því ǫllu er til lasta veit, en þó er scema miklu meirr í leyfi sett [< settr *W*] þvíat hon þykkir fegra skáldskap. Scema heitir á girzku en skrúð á norrónu. Lexeos er róða ok er scemalexeos nefnd svá sem skrúð máls eðr róðu (*TGT* 1884, 23).

> *Schemalexeos* belongs to *soloecismus* as *metaplasmus* belongs to *barbarismus* in everything that pertains to faults [of grammar]. *Schema* however is to a much greater extent classed as licence because it is considered to embellish poetry. It is called *schema* in Greek and *skrúð* in Norse. *Lexeos* [*recte*: lexis] means speech and *schema lexeos* means embellishment of diction or speech.

At this point in the *Barbarismus*—the exemplar of *Málskrúðsfræði*—Donatus claims that there are two kinds of figures, the *schemata lexeos* 'figures of diction' and the *schemata dianoeas* 'figures of thought' (Holtz, ed., 1981, 663). Donatus considers the former the domain of the grammarians and the latter as belonging to the rhetoricians (*schemata dianoeas ad oratores pertinent, ad grammaticos lexeos*, Holtz, ed., 1981, 663). Although *TGT* takes care to explain the meaning of *schema lexeos*, it leaves out any reference to the figures of thought. This might be taken as an indication that *TGT* sees itself as a grammatical rather than a rhetorical work. As mentioned above, the primary difference between the two kinds of work in this respect is that the grammatical work is hermeneutic and aimed at the interpretation of already existing discourse (poetry), while the rhetorical work aims at creating new discourse (originally speeches, but in the Middle Ages all kinds of discourse, including poetry) with the help of the rhetorical doctrine. Correctly seen as a grammatical work, *TGT* mirrors the *Barbarismus* exactly in this respect, since *Barbarismus* is essentially a listing of and commentary on the figures of diction found in Virgil's *Aeneid*, from which the text draws the vast majority of its examples. *FoGT*, by contrast, should be seen as a rhetorical work wherein one can also find figures of thought defined in the text.

The first full presentation of the doctrine of figures in the West is found in the anonymous rhetorical manual known as *Rhetorica ad Herennium*. This work on oratory dates from the second decade of the first century BC and has been called 'one of the most influential books on speaking and writing ever produced in the western world' (Murphy 1974, 18). At least from the fourth century onwards, *Rhetorica ad Herennium* was considered a work of Cicero (Taylor-Briggs 2006, 94). As a rhetorical work, *Rhetorica ad Herennium* is practical in nature and geared towards the production of discourse (speeches) rather than its analysis. The author initially stresses that theory without practice is futile and exhorts the reader to apply the precepts given (*Rhetorica ad Herennium* I, 1). By way of conclusion, the importance of practice is underlined once again (*Rhetorica ad Herennium* IV, 69). The author treats the five canons of rhetorical theory (invention, arrangement, expression, memory and delivery), but most attention is devoted to invention (*inuentio*) and expression (*elocutio*). A basic principle of rhetorical theory is the existence of a clear-cut divide between the contents of an utterance (*res*) and its expression (*uerba*) —although more advanced works such as Cicero's *De oratore* III,

19–24 (Mankin, ed., 2011) also acknowledge that the *res* and the *uerba* are indeed impossible to separate. Invention is the process through which one discovers or invents the content, while expression shapes the content by applying adequate words and sentences. The entirety of the fourth and last book of *Rhetorica ad Herennium* is given over to a detailed discussion of expression and it forms the oldest known western attempt at an exhaustive presentation of the rhetorical figures in the Latin world.

The author claims to have constructed all his examples of the various figures himself (see Calboli 1969, 46–50 on the veracity of this claim) and his prolonged justification of this procedure is of particular interest. He rejects the practice of the Greeks, which, as presented in *Rhetorica ad Herennium* (IV, 1–10), consists in using already existing examples selected from esteemed orators and poets. According to the author of *Rhetorica ad Herennium*, the Greeks argued that one should only use examples from recognised authorities, and they had four arguments in support of this view. The first was modesty: an author who concocts his own examples draws attention away from the art he is supposed to teach and towards his own abilities (*hoc est, inquiunt, ostentare se, non ostendere artem*, IV, 1), for when one can find examples among the very greatest of authorities, it would seem arrogant to set them aside and highlight one's own abilities. The second argument was testimony: examples drawn from known authorities serve as testimonies to the correctness of the precepts. Their third argument was exemplarity: the authorities of old spur the students to imitation. The fourth and final argument ascribed to the Greeks was that it requires the highest mastery of the art of rhetoric to be able to select carefully the best illustrations from the widest material possible.

The author finds the first argument ludicrous; if the Greeks do not wish to display their skills, why do they say or write anything in the first place? He compares this to a runner at the Olympic games, who, having stepped onto the racetrack and taken the starting position, refuses to run and prefers to praise the legendary runners of old. The second argument is rejected by the claim that the purpose of examples is not to testify, but to demonstrate. The author refutes the fourth and last argument (there is no refutation of the third argument at this point) by saying that anyone who has heard just a bit about the art of rhetoric, and in particular about style, will be able to recognise that which is artfully spoken, but only the true masters are able to speak artfully themselves. A skilful writer can easily discern that which is written with great skill, but a skilful selector of examples is not necessarily able to write skilfully. The author of *Rhetorica ad Herennium* also argues his case positively. The main arguments here are that an example cited by the author of an art should testify to his own mastery of that art and that fabricated examples are clearer and more illustrative than borrowed examples precisely because they are composed to illustrate a particular point. The true masters of an art, on the other hand, are able to conceal the artfulness so that it is not too obvious or readily perceptible.

After these preliminaries and a discussion of the various levels of style, the author begins his presentation of the figures in IV, 17 by introducing a distinction between the embellishment (*exornatio*) of speech and the embellishment of thought. This is followed by a long section consisting of definitions and illustrations of a great number of 'embellishments of words' (45 in all) and a smaller number of 'embellishments of meanings' (19 in all). This inventory of figures was to have a formidable influence. It often reappears in later listings of figures and is frequently reproduced in modern handbooks on rhetoric as well. The organisational principle followed in *Rhetorica ad Herennium* is not explained, and it has been suggested that a transitional section might be missing (Achard 1989, 149 n. 88). The lists seem somewhat disordered. Some figures appear to be out of place—e.g. *permissio* 'the leaving of a matter to the judgement of others' is included among the 'embellishment of words' (IV, 39)—while other figures have clearly been grouped together because of perceived similarities or dissimilarities. Thus the first four 'embellishments of words'—*repetitio*, *conuersio*, *conplexio* and *traductio*—appear to have been grouped together because all of these figures use the same word more than once for rhetorical effect, and not because the speaker is at a loss for words (IV, 21). *FoGT* also testifies to the similarity of the first three of these figures, in that it treats them as various ways of forming the figure *epimone* (ch. 23). The last ten figures among the 'embellishments of words' constitute a particularly important and clearly delineated sub-group:

> Nam earum omnium hoc proprium est ut ab usitata uerborum potestate recedatur atque in aliam rationem cum quadam uenustate oratio conferatur (*Rhetorica ad Herennium* IV, 42).

For it is characteristic of all these [ten figures] that the utterance departs from the common meaning of the words and with a certain charm is applied in another sense.

This group of ten will later be known as the tropes, and it includes among others metonymy (*denominatio*), metaphor (*translatio*) and allegory (*permutatio*).

It should be noted that *Rhetorica ad Herennium* employs Latin names for the various figures. In the preface to the fourth book the author makes a special point about the use of newly coined names. He is aware that his invented terms might sound strange initially, but prefers them because they are much more transparent than the Greek terms (IV, 10).

Another hugely influential work was Aelius Donatus's Latin textbook *Ars grammatica* (c. 350). This work was only one among a number of Latin grammars of Late Antiquity, but Donatus's compression and systematisation of grammatical material, presented in greater detail in the more encyclopaedic grammatical works, turned out to be extraordinarily useful for teachers and students alike. Donatus's *Ars grammatica* was soon divided into two works: an introductory dialogue, *Ars minor*, and a more comprehensive *Ars maior*. The aim of *Ars maior* is not to teach Latin to non-native speakers of the language, but to tutor native speakers of Latin in the language of poetry. *Ars maior* has aptly been characterised it as 'a "grammar" of Vergil's works and other texts of high canonical status' (Irvine 1994, 59). The *Ars maior* was divided into three books: the first treated sounds, letters, syllables, metrical feet, accent and punctuation; the second, the parts of speech and morphology; and the third and last book treated the virtues and vices of speech. As time passed, the first two books of *Ars maior* were eclipsed by books 1–16 of Priscian's *Institutiones grammaticae* (written c. 520), which treat the same subject matter in much greater detail. The third book of *Ars maior* contained material not treated by Priscian and continued to be copied frequently. Detached from the rest of *Ars maior*, this book circulated on its own under the name *Barbarismus* (the first word of the text), and was often transmitted as an adjunct to parts of *Institutiones grammaticae* (Holtz 1981, 505–07). A somewhat similar arrangement is found in *TGT*, the first part of which consists of material directly or indirectly derived from the first two books of Priscian's work while the second part consists of material derived from *Barbarismus*. In *Barbarismus*, Donatus presents the grammatical doctrine of virtues and vices that was current in his time. The book is divided into six chapters. Three kinds of vices are presented in the first three chapters and the (often parallel) virtues are found in the last three chapters. As its point of departure, the doctrine takes the notion of normal usage of language, referred to by Donatus as *communis sermo* (Holtz, ed., 1981, 653); *alþýðleg róða* in *Málskrúðsfræði* (*TGT* 1884, 61). A deviation from normal usage would be classified as either a vice or a virtue depending on the context in which the deviance was found. A deviance in normal speech would be considered a vice while a deviance in poetry would be regarded as a virtue. To this contextual criterion some grammarians added a causal criterion: deviations caused by ignorance or lack of linguistic abilities would be regarded as vices, while purposeful deviations from normal usage would be seen as virtues. This is not explicitly stated in *Barbarismus*, but it is spelled out with great clarity by later commentators on the *Ars maior*, such as Servius (early fifth century):

> Quaesitum est apud Plinium Secundum, quid interesset inter figuras et uitia. nam cum figurae ad ornatum adhibeantur, uitia uitentur, eadem autem inueniantur exempla tam in figuris quam in uitiis, debet aliqua esse discretio. quidquid ergo scientes facimus nouitatis cupidi, quod tamen idoneorum auctorum firmatur exemplis, figura dicitur. quidquid autem ignorantes ponimus, uitium putatur. nam sicut superius diximus, <si> sciens quis dicat 'pars in frustra secant' et causa uarietatis hoc dicat, figuram facit; si autem nescius, cum aliud uelit dicere, incongrue inter se numeros iunxerit, soloecismum fecisse iudicatur (*GL* 4, 447).

> The question about the distinction between figures and vices is raised in the writings of Pliny the Elder. For even though one should employ figures for ornament and avoid vices, the same examples are used for figures as well as for vices. There ought to be some distinction. Therefore, whatever we do knowingly, eager for something new, which can be supported by examples from suitable authors, is called a figure. Whatever we use unknowingly is considered a vice. Just as we said above, if someone knowingly says *pars in frustra secant* 'a part cut in vain', and he says it for the sake of variation, he uses a figure. But if he said it unknowingly, wanting to say something else, then he connected incongruent numbers and he is considered to have committed a solecism.

The same knowledge criterion is implied in *Barbarismus* when Donatus allows for certain deviations because of metrical constraints or as ornaments (*metri ornatusue causa*, Holtz, ed., 1981, 660). The parallel formulation in *Málskrúðsfræði* is *fyrir nauðsynja sakir eða fegrðar* (p. 86) 'out of necessities or for the sake of beauty'. The example above

Introduction xxvii

highlights the apparent paradox that a given example could illustrate a vice as well as a virtue. One instance where this can be observed is in Donatus's treatment of the pair *barbarismus per transmutationem litterae* (Holtz, ed., 1981, 654) 'Barbarism through rearrangement of letters' (a *barbarism* is defined as a vice that does not extend beyond a single word) and *metathesis* (Holtz, ed., 1981, 663), a figure that occurs if two letters of a word have changed places. In both instances Donatus gives the name form 'Euandre' as an example (instead of the expected 'Euander').[8] *Málskrúðsfræði*, in its corresponding sections, gives a poetic example where 'bort' (i.e. *burt* 'away') is used instead of 'brot' (i.e. *brott* 'away') so that it can form an internal rhyme with the verb *skorta* 'lack' (*TGT* 1884, 65, 90–91).

Virtues/vices might extend beyond a single word. A vice of this kind is called *solecismus* while the corresponding virtue is referred to as *schema*. An example of this is a sentence where the subject does not agree in number with the verb. Such lack of concord is classified among the vices in *Barbarismus* and designated *soloecismus per numeros* (Holtz, ed., 1981, 656; cf. *TGT* 1884, 77). Neither *Barbarismus* nor *Málskrúðsfræði* presents a corresponding virtuous variant, but *D* and *FoGT* fill this doctrinal gap by adding a virtuous version of this deviance called *antitosis*. *FoGT* also adds the cautious note that moderns (*ný skáld*) should not use this device (ch. 13).

Table 1: The theory of virtues and vices

	Prose/Deviation caused by ignorance	Poetry/Purposeful deviation
One word	barbarism	metaplasm
More words	solecism	schema
Mixed categories	other vices	tropes

Table 1 above shows the four possible combinations of the two parameters: virtue : vice and one word : more words. Each of these combinations carries a special name (barbarism, solecism, metaplasm and schema) and *Barbarismus* and *Málskrúðsfræði* treat each in a separate chapter. At this level, the organisational system of the deviations from normal usage presented in *Barbarismus* is so tight and logical that some of the deviations from normal usage even have

---

[8] These metatheses are probably either to be understood as Hellenisms or as archaisms (Holtz 1981, 153).

corresponding vicious and virtuous versions as illustrated above. (However, the order in which the various figures are presented within the chapters appears to be more arbitrary.) This neat system is disturbed by the addition of two mixed categories, each presented in its own chapter. The first is labelled *De ceteris vitiis* 'On other vices' in *Barbarismus*, a section which is not marked as a separate chapter in *Málskrúðsfræði*. The other chapter is designated *De tropis* 'On tropes' in *Barbarismus* and *De tropo et metaphoræ* [*recte*: metaphora] 'On the trope and the metaphor' in *Málskrúðsfræði*. These two supplementary categories contain deviations from normal usage that do not fit easily into the four preceding categories. The vices assembled in the 'other vices' category have little in common except for the fact that they are all treated under the same heading, but four of them (numbers 5–8) can be said to violate the ideal of brevity while number 9 is too elliptical. This means that *Barbarismus* and *Málskrúðsfræði* do not give an overarching definition for the 'other vices' category. The 'tropes' category fares better. The chapter devoted to this category is introduced by a definition of the trope:

> Tropus est dictio translata a propria significatione ad non propriam similitudinem ornatus necessitatisue causa (Holtz, ed., 1981, 667).

> A trope is a word transferred from its proper signification to a likeness that is not proper to it for the sake of ornamentation or necessity.

Málskrúðsfræði provides a similar definition:

> Tropus er framføring einnar sagnar af eigniligri merking til óeiginligri merkingar með nǫkkurri líking fyrir fegrðar sakir eða nauðsynjar (*TGT* 1884, 100).

> A trope is the transference of one word from its proper signification to an improper signification that has some similarity [to it] for the sake of beauty or necessity.

Roughly four and a half centuries passed between the writing of *Rhetorica ad Herennium* and *Barbarismus*. The two works differ greatly in purpose and scope as they belong to two different disciplines, *rhetorica* and *grammatica*. Each perceives and treats the various devices in different ways, as embellishments of utterances (*rhetorica*) or as deviations from normal language (*grammatica*). Both traditions illustrate these devices with examples, and both treat the flawed versions of the devices as well as the virtuous.

For Donatus the perversions occur in prose or because of ignorance, while the rhetorical tract, which treats the vices alongside the virtues, sees the vicious versions of the figures as the results of bad taste. Another difference is that the presentation in *Barbarismus* is much more systematic and well organised. The organisational neatness of *Barbarismus* was facilitated by the availability of a long tradition of grammatical writings on which Donatus could draw, and, not least, by the fact that he did not include the more complicated category of figures of thought.

The two texts that have been dealt with so far present a large number of figures, and it is to be expected that there is some overlap between them. Murphy (1974, 36–37) presents a tabular overview of the figures contained in the two texts. His chart shows that the two overlap almost completely in the case of the tropes, but less so in the case of the figures of diction and not at all in the figures of thought, which are not treated by Donatus (Murphy 1974, 34–35). It will be remembered that Donatus explicitly left these to the rhetoricians.

The expository parts of *Rhetorica ad Herennium* and *Barbarismus* were written in prose, the latter with poetic examples drawn from the canonical Latin poets of antiquity, Virgil in particular. Another branch of treatises on figures was written in verse. At least one such text, *Carmen de figuris* 'Poem on figures', was available at the time when *Barbarismus* was written, but the majority of examples seem to be much younger. *Carmen de figuris* names, defines and illustrates 61 rhetorical figures. Each figure is treated in the same way. First a name is given—*Carmen de figuris* uses Greek names—then a versified definition containing a Latin translation of the Greek name, followed by one or two examples. Three hexameter lines are devoted to each figure. The section on the fifth figure, *antimetabola* (cf. *FoGT* ch. 17), provides an example:

> Ἀντιμεταβολή
> Permutatio fit, uice cum conuertimus uerba.
> 'Sumere iam cretos, non sumptos cernere amicos.'
> 'Quod queo, tempus abest; quod tempus adest, nequeo', inquit.
> (Schindel, ed., 2001, 182)

> Antimetabola:
> 'Exchange' occurs when we transpose words.
> '[One should] select already examined, not examine selected friends.'
> 'When I am able, there is no time; when there is time, I am unable',
>   he said.

The examples are mainly versified versions of examples already current in the literature on figures. In the case of *Antimetabola* the originators of the examples have been identified as Theophrastus and Isocrates (Schindel 2001, 27–28). The anonymous author of *Carmen de figuris* does not explain why he chose to present his list of figures in versified form, but the metrical form facilitates memorisation and the presentation of technical subject matter in this manner may also have been considered something of a literary feat. *Carmen de figuris* is a rhetorical text in that its aim appears to have been the production and arrangement of meaning rather than the analysis of texts. It was written at a point in time when public speaking still held an important position in Roman life (even though the exact date of composition is unknown); it is thus likely that the author envisioned an audience of future orators rather than poets or versifiers.

In the centuries after Donatus, grammar encroaches more and more upon the territory that traditionally belonged to rhetoric, while this discipline recedes into the background. When Alcuin wrote *Dialogus de rhetorica et de uirtutibus* (c. 794), it was the first textbook of rhetoric in the classical tradition that had been written in nearly two hundred years (Knappe 1998, 12). Meanwhile, grammatical treatises continued to flourish in particular texts that were dependent on Donatus in one way or another. One example is Bede's (d. 735) *De Schematibus et Tropis* 'On Figures and Tropes'. Bede begins by declaring that the Greeks fraudulently laid claim to the invention of the figures and tropes. In order to show the falsity of their claim, he presents examples of all the figures and tropes described in *Barbarismus*. However, instead of drawing the examples from classical sources, Bede draws on the Bible. Thus he claims to have shown that all the figures were used in the Bible *before* they were used in the writings of the ancient Greeks and Romans, and hence that it is inconceivable that the Greeks invented the figures:

> Et quidem gloriantur Greci talium se figurarum vel troporum fuisse repertores! Sed ut cognuscas, dilectissime fili, cognuscant omnes qui haec legere voluerint quia sancta Scriptura ceteris omnibus scripturis ... preeminet ..., placuit mihi collectis de ipsa exemplis ostendere quia nihil huiusmodi schematum vel troporum valent pretendere secularis eloquentie magistri, quod non in illa precesserit.

> The Greeks boast that they were the inventors of these figures and tropes! But in order that you, my beloved son, and indeed all who choose to read these words may know that holy Scripture takes precedence over all other writings ... I have decided to demonstrate by means of examples gathered from its pages that there is not one of these schemes and tropes which

teachers of classical rhetoric boast of which did not appear in it first (Kendall, ed. and trans., 1991, 168–69).

Treatises on rhetoric emerge again in the late eleventh century. Of particular importance is *De ornamentis uerborum* 'On the Ornaments of Words' by Marbod of Rennes (d. 1123). Like *Carmen de figuris*, *De ornamentis uerborum* treats the subject of rhetorical figures in poetic form. Marbod's treatise contains short definitions of thirty figures of diction. In Marbod's day the *Rhetorica ad Herennium* enjoyed an immense popularity and the names of the figures in Marbod's treatise, their definition and the order in which they are presented follow the corresponding section of *Rhetorica ad Herennium*; however, the examples have been replaced by Marbod's own verse examples. The first figure of *De ornamentis uerborum*, *Repetitio*, will here serve as an example (cf. *FoGT* ch. 23):

> Repetitio est, cum continenter ab uno atque eodem verbo in rebus similibus et diversis principia sumuntur, hoc modo:
> Tu mihi lex, mihi rex, mihi lux, mihi dux, mihi vindex;
> Te colo, te laudo, te glorifico, tibi plaudo.
> Femina iustitiam produxit, femina culpam.
> Femina vitalem dedit ortum, femina mortem.
> (Leotta, ed., 1998, 4)

> Repetition is when beginnings are taken repeatedly from one and the same word in similar or diverse matters, in this way:
> You are my law, my king, my light, my guide, my protector;
> I worship you, I praise you, I glorify you, I applaud you.
> A woman caused justice, a woman offence.
> A woman gave rise to life, a woman to death.

In the first lines of his prologue, also written in poetic form, Marbod explains that the purpose of this treatise is to help future versifiers, and in his epilogue he explains that they should use his examples as models for their own poetry. His belief is that the figures are shown most effectively through verse examples, and that these should be memorised by the student, while prose definitions primarily function as glosses (Camargo 2006, 270–71; cf. Leotta, ed., 1998, 2 ll. 13–15).

Camargo, who presents an overview of the development of treatises on rhetorical figures in the wake of Marbod's *De ornamentis verborum* (2006, 268–77), mentions a number of treatises from the late eleventh and twelfth centuries. Characteristic of these texts is that they are all based on (a selection of) the repertoire of figures presented in

Rhetorica ad Herennium and generally follow the order of that classical treatise.

Around 1200, new developments take place. If the lore of the figures had been detached from larger treatises on grammar or rhetoric, it was now reintegrated into such treatises, and it also seems that the two disciplines coalesce again to some degree. Both these developments can be observed in *D* and *G*, even though they are firmly rooted in the grammatical tradition. This means that the author of *FoGT* follows a general trend when he transforms his sources in a decisively rhetorical direction. Elsewhere in Europe this development resulted in a group of hybrid texts, the arts of poetry, which have been labelled 'preceptive grammars' (Murphy 1974, 135–93). The high point of this new genre was Geoffrey of Vinsauf's *Poetria nova*. Among the many interesting features of this text, a 119 line poem on the history of the Fall and Redemption of mankind should be highlighted. In this display of virtuosity, Geoffrey illustrates all of *Rhetorica ad Herennium*'s figures of diction in the traditional order (Faral, ed., 1924, 231–34).

It was a short segment near the end of *D* that provided the main foundation for *FoGT*. Its author, Alexander de Villa-Dei, had designed *D* as a textbook of Latin grammar for intermediate students. *D* was an immediate success and it has been characterised as 'the most important pedagogical treatise of the Middle Ages' (Rosier-Catach 2009, 30). *D* was composed in metrical form, and in 2645 (often leonine) hexameters the treatise condenses a great amount of grammatical information. Alexander claims to have presented the material as gently as possible (*ut levius potero*, *D* l. 12), and medieval commentators also extol the lucidity of the work (see the quotation from the unpublished *Admirantes*-gloss in Thurot 1868, 101–02). However, the bare text as it is presented in the standard edition of the work by Reichling from 1893 (*D*) is by no means an easy read. Forcing complex grammatical subject matter, including a great number of metalinguistic *termini technici* of Latin as well as Greek origin, into hexameters can only be done at the cost of readability. Alexander and other didactic versifiers of his age were forced to use a host of special techniques to circumvent the problems caused by metrical constraints. The result is a text that is elliptical and obscure at many points (see Cizek 2009, xx–xxi). In defence of *D* and its imitators, it must be said that the intent was never for *D* to be read as it is presented in the modern standard edition of the text; rather, it was a practical work intended for use in a classroom setting. The teacher would have read out and elaborated on small segments of the work, and the students were expected to commit the verse text to memory in its entirety. An often-quoted gloss on *D* (see Cizek 2009, xx–xxi) lists the advantages of the metrical form. Verse is easier to take in, it can present materials in a neat and clear way and it is easier to retain in memory than prose.[9]

At the very beginning of *D* (ll. 7–10), Alexander recommends that the teacher use the vernacular when expounding the rules he sets forth. In manuscripts *D* is often accompanied by extensive glosses that elaborate upon the terse lines of the poem. When Reichling (1893) edited the text without glosses he therefore presented modern readers of the work with a serious obstacle to the understanding of the text. No modern edition of the glosses to *D* has been published thus far, but in recent years some early printed texts with glosses have been digitised and made available online, and easy access to these texts facilitates the appreciation of *D*. The same can also be said of Glei's (2005) helpful presentation of the work and Copeland and Sluiter's (2009, 573–83) short extracts from *D* in English translation with an introduction and comments. Also helpful is a complete translation of *D* into Spanish by Gutiérrez Galindo (1993).

The immediate success of *D* led to a vogue for treatises in verse on Latin grammar as well as other complex technical subjects. Alexander himself has been credited with writing a metrical treatise on the Arabic numerals (*Carmen de algorismos*, Halliwell, ed., 1839, 73–83) and a number of other similar texts in verse. In an effort apparently unrelated to *FoGT*, *Carmen de algorismos* was translated into Old Norse prose where it is known as *Algorismus*.[10]

Of *D*'s twelve chapters, it is only the last one on figures which will occupy us here (the previous chapters deal with morphology, syntax, metrics and accentuation). In 278 lines, ch. 12 names, defines and illustrates a large number of figures. The chapter can be divided into five distinct sections, as in the following list:

---

[9] *Sermo metricus utilis factus est ad faciliorem acceptionem, ad venustam et lucidam brevitatem, et ad memoriam firmiorem* (from Thurot 1868, 102).

[10] For studies of the Old Norse *Algorismus*, see Bekken and Christophersen (1985) and Bekken (1986). The oldest witness to this Old Norse translation is Hauksbók (AM 544 4°, c. 1302–10, Eiríkur Jónsson and Finnur Jónsson, eds., 1892–96, 417–24).

xxxiv   Introduction

Section I: Barbarisms, soloecisms and other vices

Acyrologia, cacenphaton, pleonasmus, tautologia, eclipsis, tapinosis, cacosyntheton, perissologia, macrologia, amphibologia, *alleoteta*[11] (ll. 2361–2403)

Section II: Metaplasms

Auferesis, prothesis, syncopa, epenthesis, apocopa, paragoge, *systola*, *ectasis* (four subtypes: penthemimeris, hephthemimeris, posthephthemimeris and one unnamed), dieresis, syneresis, episynalimphe, ecthlipsis, synalimpha, syncrisis, antithesis, metathesis (ll. 2404–44)

Section III: Schemata

Prolempsis, zeugma, *sylempsis* (three examples), hypozeuxis, anadiplosis, anaphora, epanalempsis, epizeuxis, paronomasia, paronomoeon, schesis onomaton, homoptoton, homoteleuton, polyptoton, hirmos, polysyndeton, dialyton (ll. 2445–96)

Section IV: Tropes

Metaphora, catachresis, metalempsis, metonomia, antonomasia, epitheton, synodoche, onomatopoeia, periphrasis, *hyperbole*, hyperbaton (five subtypes): *hysterologia, syncrisis, temesis, anastropha, parenthesis*), allegoria (seven subtypes: antiphrasis, charientismos, enigma, paroemia, sarcasmos, ironia, astismos), homozeuxis (three subtypes: icon, parabola, paradigma) (ll. 2497–2572)

Section V: [Colores]

Protheseos paralange, liptota, topographia, chronographia, hypallagium, prosopopoeia, apostropha, hendiadys, ebasis, emphasis, efflexegesis, euphonia, lepos, antitosis, antitheton, anthypophora, anticlasis, antimetabola, aposiopasis, euphemismus, synepthesis, oliopomenon, homophesis, epimone, anthropospathos, homopathion (ll. 2573–2639)

For the figures presented in sections I–IV, Alexander seems to have drawn on *Barbarismus*, and the categories of *Barbarismus* are duly mentioned and exemplified. *D* does deviate from *Barbarismus* in

---

[11] The figures with italicised names will be discussed in section 4 below.

Introduction

some cases (the deviations have been marked with italics in the list above and they will be treated in Section 4 below), but it is uncertain whether these deviations are introduced by the author or whether they were already in his source. The selection of figures presented in section V of ch. 12 cannot, on the other hand, be paralleled elsewhere, and the source(s) for this important section have yet to be determined (Grondeux 2009, 137). The figures of section V are not presented under a general heading, but in scholarship they are often referred to as the *colores* 'colours'. This term, which gained currency in Latin in the eleventh century (Murphy 1974, 39 n. 102), is sometimes used synonymously with 'figure'; at other times it refers to figures that were not included in the canonical repertoires found in *Barbarismus* and *Rhetorica ad Herennium*.

The number of lines spent on each of the *colores* varies somewhat in *D*. In some cases, such as *topographia* (l. 2577), *chronographia* (l. 2578) and *prosopopoeia* (l. 2582), Alexander deemed a single line sufficient, while he devoted six lines to *synepthesis* (ll. 2617–22). The *colores* constitute the most important foundation of *FoGT* and the full text of section V is therefore reproduced with a translation in an appendix to the present edition. To this repertoire of figures the writer added three figures found in *G* but not in *D*, one figure that has not been identified in other texts (*bethgraphia*), and three of the tropes treated in section IV of *D*'s twelfth chapter. These will be discussed in greater detail in Section 4 below.

Graecismus, ascribed to Eberhard of Béthune (fl. c. 1200), is in some respects reminiscent of *D*. The two are often mentioned in the same breath and both can be characterised as verse grammars. An important difference between the two texts is that *D* organises the material in the traditional order inherited from Antiquity, while *G*, in its present form (traditionally dated to 1212), begins with the figures. *G* is divided into 27 chapters. The first three of these are devoted to the virtues (ch. 1) and vices (ch. 2) of speech and the *colores* (ch. 3). Grondeux, in a discussion of the genesis of *G* (2000, 9–19), has argued that Eberhard's work only consisted of chs 9–24 and that the remaining sections were added not long after his death. *G* is therefore best considered a composite work. Among the added sections, we find the first three chapters on virtues, vices and *colores*. The popularity of *D* may have led to the addition of these four chapters. The assembled figures are drawn from a variety of sources, including Donatus's *Barbarismus*, Cassiodorus's commentary on the Psalms and Marbod's

De ornamentis verborum. The most striking feature of these sections is that the material has been completely rearranged. In previous texts the figures were organised into larger groups, but within the groups the figures were presented in no particular order. In *G* a clear effort was made to group together figures somehow reminiscent of one another. In section one, for instance, the first sub-heading announces metaplasms (i.e. virtuous alterations of single words). Many of the figures presented in this section are not metaplasms themselves, but only related to figures that are metaplasms, for example by analogy. A clear example can be seen in I, 13–16 of this chapter:

> *Elipsis* necat m, perimit *synalimpha* uocalem.
> Dicitur unius uerbi defectus *eclipsis*.
> Ast *aposiopasis* oratio decifiens est.
> Estque superuacui *pleonasmos* adoptio uerbi. (*G* I ll. 13–16)

> *Ellipsis* kills an *m*, *synalimpha* eliminates a vowel.
> The missing of one word is called *eclipsis*.
> But *aposiopesis* is an incomplete sentence.
> *Pleonasmos* is the adoption of a redundant word.
> (Copeland & Sluiter, trans., 2009, 588)

Only the first two figures, *elipsis* and *synalimpha*, can properly be called metaplasms, and they are treated as such in *Barbarismus* (Holtz, ed., 1981, 662 as *synaliphe* and *ecthlipsis*) and *Málskrúðsfræði* (*TGT* 1884, 90 as *sinalimphæ* and *elipsis*). The third figure on the other hand, *eclipsis*, is treated among the 'other vices' in *Barbarismus* (Holtz, ed., 1981, 659) and *Málskrúðsfræði* (*TGT* 1884, 82–83). The fourth figure, *aposiopesis*, is not treated in *Barbarismus*, but it is found in *D* among the *colores* (ll. 2612–14) and therefore also in *FoGT* (ch. 18). These four figures have clearly been grouped together because of their analogous nature. At various levels, they all illustrate the lack of one or more elements: the lack of a letter (*elipsis* and *synalimpha*), the lack of a word (*eclipsis*) and an incomplete sentence (*aposiopesis*). The last figure, *pleonasmos*, must have been added at this point because it is an example of redundancy, which can be considered the opposite of lack. In *Barbarismus* (Holtz, ed., 1981, 658) and *Málskrúðsfræði* (*TGT* 1884, 80–81) this figure is treated among the 'other vices'. At this point it should be said that the organisational efforts one can detect in *G* have not been carried out with great consequence, and Grondeux, who has outlined some of the organisational principles in this section of *G*, comments that the author of this section of *G* 'n'était décidément pas un grammairien'

(Grondeux 2001, 322). *G* contains many of the figures found in the *colores* section of *D* (and in the corresponding parts of *FoGT*), in addition to many other figures. However, *G* provides fewer examples of the various figures than *D* does, and exemplifying glosses were therefore even more necessary than in the case of *D*. A set of glosses on the first three chapters of *G* has been edited by Grondeux (2010) (*Gg*). This edition has been most useful in the work on the commentary to *FoGT*, in particular because *Dg* and *Gg* in many cases present the same examples.

D and *G* enjoyed an extraordinary popularity, but they were also criticised. John of Garland is believed to have revised both *D* and *G* (Colker 1974; Grondeux 1999) and he also attempted to replace the two with a verse grammar of his own, the *Compendium gramatice*, completed between 1235 and 1237 (Haye 1995, 15). Another effort of revision was Konrad of Mure's massive *Novus grecismus* 'The New Graecismus' (10450 ll.) from the mid-thirteenth century (Cizek, ed., 2009). None of these larger works ever attained the same popularity as *D* and *G*, and there is no indication that the author of *FoGT* was familiar with them.

3. The makeup of *FoGT*

FoGT is divided into 27 chapters. Twenty-five of these treat a single figure each, while chs 3 and 10 each treat a small handful of related figures. All chapters present figures that are found in the Latin tradition, and the commentary to this edition points to and cites the most important parallel passages in *D* and *G* and their respective commentaries (*Dg* and *Gg*). Table 2 (on the following page) presents an overview of the figures treated in *FoGT* and lists the relevant parallel passages in *D* and *G*. In the first column the (sometimes erroneous) name forms given in *FoGT* have been used, while the Latin terms used in the respective editions of *D* and *G* are given in the two latter columns. The numbers at the far left are chapter numbers in *FoGT*. They are not found in W and were first introduced in the Arnamagnæan edition (*SnE* 1848–78).

Table 2 shows that *FoGT* in general presents the same selection of figures as *D* and furthermore that *FoGT* and *D* present the figures in more or less the same order. The majority of the figures found in *FoGT* and *D* can also be found in the first chapter of *G*, but not in the same order. A few of the figures in *FoGT* and *D* can be paralleled by figures found in the second or third chapter of *G*.

Table 2: The repertoire of figures in *FoGT* and its parallels in *D* and *G*.

FoGT	*Doctrinale* (*D*)	*Graecismus* (*G*)
1 Protheseos paraloge	Proth. par. 2573–74	Proth. par. I, 27–28
2 Liptota	Liptota 2575–76	Liptote I, 58
3 Tophographia	Topographia 2577	Topographia I, 72–73
Bethgraphia	–	–
Cosmographia	–	Cosmographia I, 72–73
Cronographia	Chronographia 2578	Chronographia I, 72–73
4 Ypallage	Hypallagium 2579–81	Hypallage I, 39
5 Prosopophia	Prosopopoeia 2582	Prosopopoeia I, 106
6 Apostropha	Apostropha 2583–84	Apostropha I, 90–91
7 Endiadis	Hendiadys 2585–88	Hendiadys I, 56–57
8 Ebasis	Ebasis 2589–90	–
9 Emphasis	Emphasis 2591–93	–
10 Exflexigesis	Efflexegesis 2594	Eflexegesis I, 89
Icona	Icon 2564	–
Parabola	Paradigma 2565–69	Paradigma I, 121–22
Paradigma	Parabola 2570–72	Parabola I, 121–22
11 Euphonia	Euphonia 2595–96	Euphonia II, 7–8
12 Lepos	Lepos 2597–98	–
13 Antitosis	Antitosis 2599–2603	Antitosis I, 40
14 Antiteton	Antitheton 2604–05	Antitheton I, 68
15 Antiposora	Anthypophora 2606–07	Anthypophora I, 79
16 Aclacassis	Anticlasis 2608–09	–
17 Ansimehisa	Antimetabola 2610–11	Commutatio III, 81–82
18 Aposiopesis	Aposiopasis 2612–14	Aposiopasis I, 15
19 Euphemismos	Euphemismus 2615–16	–
20 Sineptesis	Synepthesis 2617–22	–
21 Onopomenon	Oliopomenon 2623–26	Brachylogia I, 84
22 Emophasis	Homophesis 2627–29	–
23 Epimenon	Epimone 2630–33	Epimonen I, 34–37
24 Antopazia	Homopathion 2636–39	–
25 Antropuspatos	Anthropospathos 2634–35	Anthropospathos II, 10
26 Simatrismos	–	Synacrismos I, 63–64
27 Therethema	–	Teretema I, 86–87

In some instances a discrepancy between *FoGT* and *D* can be discerned:

Chapter 3: *FoGT* has added two figures that are not found in *D*: *bethgraphia*, which has not been identified elsewhere, and *cosmographia*, which is paralleled by *G*.

Chapter 10: *FoGT* presents three subtypes of the figure *exflexigesis*. The three subtypes are also found in *D*, but there they are subtypes of the figure *homozeuxis*, a figure found neither among the *colores* of *D* nor in *FoGT*. In *Barbarismus*, Donatus treated *homozeuxis* and its subtypes among the tropes.

Chapters 24 and 25: These two figures are presented in the opposite order in *D*.

Chapters 26 and 27: These two figures are not paralleled in *D*. Both of them can be found in *G*, but not in the immediate vicinity of one another.

The author has generally structured all chapters in a similar manner. All chapters begin with the name of the figure to be defined. To make it easier for potential readers to orient themselves in the manuscript, the scribe has distinguished the initial letters of all these names with *litterae notabiliores*. The name of the figure is always followed by a finite verb, most often *vera* 'be', but also with some frequency *verða* (chs 1, 2, 4, 14 and 17). When *verða* occurs in this position it is rendered with 'occur' in the translation. In three instances another verb is used: *setja* 'put' in ch. 9, *segja* 'say' in ch. 21 and *glósa* 'gloss' in ch. 22. The finite verb is then followed by the definition of the figure. The definition is typically followed by a brief announcement of the examples, such as *sem hier* 'as here' in the case of anonymous stanzas or *sem N kvað* 'as N said' in the case of stanzas by named poets. One chapter (15) ends with the example, but generally the example is followed by a brief explanation. This general structure is varied in chapters where the author presents more than one example (usually because the figure in question has subtypes). In a few cases, most pronounced in chs 22 and 25, the author becomes carried away and elaborates on points that, even though they seem to be of marginal relevance to a treatise on figures, obviously occupied his mind. In some cases the author also passes aesthetic judgement on particular figures and gives advice on (or against) their use (such as in chs 9, 12, 13, 17, 20, 23). In one case *FoGT* also presents an etymology of the name of a figure (ch. 25). Etymologies are occasionally found in *Dg* as well, while *Gg* often gives etymological explanations.

The structure of the individual chapters may seem logical and natural, but it is by no means the only possible way of presenting the material. A glance at the extract from *D* reproduced in the Appendix will show that the variation in *D* at this point is considerable. This means that when transforming his source material into *FoGT* the author reshaped it systematically. A likely source of inspiration at this point could be *TGT*, which uses a similar structure.

4. Knowledge of *D* and *G* in Iceland and Norway

D and *G* were written in verse around 1200 and became immensely popular in a very short time. The author of *FoGT* could have acquainted himself with these works during a journey abroad, e.g. during his studies; therefore, *FoGT* in itself is not proof that *D* and *G* were known in Iceland. But evidence of the presence of these works in Icelandic libraries is provided by *máldagar* or church inventories printed in *Diplomatarium Islandicum* (*DI*). Olmer studied the book-lists contained in the *máldagar* and, among many other books, he listed the collections that had a copy of *D* and *G* (Olmer 1902 nos 63 and 100). Olmer's list contains some inaccuracies of interpretation and identification, therefore the relevant material is presented briefly here:

> In 1396 the cathedral of Hólar kept two copies of *D* and one copy of *G* among the school books: *Þessar skólabókr: Doctrinalia ij, Brito á tveim bókum, Huguicio, Grecismus* ... (*DI*, III 613) 'These school books: two *Doctrinales*, *Brito* in two volumes, Huguicio, Graecismus'. 'Brito' is *Summa Britonis*, a dictionary of difficult words in the Bible (Daly and Daly, eds., 1975) while 'Huguicio' is most likely Hugh of Pisa's *Derivationes* (Cecchini, ed., 2004), an etymological dictionary. The inventory goes on to list other school books.

> In 1397 the Augustinians at Viðeyjarklaustr kept one copy of *D* and one of *G* among their school books: *Item í skólabókum: In primis Doctrinale, Graecismus, Aurora* ... (*DI*, IV 111) 'Likewise [are kept] among the school books: first and foremost *Doctrinale, Graecismus, Aurora*'. *Aurora* is the title of a versified Bible by Peter of Riga. The inventory goes on to list other school books.

In 1461 the Augustinians at Mǫðruvallaklaustr kept one copy of *Graecismus*, listed as 'Grecissimus' among their books in Latin (*í latínubókum*, *DI*, V 288) (cf. Stotz 1996, 100 on the special form of the title).

The preserved *máldagar* thus testify to the existence of three copies of *D* and three copies of *G* in Iceland in the late fourteenth and fifteenth centuries. It is indicative of the high regard in which *D* and *G* were held that the first two inventories list these works as the first books among their school books.

In addition to the manuscripts listed in the inventories, two fragments of the Latin texts might also point to the circulation of *D* and *G* in the West Scandinavian area. 1) A half leaf of an unglossed text of *D* has recently been identified in the Hanseatic archives in Lübeck (as flyleaf of AHL 1409 (the main content of AHL 1409 is described in Asmussen et al. 2009, 255–56). According to Åslaug Ommundsen (oral communication) the fragment dates from the early fourteenth century. 2) In 1837 Finnur Magnússon sold a number of manuscripts and fragments to the British Library (see Porter 2006). Among the fragments London, BLAdd 11250 item no. 422 has recently been identified by Åslaug Ommundsen (oral communication) as a fragment of *G* (the text is from ch. 12). The fragment, a glossed double leaf, appears to be of French origin and it is unknown how it entered into Finnur Magnússon's possession.

Indirect testimony to the knowledge of *D* in Iceland can be found in *Málskrúðsfræði* of Óláfr Þórðarson's *TGT*. This text, commonly dated to c. 1250 (first attested in AM 748 I b 4°, c. 1300–25), appears to be based primarily on Donatus's *Barbarismus*, but earlier scholarship has also pointed to some similarities between *Málskrúðsfræði* and *D*, and concluded that the two texts must have drawn on a common source (see Holtsmark 1960, cols 417–18; Louis-Jensen 1981, 333). Neither Holtsmark nor Louis-Jensen described the similarities in great detail. In a more thorough analysis, Wellendorf (forthcoming) argues that the author of *Málskrúðsfræði* drew directly on *D* rather than on the source of *D*. Instead of assuming that an unknown work, of which no trace has been found thus far, had a pervasive influence on *D* and *Málskrúðsfræði*, it must *a priori* be considered more likely that a well known and popular work, that was the staple of grammatical teaching below the university level in the thirteenth century throughout Northwest Europe, had a formative influence on *Málskrúðsfræði*. That being said, *Málskrúðsfræði* explicitly refers to Donatus and his work on three occasions (*TGT* 1884, 59–60, 72 and 101), while there are no references to *D*.

The instances of agreement between the two works will be presented briefly below. *D* spread quickly throughout Northern Europe so it is not inconceivable that a copy made its way to Iceland as early as the mid-thirteenth century when *Málskrúðsfrœði* was written. Neither is it inconceivable that Óláfr, who was born in 1210, was exposed to *D* during his schooling or while abroad. Since students generally learned *D* by heart, it is not necessary to posit that Óláfr had a copy of *D* at hand when he wrote *Málskrúðsfrœði*; he could have worked from memory. The similarities between *Málskrúðsfrœði* and *D* concern mostly the ordering and selection of figures, but occasionally the definitions. The list on p. xxxiv above shows that sections I–IV of the twelfth chapter of *D* and *Barbarismus* present the same repertoire of figures, but that there are some points of divergence (marked with italicised letters). These will be commented upon briefly here:

Alleoteta

Alleoteta is the last figure mentioned among the 'other vices' in *Málskrúðsfrœði*. It is defined as follows: *Alleotheta er þat ef skipt er tǫlum eða fǫllum eða kynjum, sem fyrr er ritat í Soloecismos* (*TGT* 1884, 85) '*Alleoteta* is when numbers, cases or genders are changed, as was written earlier in [the section on] *Soloecismus*'. No example is given. Ólsen (1884, 85n.) has noted that *alleoteta* is not found in *Barbarismus*. However, in *Doctrinale* it occurs in exactly the same place as in *TGT*, namely as the last of the 'other vices'. *D*'s definition agrees with that of *Málskrúðsfrœði*: *confundit casus, numeros, genus alleoteta* (*D* l. 2404) '*Alleoteta* confuses cases, numbers, gender'.

Systola and *ectasis*

Systola and *ectasis* are presented in this order in *TGT* (1884, 88–89) and *D* (ll. 2412–26). *Barbarismus* presents them in the opposite order (Holtz, ed., 1981, 661–62).

Ectasis

TGT defines the figure *ectasis* (written *eptasis*) as follows: *Eptasis er gagnstaðlig sistole ok gerir skamma samstǫfu langa, sem fyrr er ritat:* [example]. *Þessi figúra hefir margar kynkvíslir í versum, en í skáldskap er hon sjaldan, nema ofljóst sé ort* (*TGT* 1884, 89) '*Ectasis* is the opposite of *systole* and lengthens a short syllable, as written earlier: [example]. This figure has many subdivisions in [Latin] verses, but is rarely found in [Norse] poetry, except in *ofljóst*'. *Barbarismus* omits the second part of the definition and simply writes: *Ectasis est extensio syllabae contra naturam uerbi, ut* [example] (Holtz, ed., 1981, 661) '*Ectasis* is the lengthening of a syllable contrary to the nature of the word, as: [example]'. *D* defines the figure as well, but then continues to list many subdivisions in an unusually long section (ll. 2413–26). The subdivisions carry long and arcane names (such as *posthephthemimeris* in l. 2419) and are illustrated with Latin verses. These figures are rarely, as *TGT* observes, used in Old Norse poetry.

Sylempsis

This figure is subdivided into three unnamed branches in *TGT* (1884, 93; written *silemsis*). The same branches are found in *D* (ll. 2456–62). The text of the parallel section of *Barbarismus* varies considerably between the editions of Holtz (1981, 664) and *GL* (4, 397), but none of them matches *Málskrúðsfrœði* as closely as *D*.

Hyperbola and *hyperbaton*

Málskrúðsfrœði (*TGT* 1884, 110–11) and *D* (ll. 2524–40) define these two figures in the same order, while *Barbarismus* treats them in the opposite order (Holtz, ed., 1981, 670–71).

Subtypes of hyperbaton

Barbarismus (Holtz, ed., 1981, 670–71) lists and exemplifies five subtypes of *hyperbaton*: 1) *hysterologia*, 2) *anastrophe*, 3) *parenthesis*, 4) *tmesis* and 5) *synchysis*. *Málskrúðsfrœði* (*TGT* 1884, 110–13) and *D* (ll. 2529–40) list the same subtypes, but present them in a different order, namely: 1, 5, 4, 2 and 3.

Paradigma

Louis-Jensen (1981, 333) has pointed out that *Málskrúðsfrœði* and *D* agree in their definition of this figure, which goes against *Barbarismus*. *Málskrúðsfrœði* defines: *Paradigma samjafnar fyrst nǫkkura hluti ok síðan greinir hon þá í líking* (*TGT* 1884, 118) 'First *paradigma* compares some things, then it gives an account of the similarities'. This agrees with *D*: *Hic paradigma facit, qui primum comparat et post assignat simile* (ll. 2570–71) 'He makes a *paradigma* who first compares and then assigns the similarity'. *Barbarismus* on the other hand defines the figure as follows: *Paradigma est enarratio exempli hortantis aut deterrentis* (Holtz, ed., 1981, 674) '*Paradigma* is the telling of an exhortative or deterring example'.

Parabola and paradigma

Málskrúðsfræði's last sections, on *parabola* and *paradigma* (*TGT* 1884, 117–19), differ in tone and method from the preceding sections of the text. Throughout, *Málskrúðsfræði* follows *Barbarismus* in exemplifying the figures discussed with examples of a secular nature, but the last two examples are markedly clerical in their tone. *Barbarismus* illustrates these figures with Virgilian examples (Holtz, ed., 1981, 674), while *Málskrúðsfræði* uses examples drawn from the realm of biblical typology. Both of these examples are accompanied by relatively detailed information on exegetic interpretive matters. This learned approach does not have much in common with the preceding sections of *Málskrúðsfræði* and reads more like a section from *FoGT*.

In the preceding paragraphs, a number of instances have been identified where *TGT* differs from *Barbarismus* and concurs with *D*. This agreement between *TGT* and *D* is most easily explained by suggesting that the author of *TGT*, in addition to the material he obviously drew from *Barbarismus*, also included material from *D*. If this supposition is correct, it raises the question of what kind of relationship exists between *TGT* and the *D*-based *FoGT*. It is tempting to regard them as a single work, in particular because of the similarities between the contents of the last two figures of *TGT* and *FoGT*, but internal evidence from *FoGT*, as outlined above, as well as the manuscript evidence, speak against this hypothesis. Even though W has a smooth transition between the two treatises, the oldest ms. of *TGT*, A (AM 748 I b 4°, c. 1300–25), explicitly ends *TGT* at the point where *Barbarismus* ends. In the light of these facts, the most likely conclusion is that the two treatises have distinct origins, but that they drew partly on the same source text, namely *D*. One can thus assume that *D* was known in Iceland before c. 1300–25, perhaps even in the mid-thirteenth century when Óláfr Þórðarson wrote *TGT*.

5. The nature and origin of the poetic examples in *FoGT*

a. Named poets and poems

There are 62 individual stanzas or part-stanzas cited by the author of *FoGT* and, of these, 47 are not ascribed to any named poet. While it is possible that some of these are by poets whose identity we do not know, it is likely that the majority are compositions of the author of *FoGT* himself or of someone composing to his direction. The reasons for thinking so are discussed below. Not all of the fifteen remaining stanzas are actually attributed to a named poet, but in some cases we can identify the composer because the stanza occurs in other sources. Stanzas 35 and 36 of *FoGT*, which are unattributed in the treatise, are sts 14 and 12, respectively, of Snorri Sturluson's *Háttatal*. It is possible that the writer of *FoGT* did not name Snorri as their author because he considered the latter's authorship to be common knowledge among fourteenth-century Icelanders interested in poetics. Another very well known poet, unnamed in *FoGT*, is Einarr Skúlason, one of whose verses is cited as st. 56. Einarr was a skald whose works are frequently cited in *Snorra Edda* and elsewhere in the grammatical literature.[12] Again, the author of *FoGT* may have reckoned with his audience's familiarity with Einarr's poetry and not felt the need to mention his name. Stanzas 24 and 25 are said to belong to a *Nikulásdrápa* 'Poem with refrain in honour of St Nicholas', and, judging by its subject-matter, stanza 6 belongs there as well. The author of *FoGT* does not name the composer of *Nikulásdrápa*. Perhaps he and his audience knew who it was, seeing that interest in St Nicholas was high in Iceland and particularly in the northern monasteries, where at least one prose saga of the saint, by Bergr Sokkason, was written in the fourteenth century.

All eight of the named poets cited in *FoGT* are mentioned only by their personal names without patronyms, suggesting that the author expected his audience to be familiar with them. A similar practice is followed much of the time in *TGT*, though there the poet's personal name is often accompanied by a nickname, like Auðunn illskælda 'Bad-poet' or Halldórr skvaldri 'Prattler'. The named poets of *FoGT* are Þorleifr (st. 1), that is, Þorleifr jarlsskáld 'Jarl's poet' Rauðfeldarson; Eiríkr viðsjá 'the Circumspect', whose patronym is unknown (st.

---

[12] Einarr's poetry is also cited in *Skáldskaparmál*, *TGT* and in the *ókend heiti* section added to W, as well as in *LaufE*; cf. Nordal's assessment of his key role in the skaldic canon (2001, 233–34).

2); Snorri (st. 18), that is, Snorri Sturluson; Óláfr (sts 19 and 20), probably but not certainly Óláfr hvítaskáld 'White Poet' Þórðarson, author of *TGT*; Bragi skáld (st. 23), that is, Bragi Boddason, an early Norwegian poet; Þorleifr (st. 27), that is, Þorleifr skúma 'Dusky' Þorkelsson; Eilífr (st. 28), probably but not certainly Eilífr kúlnasveinn 'Fellow with lumps' (?); and Arnórr (st. 32), Arnórr jarlaskáld 'Jarls' poet' Þórðarson. The only named poet whose patronym is given is Eyjólfr Brúnason; however, he is not the composer of a stanza cited in *FoGT* but the addressee of st. 18 by Snorri Sturluson. The treatise names him and tells the audience that he was a good poet and a good farmer, though not a wealthy one. It is possible that the author of *FoGT* did not expect his audience to know anything about Eyjólfr, unlike the other poets he mentioned, and so provided some information to fill them in on his background.[13]

Leaving aside for a moment the anonymous stanzas that cannot be identified as either the work of a known poet or the one poem *FoGT* identifies by name, *Nikulásdrápa*, we see that the skaldic canon familiar from *Snorra Edda* and *TGT* is still represented to some extent in *FoGT* through citations from the poetry of Bragi Boddason, Arnórr jarlaskáld, Einarr Skúlason, Snorri Sturluson, and possibly Eilífr kúlnasveinn and Óláfr Þórðarson. Of these Bragi's stanza (*Ragnarsdrápa* 3) is probably cited from a version of *Skáldskaparmál* familiar to the author of *FoGT*, though this could not have been the version in W (see below), and Arnórr's couplet appears also in *TGT*; Snorri's two stanzas from *Háttatal* and several of the prose parts of that work must also have been known to the *FoGT* composer. Indeed, the presence of a version of all parts of *Snorra Edda* in W makes it likely that at least one text of this four-part work was available at Þingeyrar or in its vicinity. Stanza 28, attributed to an Eilífr and unique to *FoGT*, is probably by the same person named as Eilífr kúlnasveinn in *Skáldskaparmál*, where three *helmingar* and a couplet from a poem about Christ are attributed to him.[14] The single stanza by Einarr Skúlason

---

[13] Only one *helmingr* by Eyjólfr survives in the poetic record, and that is found only in *LaufE*. See introductory commentary to st. 18 (pp. 70–71).

[14] His dates are unknown, but the style and subject matter of his poetry suggests the second half of the twelfth century. Nordal (2001, 87–88) assumes that the late tenth-century skald Eilífr Goðrúnarson was the composer of st. 28, but this is most unlikely, given the considerable similarity of both style and subject matter between st. 28 and the four fragments about Christ in *Skáldskaparmál*.

Introduction xlvii

does not appear in either *Snorra Edda* or *TGT*, however, and the two couplets from a poem on Thomas Becket, if they are by Óláfr Þórðarson and not by some other Óláfr,[15] are not recorded elsewhere. Snorri's *lausavísa* for Eyjólfr Brúnason is yet another stanza unique to *FoGT*.

None of the other named poets cited in *FoGT* can be considered canonical in the grammatical tradition, though one must note that the *helmingr* of Þorleifr jarlsskáld, which also appears in *TGT*, but to exemplify the fault of *solecismus*, was probably suggested to the author of *FoGT* from that work, where the example is garbled. This *helmingr* appears nowhere else in the skaldic corpus. Two poets whose works are unrepresented elsewhere in the grammatical tradition are Eiríkr viðsjá and Þorleifr skúma. Þorleifr's stanza is the only surviving example of his poetry, and it is recorded in manuscripts of *Jómsvíkinga saga* and in *Fagrskinna*, as well as in *FoGT* and *LaufE*. Aside from Eiríkr viðsjá's stanza recorded in *FoGT*, this same verse together with six others by Eiríkr are found only in *Heiðarvíga saga*, a connection that is significant in terms of the *FoGT* author's likely northern geographical and intellectual milieu at Þingeyrar in Húnavatnssýsla where the saga may have also been composed (so Nordal in ÍF 3, cxxxiv–cxliv). It is further significant in this context that the first line of a stanza by Gestr Þórhallsson (Gestr Lv 2^{III}), who also appears as a character in *Heiðarvíga saga*, has been preserved as the very last line of p. 168 of the unique additional section of *ókend heiti* in W, after which there is a lacuna of two leaves (*SnE* 1924, 105). The full *helmingr* to which this line belongs is preserved in the Y version of *LaufE* (*LaufE* 1979, 371),[16] along with a preceding prose quotation of a sentence in the saga that introduces Gestr Lv 1^{III}. Faulkes (*LaufE* 1979, 58) has argued that this suggests that the verse is likely to have derived from a manuscript of the saga, rather than from a version of *Snorra Edda*. It is possible that the author of *FoGT* may also have had access to a manuscript of the saga.

Another way in which the stanzas of *FoGT* associated with known poets can be assessed is in terms of their chronological and ethnic or regional spread across the Old Norse poetic corpus, compared with the

---

[15] If the author of these couplets was the thirteenth-century skald Óláfr svartaskáld 'Black Poet' Leggsson, then he also seems to form part of the grammatical tradition. Although only fragments of his output have survived, a number of them have been preserved in *TGT* and *LaufE*.
[16] *SnE* 1924 fills this lacuna in W with the text of *LaufE*.

citations from *Snorra Edda* and *TGT*. To consider the ethnic origin of the poets first, it is only in *Snorra Edda* that we find a significant number of Norwegian skalds represented, and that is because Snorri includes several poems and *lausavísur* by very early skalds. While both *TGT* and *FoGT* include mention of the Norwegian Bragi Boddason, doubtless in view of his iconic status as the first skald, and *TGT* also mentions Starkaðr gamli 'the Old', the latter associated with Danish rulers, poetry from the late ninth and early tenth centuries has little coverage in *TGT* and even less in *FoGT*. The later tenth century is reasonably well represented in both treatises, however, and here the poets cited in *TGT* are mostly Icelanders from the west and north of the island, as Gísli Sigurðsson has noted (2000, 108–13). Some of *TGT*'s sources are obscure and are not mentioned elsewhere. For the eleventh and twelfth centuries, *TGT* relies on a number of citations from important Icelandic skalds who served foreign rulers as their court poets: Arnórr jarlaskáld, Einarr Skúlason, Þjóðólfr Arnórsson, Markús Skeggjason and Sigvatr Þórðarson. Egill Skallagrímsson, who is cited several times in *TGT*, is an exception here both chronologically, as he belongs to the tenth century, and because he does not figure in historical writings, where the poetry of the other chief poets is largely preserved. As Nordal has observed (2001, 84): 'Óláfr's canon is the same as that used in the established skaldic canon of historical saga writing, in the kings' sagas and *Sturlunga saga*, and in *Snorra Edda*. These are the poets who are cited in the learned literature'. Óláfr adds Snorri Sturluson to his canon, and, if he composed the anonymous stanzas in *TGT*, he also silently adds himself.

FoGT cites many fewer named sources than *TGT*, and it is, of course, a rather shorter work. Its later tenth-century coverage is not dissimilar to that of *TGT*, though the sample is small. However, all three poets whose work can be dated to the second half of the tenth century or the very early part of the eleventh, Þorleifr jarlsskáld, Eiríkr viðsjá and Þorleifr skúma, are from northern Iceland, indicating again a particular northern interest on the author's part. *FoGT*'s coverage of the chief poets of the eleventh and twelfth centuries is noticeably restricted compared with both *SnE* and *TGT* and comprises only a single couplet by Arnórr jarlaskáld, also cited in *TGT*, and a stanza by Einarr Skúlason, which is quoted anonymously. Tribute is again paid to Snorri Sturluson by quoting three stanzas by him, two of them anonymously. The date and provenance of the stanza by an Eilífr are uncertain, but on internal grounds of style and subject matter the verse is likely to be from the second half of the twelfth century, while the couplets attributed to an Óláfr about Thomas Becket are probably of the thirteenth century, and the same may be true of the three *helmingar* from a *Nikulásdrápa*.

FoGT cites *Ragnarsdrápa* 3 by Bragi Boddason (st. 23) as an example of the figure *ebasis*, which the treatise defines as a departure from the subject matter 'when the poet drifts off course' (*þá er skáldið reikar afvegis*). This statement is puzzling, given that the wider context of *Snorra Edda* indicates that *Ragnarsdrápa* was a shield poem in which Bragi described scenes, including the killing of Jǫrmunrekr by the brothers Hamðir and Sǫrli, that he saw depicted on a shield that his patron, Ragnarr, had given him. The full citation of the four stanzas and a *stef* 'refrain' on this subject in three manuscripts (R, T^x and C) of *Skáldskaparmál* (*SnE* 1998, I 50–51) make this circumstance clear. The prose text of *FoGT* indicates that its author thought the main subject of *Ragnarsdrápa* was direct praise of Ragnarr himself, and that the legend of Hamðir and Sǫrli was a deviation from that, occasioned as an indirect compliment to Ragnarr loðbrók, who was considered a descendant of the legendary family of the Niflungar in some sources, including *Skáldskaparmál*. A question of interest here is what version of *Snorra Edda* the author of *FoGT* would have known, seeing that none of the stanzas about Hamðir and Sǫrli are in the W version of *Skáldskaparmál*. Clearly the author of *FoGT* knew the verse quoted from somewhere, but it may have been from a source in which the three other stanzas and, in particular, the *stef*, were missing. At any rate, the author does not seem to have been aware of the wider subject or subjects of the *drápa*.

b. The anonymous stanzas

If the number of stanzas by known poets in *FoGT* is meagre, the treatise makes up for its restraint in this regard by citing a very large number of stanzas that are unattributed to either poet or poem. There are several cogent reasons to think that many of these are the work of the author of *FoGT* himself or, if not by him, then by someone working to his direction. It has been mentioned already that the abundance of these anonymous stanzas is something that distinguishes *FoGT* from its predecessors among the grammatical treatises, even though some citation of unattributed verses occurs in both *Snorra Edda* and, somewhat more plentifully, in *TGT*.[17] It is quite likely that the author of *FoGT* was influenced by some of the preceptive arts of poetry of the thirteenth century, such as Geoffrey of Vinsauf's *Poetria nova* (c. 1215), both in composing his own examples to demonstrate his arguments and in developing long expositions of the significance of the citations themselves within the prose commentary.[18] Geoffrey does both these things, as does the author of *FoGT*. Neither can be paralleled in the earlier Icelandic grammatical treatises. Many of the anonymous stanzas, if the work of the author of the treatise or a colleague, are likely to date from the period c. 1320–40 and are thus more or less contemporary with such poems as *Lilja* 'Lily' and Abbot Arngrímr Brandsson's *Guðmundardrápa* (Arngr *Gd*^{IV}, securely self-dated in st. 47 to the year 1345). The language and subject matter of some of the anonymous stanzas in *FoGT* are often reminiscent of these two poems, particularly the former.

The anonymous stanzas can be classified using several different criteria. There is a group that is clearly modelled on the Latin examples given in either *D* or *G* or in related commentaries and must have been invented specifically for the purpose of reproducing in Icelandic dress the figures recommended in *FoGT*'s source texts. These examples can be divided into two sub-groups, comprising on the one hand stanzas or part-stanzas that imitate Latin verse examples with exactly or almost exactly parallel Icelandic constructions, and, on the other, those that provide a more broadly-based analogy, as, for example, in st. 51, *Sæll er sienn í milli*, which illustrates the figure *homophesis*, a form of obscurity, and is dependent on a definition in *D* which provides examples from the technical language of astrology. *FoGT* provides a stanza that depends on the exegesis of two Old Testament prophecies, and supplies a prose interpretation of the verse based on the writings of Christian Church fathers.

---

[17] Snorri's own 102-stanza encomium, which exemplifies the different verse-forms of Old Norse poetry, is not actually attributed to him within the prose text of *Háttatal*, though there are several medieval attestations to his authorship elsewhere (cf. *SnE* 2007, vii–viii).

[18] Although no manuscript of the *Poetria nova* is recorded as existing in medieval Icelandic book collections, it is very likely that the text was known in Iceland by the early fourteenth century. It must now be taken as certain that the poet of *Lilja* (Anon *Lil*^{VII}) knew and was influenced by the *Poetria nova* (cf. Foote 1982 [1984]; Chase 2007, 2, 580–85, 637–38) and the date of composition of *Lilja* (c. 1340) is more or less contemporary with that presumed for *FoGT*.

The first sub-group, of close parallels, includes sts 11, *Framan unnu gram gunnar*; 12, *Mari sendu vers vinda*; 13, *Blies um hváfta hása*; 21, *Skálm vann og hjalt hilmi*; 22, *Þýddiz karl inn klædda*; 33, *Þá, er eg leyfi mey mjóva*; 34, *Sveit fylla ein alla*; 43, *Mætum stend eg að móti*; 45, *Eigi er ván, að eg vága*; 46, *Það saung og í gröf geinginn* (second *helmingr*) and 47, *Víngarðr hafði öl-Giefn orðið*. Detailed support for the correspondence between the Latin sources and the Icelandic rendition will be found in the commentary to this edition. In general, the execution of the Icelandic examples is extremely clever and, in some cases, of real poetic merit. In order to provide parallels, however, a rather strained syntax or lexical meaning of Icelandic words is sometimes required.

The second sub-group of more broadly-based parallels occurs mostly towards the end of *FoGT* and, typically, in full eight-line stanzas rather than in couplets or *helmingar*, as is the case with many of the first sub-group. In some cases pairs or even larger groups of stanzas are involved. Relevant stanzas include 48 and 49, which illustrate the figure *oliopomenon*, defined in *D* as one in which a series of important events is expressed in few words. *D* gives as an example a series of short clauses encapsulating the history of the Trojan war. The author of *FoGT* produces two *dróttkvætt* stanzas, each consisting of four couplets, illustrating which he calls *ávarp theologie* 'a summary of the Bible', and describing eight key events in the life of Christ. As he does frequently, the *FoGT* author gives examples from Christian literature rather than from classical history or the liberal arts, which his exemplars use. In this pair of stanzas *FoGT* provides functional equivalence of subject matter and style to its Latin exemplar. Other examples in this sub-group are sts 50, *Hugsan flýtir lysting ljóta*; 51, *Sæll er sienn í milli*; 57, *Ádám sá, þann alt í heimi*; 58–60 and the first part of 61, *Hverr deyr? Hjarðar stýrir*. Details of the relationship of these stanzas with their Latin exemplars will be found in the commentary to this edition. The three sts 58–60 are particularly interesting in this context and reveal how cleverly and subtly their creator worked to establish equivalences between his sources and his Icelandic examples. These three stanzas are said to illustrate the figure of *synacrismos*, which the prose text defines as the collection of praise or vices in one chapter and clause or verse in Latin but in one or more stanzas of Old Norse poetry. In fact all the examples in the three stanzas are of praise of Old Testament characters and the Christian

God, but each stanza contains in addition a number of stereotyped and deliberate metrical faults, thus illustrating both praise and vices.[19]

A third group of anonymous stanzas in *FoGT* may be distinguished from the two sub-groups discussed above. These are presented as illustrations of Latin rhetorical figures but, although they bear some relation to the Latin models and are likely to have been composed specifically for *FoGT*, they are probably as much developments of indigenous categories of Old Norse poetry as they are attempts to approximate Latin figures. All of them involve the use of established and often complex verse-forms for which precedents and technical terms already existed in the earlier manuals of *Snorra Edda* and/or *TGT*. In most cases the prose text of *FoGT* draws attention to the Icelandic precedents for the use of these poetic ornaments.

In this category belong sts 29, 30 and 31, which are said to illustrate the figure of *euphonia*, the alteration of speech sounds to make them more pleasing to the ear. The prose commentary mentions that Óláfr Þórðarson also discussed this issue and, in the three stanzas themselves, presents a series of couplets which all play on words that are etymologically connected but have different stem vowels on account of recent phonological changes in the Icelandic language. The verse-form used here is *áttmælt* 'eight times spoken'. Another extensive set of stanzas in this group is 37–41, which is preceded by sts 14 and 12 of Snorri's *Háttatal*. All these stanzas, including Snorri's, are presented as illustrations of the figure *antitheton*, defined in the treatise as occurring if the last words of a stanza correspond to the first and where other possible ways of dividing clauses within metrically correct stanzas are found. These stanzas constitute a virtuoso performance by their composer, as various ways are found to split a series of semantically related clauses, and several different verse-forms are used to achieve this end, including *hrynhent* 'flowing rhymed', the variety of *tøglag* 'journey metre' called *inn nýi háttr* 'the new verse-form' in *Háttatal* (*Háttatal* 73, *SnE* 2007, 31), and *runhent* 'end-rhymed'. Although it has been suggested that some of the variant verse-forms presented here were likely to be new creations of the *FoGT* composer (so Ólsen in *FoGT* 1884, 275 n. 7; Longo 2006), most of them probably had precedents in the vernacular tradition. Stanzas 52–55 illustrate different types of repetition, which the prose

---

[19] We are grateful to Kari Ellen Gade for analysing the metrical faults in these three stanzas and pointing out their significance.

commentary of *FoGT* attempts to align with the indigenous technical terms of *dunhenda* 'echoing rhyme', *iðurmæltr* 'repeatedly spoken' and *greppaminni* 'poets' reminder', although the stanzas presented do not correspond precisely to these native verse-forms. The final two stanzas in the treatise, 61–62, are said to illustrate the figure of *teretema*, a series of questions and answers about the same subject. This is rather similar to the native figure *greppaminni*, but the stanzas are in fact in a form of *sextánmælt* 'sixteen times spoken', as exemplified in *Háttatal* 9 (*SnE* 2007, 9).

For the most part, the author of *FoGT* provided Icelandic poetic examples that were consistent with the rhetorical purpose his Latin exemplars attributed to their illustrative material. However, in a small number of cases the Icelandic examples do not approximate very well to their Latin counterparts. Two of the anonymous stanzas, 42 and 44, are of this kind. Stanza 42, *Þier giet eg, karl, ef þú kærir*, is intended to illustrate *FoGT*'s definition of the figure *anthypophora*, which the prose text says comes about if a man responds to charges that someone has prepared against him at an assembly, thinking of an Icelandic legal situation. The stanza illustrates just such a circumstance, but both the Icelandic definition and the illustration are rather far from the normal sense of the Latin figure, which involves making an anticipated response to a tacit objection. Stanza 44, *Sveit lifir ill til átu*, picks up on the sense of the adage used in *D* to illustrate the figure of *antimetabola*: *non, ut edas, vivas, sed edas ut vivere possis* 'you should not live so that you may eat, but eat so that you may live', but does not reproduce the essence of the figure itself, which is a demonstration of how meaning can change if one changes the arrangement of words, as in the adage. *FoGT* understands the figure as changing sense by using words of obscure signification, and introduces the coinage *þokumenn* 'fog-men' for this purpose, explaining how this term refers to people who waste their money on food and drink and do not see the light of proper behaviour.

c. Dominant themes of the anonymous stanzas and their prose exegesis

Unlike its predecessors, *FoGT* exemplifies the rhetorical figures of its Latin sources with a high proportion of stanzas that refer to the Christian religion and assumes an audience familiar with the beliefs and rituals of the Christian Church, as well as the principles of exegesis and allegorical interpretation of sacred texts that are invoked right at the end of *TGT* but are otherwise not used in earlier Icelandic grammatical treatises. If *FoGT* was the product of a member of the Þingeyrar monastic community or a related religious house, such an emphasis would not be surprising. Another consideration is that the author of *FoGT*, writing in the first half of the fourteenth century, must have been aware that most of the skaldic poetry composed in Iceland in his day was religious in character. His manual was thus in tune with contemporary poetic practice, whereas earlier manuals had rather stressed secular poetry, though in both *Snorra Edda* and *TGT* some poetry with Christian subjects is included, but in neither of these earlier treatises does it dominate.

The stanzas that address religious themes include some poetry by known skalds together with a much larger number of anonymous compositions. This group of subjects can be divided between those that deal with Christian ritual, dogma or exegesis, those that are specifically hagiographical and a third group of moralising stanzas in which the voice of the preacher can be detected. The first group predominates and includes sts 4, *Fingr vann eigi eingan*; 8, *Allr lýtr heimr undir hylli*; 9, *Sjálfráði dó síðan*; 15, *Vatn kalla mig*; 16, *Grœnn kvað viðr á víði* and 17, *Vátr kvað marr á móti*; 28, *Báru mœta móti*; 44, *Sveit lifir ill til átu*; 46, *Það saung og í gröf geinginn*; 48, *Beraz liet frá mey mætri*; 49, *Píndr reis upp með anda*; 51, *Sæll er sienn í milli*; 52–55, *Eg em synda bót ... Eg blessa þig*; 56, *Máni skínn af mæni*; 57, *Ádám sá, þann alt í heimi*; 58, *Ábiels lofar ævi*; 59, *Trúa lofar Ábráms ævi*; 60, *Moysen lofar ljósan* and 61, *Hverr deyr? Hjarðar stýrir*. There is a smaller group of hagiographical stanzas that celebrate the lives of particular saints who were popular in Iceland, including sts 6, *Firð stóð í bygð breiðri* (St Nicholas); 19, *Þier fremiz þí með tíri* and 20, *Teitr giefr, Thómas, ýtum* (St Thomas Becket); 24, *Öll þing boða eingla* (St Nicholas) and 25, *Jón laut í höll hreinum* (St Nicholas, John the Baptist); 62, *Hverr fell?* *Hörða stillir* (St Óláfr Haraldsson). The third group, which shows the influence of the arts of preaching, comprises sts 10, *Hákon rieð fyr hauðri*; 11, *Framan unnu gram gunnar*; 14, *Grund, taktu, bölvi blandin*; 26, *Píndr er stuldr, þar er standa* and 50, *Hugsan flýtir lysting ljóta*.

Some other thematic issues can be detected across the stanzas of *FoGT* and in its prose commentary. Aside from the group of anonymous stanzas that provoke discussion of indigenous technical terms, mentioned in section 5 b above, a significant interest in history and government can be discerned (sts 10, 11, 27, 32, 35, 36, 37, 39, 40 and

Introduction

62) as well as an interest in the law (sts 11, 26, 42 and 43), and this latter interest is supported by some overlap in vocabulary between the prose text of *FoGT* and legal writings like *Jónsbók*, a work that is known to have been copied at Þingeyrar in the mid-fourteenth century. A further thematic interest is in male-female relations, often with a suggestively sexual element, witnessed by sts 5, 22, 33, 45 and 47.

At several places in the treatise, the author of *FoGT* offers prose explanations of varying lengths on the stanzas he quotes. Many are devoted to religious ideas and are very much in the tradition of biblical and doctrinal exegesis familiar from the Latin commentary tradition and from Latin and vernacular sermon literature. Others involve commentary on Icelandic grammatical technical terms and incorporate the author's opinions on the desirability or undesirability of certain figures. The first, relatively short excursus comes after st. 15 and explains how Alms-giving (*Ölmusugjöfin*) calls itself the water of Christ in the stanza and how the equivalence between the two terms is developed throughout the verse. This is followed by a much longer explanation of the Biblical background to the paired sts 16 and 17, which the prose commentary says (erroneously) are based on the Apocryphal Book of Baruch. After quoting the verses, the commentary then claims that the forest and the sea of the poetry should be understood historically as signifying the Jews and the Chaldeans. The treatise's discussion of the figure of *ebasis*, which is exemplified both by *Ragnarsdrápa* 3 (st. 23) and by two *helmingar* from *Nikulásdrápa* (sts 24-25), has been mentioned above in Section 5 a. The discussion is of interest not only because it throws light on the author's apparently limited understanding of *Ragnarsdrápa*, but also for his attitude to the use of examples from other narratives to illuminate a specific subject: they may be used out of necessity or for ornament or for the ascription of blame but otherwise should be avoided at all costs!

After st. 27, by Þorleifr skúma, which employs a variety of periphrases to describe an oaken club and its likely effect on various intended victims, the commentary introduces the idea that this switching of images, which it does not approve of, at least for grand poems (*stórkvæðum*), can be called *finngalknað* 'monstrous', and draws attention to Óláfr Þórðarson's earlier use of this technical term. This, in its turn, was dependent on Snorri Sturluson's disapproval of such changes of imagery in *Háttatal* (*SnE* 2007, 7), though there Snorri uses the term *nykrat* rather than *finngalknað* to refer to them. *FoGT* also brings Óláfr's views into the discussion again in connection with the three sts 29, 30 and 31 that exemplify the figure of *euphonia*, drawing on the precedent of Óláfr's writing about unpleasing conjoined characters (*límingarstafir*). This excursus has been discussed above in Section 5 b. Further comments and value-judgements about indigenous verse-forms and other stylistic devices are found concentrated around sts 35–41, a group also discussed above. Here the author declares his appreciation of the device called *stælt* 'inlaid', which is exemplified by two stanzas by Snorri Sturluson (35 and 36, *Háttatal* 14 and 12), and mentions another term, *langlokur* 'long enclosures', which appears in *Háttalykill* and, in the form *langlokum*, in ms. R of *Snorra Edda*, though not in the main scribe's hand, and in the list of names of verse-forms that precedes *Háttatal* in U. The paragraph preceding sts 52–55 has a discussion of the figure *epimone* in which the same word is used more than once, drawing a distinction between its use to reinforce meaning in theological writings and its function in Icelandic poetry, where it is used for the sake of beauty (*fyrir fegrðar sakir*) in verse-forms like *dunhenda* and *iðurmæltr*.

The author's explanation of the 'fog-men' (*þokumenn*) stanza (44) introduces another cluster of moralising or exegetical excursuses. Although he probably coined the term *þokumaðr* in imitation of the Latin word *nebulo* 'worthless person, wretch', the *FoGT* author expands its implications in homiletic fashion in the prose gloss to the stanza. The excursus to st. 51, *Sæll er sienn í milli*, is by far the longest and most complex in *FoGT*. David McDougall (1988) has shown that it draws on two excerpts from patristic commentaries which the grammarian probably derived directly or, most likely, indirectly from the eighth-century homiliary of Paul the Deacon. The commentary that follows st. 56, Einarr Skúlason's *Máni skínn af mæni*, is indebted to commonplace scientific or encyclopedic information about the relationship between the sun and the moon that formed part of the medieval literature on computus (cf. Clunies Ross and Gade 2012). The final excursus of any length in *FoGT* comes after st. 57, which exemplifies the figure termed *anthropospathos*, in which what belongs to mankind is attributed to the Godhead. The treatise advises its audience not to understand this transfer literally, but only in a figurative sense, giving a number of examples of human physical movements and their figurative senses when applied to God.

Introduction

lvii

6. The present edition: guiding principles

a. Normalisation of the Icelandic text

Various kinds of evidence indicate that *FoGT* is a work of the first half of the fourteenth century, most probably composed between 1320 and 1340, and extant in a single manuscript, W, of c. 1350. This edition has normalised the text to reproduce orthographically the presumed state of the Icelandic language in this period. Some of the poetry cited in *FoGT* dates from various periods before 1300, and in a few cases from much earlier than that. In spite of this anomaly, a decision was made to normalise all the poetry cited in *FoGT* to the same fourteenth-century standard for the sake of uniformity of presentation.

A concise analysis of the paleographical, orthographic and linguistic characteristics of the W manuscript as a whole can be found in Hreinn Benediktsson 1972, 17–18 and confirms the scribal hand as of the fourteenth century but not later than its third quarter. In general, many of the same principles of normalisation, affecting orthography, syntax and morphology, have been followed here as are outlined in section 9 of the Introduction to *SkP* VII (Gade 2007a, lxv–lxvii), which may be consulted for further reference, along with Björn K. Þórólfsson (1925) and relevant sections of *ANG* and Nygaard (1906). However, some of the fourteenth-century changes exemplified in these authorities are not found in *FoGT*. These include loss of *er* after *þá* 'when', *þar* 'where', *þegar* 'as soon as' and *síðan* 'after' (Nygaard §265, Anm. 2a) and loss of *að* 'that' after *svá* 'so that', *þó* 'although' and *því* 'because' (Nygaard §265, Anm. 2b). There is only one example of the loss of the relative particle *er* following a demonstrative in *FoGT*, and that is in st. 57/1 *Ádám sá, þann alt í heimi*. There is no indication that desyllabification of *-r* > *-ur* (*ANG* §161a) has occurred and *rl* has not changed to *ll*. Examples of normalisations of orthography, syntax and morphology are given below.

The normalisation of the many technical terms derived from Greek via Latin has posed a particular problem. In most cases these terms would have been transparent to speakers of Greek, but not to a Western medieval audience of treatises of figures, whether in Latin, Old Norse or some other Western language. An additional complicating factor is that many of the names were distorted during their transmission. The figure called *antiposora* (ch. 15) can be used as an example. It is defined as a reply to an anticipated, but not spoken, accusation. To an Old Norse reader of *FoGT*, there would be no obvious connection between the name of the term and the figure it describes, even if the sound of the name itself might have evoked the notion of a rhetorical figure, and someone might have recognised *anti-* as meaning 'against'. The Greek name of this figure is *anthypophora* (ἀνθυποφορά), a compound consisting of the elements *ant-* 'against' and *hypophora* 'objection'. The last part of the compound is itself a compound and consists of *hypo* 'under' and *phora* 'utterance'. To a speaker of Greek the name of the figure fits well semantically with the device it names. The typical Old Norse reader, on the other hand, would have had no way of knowing this. In the main text, therefore, the names of the figures have not been altered from their manuscript form. Access to dictionaries and reference works give us an advantage over medieval readers and in most cases it has been possible to determine the original/traditional forms of the names of the figures. Consequently it was deemed unnecessary to perpetuate the use of the garbled forms of the main text in the translation and the commentary. The names of figures and other technical terms of Latin and Greek extraction have therefore been restored in the translation and commentary. The index includes both the forms of *FoGT* and the corrected forms. It is evident that the Latin audience of the collections of rhetorical figures such as those found in *D* and *G* also occasionally misunderstood the names of the figures. In the case of *anthypophora*, *Gg* (p. 91) explains that this is a compound of *anti*, interpreted correctly as *contra* 'against', and *phora* misinterpreted as *ferre* 'bring, bear'. *Gg* does not account for the middle element of the term (*hypo*).

A. Normalisations relevant to fourteenth-century texts

I. *Phonology*

1) *Vowels in stressed syllables*

   i) é > ie (*ANG* §103; Björn K. Þórólfsson 1925, xiv): *réð > rieð* 'ruled', *þér > þier* 'to you'.

   ii) e > ie | k, g, h- to denote palatal stops, but after h- only where e does not derive from short æ (*ANG* §103): *einkend > einkiend* 'specific to', *gefa > giefa* 'to give', *hekk > hiekk* 'hung'.

   iii) e > ei | -ng (*ANG* §102; Björn K. Þórólfsson 1925, iv, Stefán Karlsson 2004, 14): *engi > eingi* 'no, none', *lengi > leingi* 'long'.

iv) ǿ > æ (*ANG* §120): *grǿnn* > *grænn* 'green', *dǿmi* > *dæmi* 'example'.

v) ǫ, ø > ö (*ANG* §115, 2; Björn K. Þórólfsson 1925, xviii–xix): *hǫll* > *höll* 'hall', *ǫðruvís* > *öðruvís* 'otherwise, differently', *sløkkvir* > *slökkvir* 'quenches', *ørlǫg* > *örlög* 'fate, fortunes'.

vi) ö > au | -ng, nk (*ANG* §105): *krönk* (neut. pl.) > *kraunk* 'hurtful', *söng* > *saung* 'sang'.

2) *Consonants*

i) ð > d | [+short syllable] l, n, m- (*ANG* §238, 1b): *talði* > *taldi* 'counted, told'.

ii) ð > d | b, lf, lg, ng, rg- (*ANG* §238, 1b): *skelfða* > *skelfda* 'trembled'.

iii) pt > ft (*ANG* §247): *hváptr* > *hváftr* 'mouth, maw', *eptir* > *eftir* 'after, behind'.

iv) t, k > ð, g | [- stress]- (*ANG* §248; Björn K. Þórólfsson 1925, xxvii, xxxii): *ek* > *eg* 'I', *at* > *að* 'that'.

v) ts ⟨z⟩ > ss (*ANG* §274, 2): *bleza* > *blessa* 'bless'.

II. *Morphology*

1) Mediopassive voice: -sk > -z (*ANG* §544): *kallask* > *kallaz* 'is called'.

B. Occasional syntactic change

1) Loss of the relative particle *er* in the combination demonstrative + relative particle (Nygaard 1906, §261): Anon *FoGT* 57/1 *Ádám sá, þann alt í heimi* 'Adam saw the one who everything in the world'.

b. Reproduction of the text and the translation

Prose text and translation

The prose text is based on digital images of W. In general, the text of *FoGT* is clearly legible, but in some instances holes and other damage to the manuscript have rendered letters and sometimes even words illegible. All problematic passages have been checked against the manuscript. Earlier transcriptions of the text, in particular those of Ólsen (1884) and Johansson (2007), have been helpful throughout. All previous editions have been consulted in those cases where uncertainty about the text remains, and their suggestions/readings are noted in the commentary. Concerning normalisation, the guidelines for fourteenth-century poetry found in the new edition of skaldic poetry (*Skaldic Poetry of the Scandinavian Middle Ages*) have been followed. Since the orthography of W in many cases is quite traditional/classical, the normalisation has resulted in a modernisation of the text. All changes made to the text have been noted in the critical apparatus found at the bottom of the text page and are discussed in the textual commentary. In the cases where a manuscript reading does not contain a recognisable Old Norse word, is damaged or when the exact manuscript reading is judged to be of interest to the reader, the reading has been enclosed in single quotation marks and rendered semi-diplomatically with expanded abbreviations and a normalised set of graphemes.

The technical subject matter and the sometimes convoluted prose style of the author have in some cases rendered the text difficult to understand. No attempt has been made to even out this aspect of the text in the translation, as faithfulness to the Old Norse text has been the main goal. In determining the meaning of problematic passages, the two earlier translations of the text have proved helpful. These are the Latin translation in the Arnamagnaean edition of *Snorria Edda* (*SnE* 1848–87, II 191–249) and Longo's Italian translation (*FoGT* 2004, 59–81). Passages that have posed particular problems of translation are discussed in the commentary.

Poetry and its translation

In this edition the same principles have been followed as guide the ongoing new edition of *Skaldic Poetry of the Scandinavian Middle Ages* (*SkP*). These are set out in the General Introduction to *SkP* I (2012). It is anticipated that this edition will become the standard for future research and study, though Finnur Jónsson's 1912–15 edition (*Skj*) will retain its place as a valuable reference tool. The poetry by known skalds in *FoGT* will be published in several different volumes of *SkP*, depending on where that poet's works are located, while the anonymous stanzas and some of those by named skalds will be published in Volume III, *Poetry from Treatises on Poetics*. In order to be consistent with the new edition, all sigla for poems and poets conform to those of *SkP* (not Finnur Jónsson's edition) as do manuscript sigla cited. The latter, in cases of medieval manuscripts, are in accordance with the sigla of *ONP*. A list of manuscript sigla used in this edition can be found on p. lxiv.

For most of the poetry cited in *FoGT* there is only one manuscript, W, but some of the stanzas by known skalds are extant in several manuscript witnesses. In all cases in this edition, W's text of a stanza has been reproduced, unless a reading does not make sense or is defective in some other way. If other, better manuscript readings exist where W's text is problematical, these have been adopted. Variant readings are noted at the foot of each text page and, where W's text has had to be emended to make sense, the manuscript reading is given at the foot of the page. Emendation is conservative, and conjectures are avoided, unless metrical or alliterative criteria support them. Manuscript orthography has been normalised to fourteenth-century standards, as described above.

The treatment of *FoGT*'s poetic texts follows the practices of *SkP*. To assist the reader, a prose word order for each text is given either at the foot of the text page on which the verse occurs or at the foot of the facing translation page. The English translation of the poetry, set in its prose context, faces the Icelandic text. The translation is as literal as it is possible to be without seeming strange. In some cases, the literal sense of a word or phrase is difficult to translate and here an approximate sense is given with the literal sense in square brackets, for example 'courtship [*lit.* wooing words]'. Kennings are treated fully. All base words and determinants are translated in full, for example *neytir vargs unda* appears as 'the user of the wolf of wounds', while the kenning referent, which is not explicit in the poetic text, is given in the translation in small capitals enclosed in square brackets, in this case '[AXE > WARRIOR]'. In cases of complex kennings with more than one referent, the use of > indicates the direction that interpretation should follow from the centre of the bracketed interpretation outward. In some cases, in this edition principally in kennings for God or Christ, an equals sign (=) is used with the referent given in roman type to indicate that this kenning referent is unique. For example, in st. 28 the kenning *siklingr skýja* 'the prince of the clouds' has been represented by the notation '[= God (= Christ)]', to show that such a kenning can refer only to God, but in this case as the Second Person of the Godhead, because the stanza is about Christ's entry into Jerusalem on Palm Sunday. Notes on individual points of interest or difficulty in the poetry are found within the commentary, keyed to relevant pages and lines, as are comments on interpretations proposed by earlier editors.

c. Commentary

The commentary to the prose text focuses on points of interpretation of the literal meaning of the text. Throughout the text has been compared with *D*, *G* and with glosses to these two texts (*Dg* and *Gg*). Ólsen showed conclusively that the author of *FoGT* used such glosses when he created his text. The exact set(s) of glosses the author had access to has not been determined, but a perusal of various glossed texts of *D*, Grondeux's study of glosses on *G* (2000) and her 2010 edition of such a set of glosses (*Gg*) have shown that while the contents of the glosses and the amount of glossing vary from text to text, other elements—in particular core examples of the various figures—remain stable from one text to another. It was found that the set of glosses that accompany *D* in a 1494 print from Venice by Manfredus de Bonellis was most helpful. This widespread set of glosses is ascribed to Ludovicus de Guaschis (see Reichling 1893, lxiii–xliv). Even though this gloss is younger than *FoGT*, comparison between the two texts shows that the gloss contains many features that were also present in the set of glosses on *D* to which the author of *FoGT* had access. Glosses on *G* (*Gg*) are drawn from Grondeux's edition which is primarily based on a fifteenth-century manuscript (Paris, BnF lat. 14746). The gloss contained in this manuscript is much more detailed than anything found in *FoGT*, but again some of its features were also present in the tradition to which the author of *FoGT* had access. To avoid unnecessary anachronisms, *Dg* and *Gg* are chiefly cited in those cases where they provide parallels to the material presented in *FoGT* and they primarily serve to show that the author of *FoGT* drew on a widespread and well-established tradition of glossing.

The wordlists and citations made available online by *A Dictionary of Old Norse Prose* (*ONP*) were very helpful when preparing the commentary.

7. Previous editions of *FoGT*

There have been five earlier editions of *FoGT*. The first was that of Rasmus Rask (1818) in his edition of *Snorra Edda* (*SnE* 1818, 335–53). Rask did not consider *FoGT* an independent text but a part of

Introduction   lxiii

TGT, entitled *Fígúrur í ræðunni*. The second edition was that of Sveinbjörn Egilsson from 1848 in *Edda Snorra Sturlusonar* (*SnE* 1848, 200–12), in which *FoGT* was entitled *Seinni viðbætir við málskrúðsfræðina* and the third the Arnamagnæan Commission's edition (*SnE* 1848–87 II 190–249; III 152–63), whose editor-in-chief was Jón Sigurðsson, but to which Sveinbjörn Egilsson contributed the facing Latin translation in Volume II (1852) and a number of Latin notes in Volume III (1880–87). In that edition *FoGT* is entitled *IV* (*Málskrúðsfræði*). The fourth edition and the best known (*FoGT* 1884) is by Björn Magnússon Ólsen, and this includes an Introduction, notes to the text and separate editions and interpretations of the stanzas. The fifth edition is the unpublished doctoral dissertation from the University of Palermo of Michele Longo (*FoGT* 2004), which includes an Italian translation and commentary on the text, including that of the poetry. Longo's edition is not, however, based on a fresh transcript of W, but uses *SnE* 1848–87 II as its base text for the most part. The stanzas have been edited separately from the prose text by Finnur Jónsson (*Skj* A II 163–67 and 214–19; *Skj* B II 180–85 and 231–36) and by E. A. Kock (*Skald* II 94–96 and 120–22).

SIGLA

7	Holm perg 7 4°
291	AM 291 4°
510	AM 510 4°
743^x	AM 743 4°^{x}
2368^x	GKS 2368 4°^{x}
A	AM 748 I b 4°
C	AM 748 II 4°
Flat	GKS 1005 fol
FskA^x	AM 303 4°^{x}
FskB^x	OsloUB 371 fol^x
H	AM 66 fol
Holm18	Holm perg 18 4°
Hr	GKS 1010 fol
Mork	GKS 1009 fol
R	GKS 2367 4°
T^x	Traj 1374^x
U	DG 11
W	AM 242 fol

THE FOURTH GRAMMATICAL TREATISE

1 PROTHESEOS PARALOGE verðr þá er önnur prepositio stendr þar er p. 111
önnur ætti viðkæmiliga að vera, svá sem Þorleifr kvað: l. 18

> Höfðu vier í þier, Hákon, (1)
> er að hjörþingi gingum,
> —þú rautt Sköglar skýja
> skóð—forvistu góða.

Hier er 'í' sett óviðkæmiliga svá sem þeir hefði í Hákoni forystu góða þá sem þeir höfðu af honum. Verðr og þessi fígúra hvervetna þar sem um fyrirsetning er skift.

2 LIPTOTA verðr á þrjár leiðir. Stundum merkir hon framar en skilning orðanna stendr til, sem Eiríkr viðsjá kvað:

> Styrr liet snart og Snorri (2)
> sverðþing háið verða,
> þar er geir-Nirðir gierðu
> Gíslungum hlut þungan.
> Enn var eigi minna
> ættskarð, það er hjó Barði.

Og skal svá skilja að það ættskarð er Barði gierði var meira en hitt er áðr er greint.

Stundum er liptota útþanning orðanna sú er alt merkir, þar er sumt er talið, sem hier:

> Sprungu eigi eingir (3)
> út ór—... sútir—
> bæjum, þvíað hyrr á hávar
> heitr giekk fira sveitir.

W **1** Protheseos] 'rotheseos' *W*   **3** Höfðu] *AW(103) begin* | í þier] *W A*, þá er *W(103)*   **4** hjörþingi] *W*, hjörrógi *A W(103)* | gingum] *W*, drógumz *A*, drógum *W(103)*   **6** forvistu] 'forostu' *W*, 'forustu' *W(103)*, 'forystu' *A* góða] *A W(103) end*   **7** óviðkæmiliga] viðkæmiliga *W*   **12** Styrr] *Holm18 begins* | snart] *W*, snarr *Holm18*   **13** háið] *Holm18*, 'haað' *W*   **14** geir-Nirðir] geirníðir *W*, gnýverðir *Holm18*   **15** Gíslungum] *W*, Gíslunga *Holm18*   **16** var] *W*, varð *Holm18* | minna] *W*, in minna *Holm18*   **17** ættskarð] *W*, eitt skarð *Holm18* | Barði] *Holm18 ends*   **22** eingir] eingar *W*   **23** ...] *empty space in W*   **24** hávar] 'havvi' *W*   **25** sveitir] sveiti *W*

1 PROTHESEOS PARALANGE occurs when one preposition is used where another would have been appropriate, as Þorleifr said:

(1) We had good leadership in you, Hákon, when we went to the sword-assembly [BATTLE]; you reddened the harmer of the clouds of Skögul ‹valkyrie› [SHIELDS > SWORD].

Here 'in' is used inappropriately, as if they had the good leadership in Hákon which they had from him. This figure also occurs whenever the preposition is changed.

2 LIPTOTA occurs in three ways. At times it signifies more than the meaning of the words implies, as Eiríkr viðsjá said:

(2) Styrr and Snorri caused a swift sword-assembly [BATTLE] to be fought, where the spear-Nirðir ‹gods› [WARRIORS] made the lot of the Gíslungar heavy. Yet the notch in the family, that Barði cut, was not smaller.

And this is to be understood in such a way that the notch Barði hewed in the family was greater than the other which is mentioned earlier.

Sometimes *liptota* is a stretching out of the words in order to signify the whole, when a part is mentioned, as here:

(3) Not none [= very many] ran out from the farmsteads, because hot fire spread towards the distinguished groups of men; ... sorrows.

---

1 Vier höfðu[m] góða forvistu í þier, Hákon, er gingum að hjörþingi; þú rautt skóð skýja Sköglar.
2 Styrr og Snorri liet[u] snart sverðþing verða háið, þar er geir-Nirðir gierðu Gíslungum þungan hlut. Enn ættskarð, það er Barði hjó, var eigi minna.
3 Eigi eingir runnu út ór bæjum, þvíað heitr hyrr giekk á hávar sveitir fira; ... sútir.

Hier er sagt að eigi eingir menn rynni af bæjum þar sem allir *runnu*. Sumstaðar merkir 'eigi eingi' 'nökkurn' eða 'mikinn', sem hier:

    Fingr vann eigi eingan   (4)
    eins með vatni hreinu
    Guðs á virðum víða
    vinning að því sinni.

Hier er 'eigi eingi' settr fyrir 'nökkurum' eða 'miklum vinningi'. Stundum standa tvær neitingar fyrir einni játan, sem hier:

    Eg veit, að ní neitar   (5)
    Nytju l*o*gs, því er flytja
    meiðar geirþings...
    Gunnr, fjarðloga runni.

Hier segir skáldið að konan sú er manni játaðiz fyrir flutning förunauta sinna neitaði ní.

3 TOPHOGRAPHIA | er það ef skáldið segir frá stað þeim er tíðendin   p. 112
gierðuz, þau er hann vill frá segja, sem hier:

    F*i*rð stóð í bygð bre*i*ðri   (6)
    borg Pátera sorgum,
    mest áðr lýðr, frá losta
    l*í*t gættr, í bý fættiz.

Hennar f*ó*stsystir er BETHGRAPHIA er frá húsi er sagt:

    Leygs svelgr, en etr eigi,   (7)
    íugtanni lið manna;
    ganga m*e*nn ór mun*n*i
    margreftum fletvargi.

Hier talar skáldið af smíð hússins.

W **1** runnu] rynni *W*   **10** logs] 'l*o*gs' *W*   **11** ...] *a word appears to be missing in* *W*   **17** Firð] Frið *W* | breiðri] 'breðri' *W*   **20** lítt] 'lut' *W*   **21** fóstsystir] 'f[...]stsyst*i*r' *W*   **24** menn] 'm[...]n' *W* | munni] 'mun[...]' *W*

4 Fingr eins Guðs vann víða að því sinni eigi eingan vinning á virðum með hreinu vatni.

Here it is said that not no men ran from the farmsteads, whereas all were running.

In some places 'not none' denotes 'some' or 'great', as here:

(4)   The finger of the one God gained widely at that time not one [= great] advantage for men with pure water.

Here 'not none' is used instead of 'some' or 'a great advantage'. At times two negations replace one affirmation, as here:

(5)   I know that the Gunnr ‹valkyrie› of the flame of Nytja ‹river› [GOLD > WOMAN] does not deny to the bush of the fjord-flame [GOLD > MAN] that for which the . . . trees of the spear-assembly [BATTLE > WARRIORS] plead.

Here the poet says that the woman, who consented to the man on account of the pleading of his companions, did not say no.

3 TOPOGRAPHIA is when the poet mentions the place where the events occurred that he wants to describe, as here:

(6)   The city of Patara stood in a broad settlement, removed from sorrows, until the people, not at all guarded against lust, diminished greatly in the town.

Her foster-sister is BETHGRAPHIA, when a house is described:

(7)   The bear of the [hearth-]flame [HOUSE] swallows, but does not eat, the band of men; men issue from the mouth of the many-raftered bench-wolf [HOUSE].

Here the poet speaks about the structure of the house.

5 Eg veit, að Gunnr l*o*gs Nytju neitar ní runni fjarðloga því er ... meiðar geirþings flytja.
6 Páteraborg stóð í brei*ð*ri bygð, fi*r*ð sorgum, áðr lýðr, l*í*tt gættr frá losta, fættiz mest í bý.
7 Íugtanni leygs svelgr, en etr eigi, lið manna; m*e*nn ganga ór mun*n*i margreftum fletvargi.

COSMOGRAPHIA er það er skáldið segir frá heimsins skipan, skapan, stöðu eða hætti eða setningu, sem hier:

Allr lýtr *h*eimr undir hylli (8)
heilags friðar deilis.

5   CRONOGRAPHIA er það ef sagt er á hverjum tíma tíðendin gierðuz, þau
er hann vill frá segja, sem *hier*:

Sjálfráði dó síðan (9)
sólar fróns að nóni,
sá er hiekk, en dag dökkti,
10 döglingr, á jarnnöglum.

Svá er og in sama fígúra þó að skáldið segi hvað samtíða er eða hverir höfðingjar löndum stýra, sem hier:

Hákon rieð fyr hauðri (10)
handsterkr, þ*a*r er Guð merkti
15 refsiþátt inn rietta
rangri þjóð a*ð* angri.
Laust með elding æstri
alvirkr höfuðkirkju
himnagarðs *að* hjörðum
20 hirðir glæpsku firðum.

4 YPALLAGE verðr það er sá er kallaðr þolandi sem að riettu er gierandi, eða sá gierandi sem að riettu er þolandi, sem hier:

Framan unnu gram gunnar (11)
†grafins seiðs† framir meiðar;
25 biðu Jótar lið ljótan
lagagangs daga strangra.
Lofag sjaldan hóf haldið;
hataz dygð, *rataz lygðir;

W **3** heimr] '[. . .]imr' *or* '[. . .]nnr' *W* **6** hier] *add.* **14** þar] 'þ[. . .]r' *W*
16 að] af *W* **19** að] og *W* **28** rataz] hrataz *W*

8 Allr *h*eimr lýtr undir hylli heilags deilis friðar.
9 Döglingr fróns sólar, sá er hiekk á jarnnöglum, dó síðan sjálfráði að nóni, en dag dökkti.

COSMOGRAPHIA is when the poet speaks about the order of the world, its creation, state or nature or design, as here:

(8) The whole world bows before the grace of the holy distributor of salvation [= God].

CHRONOGRAPHIA is if it is specified at what time the events occurred that he wants to describe, as here:

(9) The king of the land of the sun [SKY/HEAVEN > = God (= Christ)], who hung on iron nails, then died of his own volition at nones, and the day grew dark.

It is also the same figure when the poet tells what is contemporaneous or which chieftains rule the lands, as here:

(10) Strong-handed Hákon ruled over the land where God showed the just law of punishment to the distress of the sinful people. The shepherd of the heavens' stronghold [= God], most careful for the flocks freed from sin, struck the cathedral [lit. head church] with raging lightning.

4 HYPALLAGE occurs when he is called passive who is in fact active, or he [is called] active who is in fact passive, as here:

(11) The trees of the †seiðs grafins† [GOLD? > MEN], outstanding in [lit. of] battle, overcame the prominent prince; the Jótar (Jutlanders) experienced an ugly situation of legal proceedings during harsh times. I seldom praise moderation preserved; virtue is destroyed, lies are

10 Handsterkr Hákon rieð fyr hauðri, þar er Guð merkti inn rietta refsiþátt að angri rangri þjóð. Hirðir himnagarðs, alvirkr að hjörðum firðum glæpsku, laust höfuðkirkju með elding æstri.
11 Meiðar †seiðs grafins†, framir gunnar, unnu framan gram; Jótar biðu ljótan lið lagagangs strangra daga. Lofag sjaldan haldið hóf; dygð hataz, lygðir *rataz; megindjarfir valdar tregs vegs halda veginn arf.

tregs halda vegs valdar
veginn arf megindjarfir.

Hier er arfrinn veginn kallaðr, sá er maðr var frá veginn sá er með
riettu hielt, er þeir tóku er hann drápu. Og í öðrum stað er sama fígúra:

5 Mari sendu vers vinda (12)
 veitendr Góins leita.

Hier er sagt að vindarnir væri sendir skipinu þar sem að riettu var
skipið sent vindunum; það er að skilja: út sett í þeirra vald eða stjórn.
Og í öðrum stað segiz svá:

10 Blies um hváfta hása (13)
 höfuðskrípamanns pípa.

Hier er pípan kölluð blása, sú sem í var blásið, og þykkir hon jafnan
ljót fígúra, þó að hon finniz í skáldskap sett fyrir sakir skrúðs eða
nauðsynja.

15 **5 PROSOPOPHIA** er ísetning nýrrar persónu og verðr á þrjár leiðir. Sú er
in fyrsta ef skáldið segir að lífligr hlutr tali til líflauss hlutar, sem hier:

 Grund, taktu, bölvi blandin, (14)
 bót fyr glæpsku ljóta!
 Þier mun óhlýðni ærin,
20 Ísland, búa p*ís*lir!
 Þú mátt ófrið óttaz,
 óþýð*, nema vel hlýðið,
 fold, þeim er sverðum sjaldan
 —siðir breytiz hier—neyta.

25 Hier talar skáldið nefndri fígúru, eggjandi undirmenn að hlýða vel
forstjórum sínum og nefnir landið í stað þeirra er þa*ð* byggja.
 Frá líflausum til lífligs hlutar, sem hier:

W **20** píslir] 'p[...]lir' *W* **22** óþýð] óþýðr *W* **26** það] þau *W*
12 Veitendr leita Góins sendu vinda mari vers.
13 Höfuðskrípamanns pípa blies um hása hváfta.

abroad; the very bold possessors of slow honour [CONTEMPTIBLE MEN] keep hold of the slain [man's] inheritance.

Here the inheritance—which was taken from the slain man who rightfully owned it by those who killed him—is called slain. The same figure is found another place:

(12) The givers of the mound of Góinn <snake> [GOLD > GENEROUS MEN] sent winds to the horse of the sea [SHIP].

Here it is said that the winds were sent to the ship, when the ship was actually sent to the winds; viz. placed under their power or rule. And in another place it is said thus:

(13) The lead minstrel's flute blew across hoarse cheeks.

Here the flute which was blown into is said to blow, and this always seems an unattractive figure, even though it is found in poetry for the sake of ornament or necessities.

5 PROSOPOPOEIA is the insertion of a new person, and it occurs in three ways. The first is when the poet says that something living is speaking to something lifeless, as here:

(14) Country, imbued [lit. mixed] with evil, do penance for [your] ugly sin! Iceland, great [lit. sufficient] disobedience will lay punishments in store for you! You can fear hostility, rough land, unless you obey well those who seldom use swords; may morals here change!

Here the poet speaks using the above-mentioned figure, exhorting subjects to obey their rulers fully, and names the land instead of those who inhabit it.

When something lifeless speaks to something living, as here:

---

14 Grund, blandin bölvi, tak bót fyr ljóta glæpsku! Ísland, ærin óhlýðni mun búa þier píslir! Þú mátt óttaz ófrið, óþýð* fold, nema hlýðið vel, þeim er sjaldan neyta sverðum; siðir breytiz hier.

Vatn kalla mig (15)
—vil eg efla þig,
hoddveitir—frams
hauðrfjörnis grams:
5   eg hreinsa alt,
eg vermi kalt,
eg birti sjón,
eg bæti tjón.

Hier er sagt að Ölmusugjöfin kalli sig vatn Krists og telr upp dygðir
10 sínar, eggjandi manninn til mildinnar, þvíað svá sem vatnið slökkvir
líkamligan eld, slíkt ið sama slökkvir ölmusan syndabruna og þvær á
þá leið sál sem vatnið búkinn.
Frá líflausum hlut verðr prosopophia til líflauss hlutar sem segir í
Barruk, að sjór og skógr bjugguz í grend, og vildi hvárr annan upp
15 taka. Af því hljóp sandr í sjóinn og eyddi svá hans yfirgang, en logi
brendi upp allan skóginn. | Hier er svá um kveðið: p. 113

Grænn kvað viðr á víði (16)
—varð skrjúpr í því—djúpan:
'Út man eg rýma [. . .]
20 ríkis míns af þínu;
betr samir bolr með skrauti
blóms en unnir tómar;
skóg man *eg u*pp yfir ægi
angrlestan rótfesta.'

25 Vátr kvað marr á móti: (17)
'Man eg vald yfir þier halda;
skal hrís um lög ljósan
—lamið rót er þá—fljóta.'
Sandr luktaði sundum,
30 sjór fekk af stað ekki,
en sterk*r* um b*o*l bjarkar
bani hvess viðar gandi.

W 3 hoddveitir] *corrected in W from* hold- *to* hodd- 19 . . .] *hole in W* 23 eg
upp] '[. . .]pp' *W* 31 sterkr] sterk *W* | bol] 'bǫl' *W*

15 Kalla mig vatn frams grams hauðrfjörnis; eg vil efla þig, hoddveitir: eg
hreinsa alt, eg vermi kalt, eg birti sjón, eg bæti tjón.
16 Grænn viðr kvað á djúpan víði—varð skrjúpr í því—: 'eg man rýma út ...

(15) I call myself water of the outstanding king of the earth-helmet [SKY/HEAVEN > = God (= Christ)]; I want to strengthen you, gold-giver [GENEROUS MAN]: I cleanse everything, I warm what is cold, I brighten vision, I repair loss.

Here it is said that Alms-giving calls herself the water of Christ, and enumerates her virtues, urging the man to generosity, because, just as the water quenches bodily fire, in the same way alms quench the fire of sins and wash the soul in the same way as water washes the body.

Prosopopoeia occurs when something lifeless speaks to another lifeless thing, as it says in Baruch, that the sea and the forest lived close by one another and each wanted to take over the other. For that reason sand rushed into the sea and thus put an end to its transgression, while fire burnt up all the forest. Here this is referred to thus:

(16) The green wood said to the deep sea—in that it was weak—: 'I want to expand the . . . of my kingdom from yours; a tree-trunk with ornament of blossom looks better than empty waves; I will fasten a forest by its roots up over the sorrow-damaged ocean.'

(17) The wet sea spoke in reply: 'I will keep power over you, brushwood will float upon the shining sea; the root will then be smashed.' Sand blocked channels, the sea got nothing of the land [lit. place], but the strong killer of every tree [FIRE] gaped around the birch tree's trunk.

ríkis míns af þínu; bolr með skrauti blóms samir betr en tómar unnir; *eg* man rótfesta skóg *u*pp yfir angrlestan ægi'.
17 Vátr marr kvað á móti: 'eg man halda vald yfir þier; hrís skal fljóta um ljósan lög; rót er þá lamið'. Sandr luktaði sundum, sjór fekk ekki af stað, en sterk*r* bani hvess viðar gandi um b*o*l bjarkar.

Skógr merkir júða, en sjór chaldeos. Þjóðir þær sem eyddu ríki chaldeorum merkja sand, en guðspjallig *kienning* eldinn, sú er í stað kom lögmáls júða.

6 APOSTROPHA er sú fígúra ef maðr talar til fráveranda manns svá sem við hjáveranda mann og setr sitt nafn í fyrstu skilningu að riettu, en þess í annarri er hann talar til. En þó finnz öðruvís giert, sem Snorri kvað:

Eyjólfi ber þú, elfar (18)
úlfseðjandi, kveðju
heim, þá er honum sómi
heyra bezt með eyrum,
þvíað skilmildra skálda
skörungmann lofag örvan;
hann lifi sælstr und sólu
sannauðigra manna.

Þessi Eyjólfr var Brúna sonr, skáld einkar gott og búþegn góðr, en eigi fieríkr. Sama fígúra er og ef maðr talar til heilagra manna sem Óláfr kvað:

Þier fremiz þí með tíri (19)
þú ert næst Guði hæstum.

Og í öðrum stað:

Teitr giefr, Thómas, ýtum (20)
trúarbót fyr sið ljótan.

Er þessi fígúra *jafnan sett í briefum er menn sendaz í millum eða þeim prologis bóka er einhverjum eru ætlaðar til riettingar eða framburðar.

7 ENDIADIS er sú fígúra er tveir sundrlausir hlutir eru merktir fyrir einn óskiftiligan hlut, eða einn óskiftiligr hlutr er settr fyrir tveim

---

W 2 kienning] *add.* 24 jafnan] er jafnan *W* 27 er[2]] 'en*n*' *W*
18 Úlfseðjandi elfar, ber þú Eyjólfi kveðju heim, þá er sómi honum bezt heyra

The forest signifies the Jews, and the sea the Chaldeans. The peoples who destroyed the kingdom of the Chaldeans signify the sand while the evangelical teaching, which supplanted the law of the Jews, signifies the fire.

6 APOSTROPHA is that figure by which one addresses an absent person as if to someone present, and rightly uses one's own 'name' in the first person, and the 'name' of the person one speaks to in the second. Yet it can also be found in a different way, as Snorri said:

(18) Feeder of the wolf of the river [lit. 'wolf-feeder of the river'] [SHIP > SEAFARER], carry home [my] greeting to Eyjólfr, which it befits him best to hear with [his own] ears, since I praise the energetic leader of poets, generous with knowledge; may he live the happiest of truly rich men under the sun.

This Eyjólfr was the son of Brúni, an exceptionally good poet and a good farmer, although not a wealthy one. It is also the same figure if one addresses saints, as Óláfr said:

(19) Thus you gain distinction with glory, you are nearest to God the highest.

And in another place:

(20) Cheerful Thomas, you give to men the remedy of faith instead of ugly custom.

This figure is always used in letters exchanged by people and in those prologues of books which are destined for correction or publication by someone.

7 HENDIADYS is that figure where two separate entities signify one indivisible entity, or one indivisible entity is used for two divisible

með eyrum, því að lofag örvan skörungmann skilmildra skálda; lifi hann sælstr
sannauðigra manna und sólu.
19 Því fremiz þier með tíri, þú ert næst Guði hæstum.
20 Teitr Thómas giefr ýtum trúarbót fyr sið ljótan.

skiftiligum hlutum, og er hon undir dregin samfesting laussa hluta og leysing fastra hluta, sem hier:

 Ská*l*m vann *og* hjalt hilmi   (21)
 hoddbeiðöndum reiðan.

Hier er óskiftiligr hlutr, sverðið, merkt fyrir skálm og hjalt, *sundrlausa hluti. Og enn segir svá:

 Þýddiz karl inn klædda   (22)
 kona mín og þörf sína;
 eg sá karl og klæði
 koma inn í því sinni.

Hier er klæddr maðr settr fyrir sjálfum sier og þeim klæðum er hann gaf konunni að fá sinn vilja, og í annað sinn er sagt að sierhvárt kom inn, karl og klæði, þar sem klæddr maðr kom inn, og heitir sú endiadis sundrlaus er fastir hlutir eru settir í stað laussa hluta. En sú endiadis heitir samföst er lausir hlutir eru settir í stað fastra hluta, svá sem hier má skilja á þessum dæmum, er hier standa áðr ritin.

8 EBASIS er afganga efnisins þá er skáldið reikar afvegis, sem Bragi skáld gierði þá er hann setti í þá drápu er hann orti um Ragnar konung, þær vísur er segja um fall Sörla og Ha*m*dis, sona Jónakrs konungs og Guðrúnar Gjúkadóttur, er þeir fellu fyrir mönnum Erminreks konungs, og er sjá vísa ein af þeim:

 Knátti eðr við illan   (23)
 Erminrekr að vakna
 með dreyrfáar dróttir
 draum í sverða flaumi.
 Rósta varð í ranni
 Randvies höfuðniðja,

W **3** Skálm] 'Ska*m*m' *W* | og] ef *W* **5** sundrlausa] 'sundr|sundr lausa' *W*
19 Hamdis] 'hanðis' *W* **22** Knátti] *R Tˣ C begin* | Knátti *R Tˣ C*, 'Knatt' *W* eðr] *R Tˣ*, ørr *W*, áðr *C* **23** Erminrekr] *W*, 'iormvnreckr' *R*, 'Jormunrecr' *Tˣ*, 'ermenrekr' *C* **24** dreyrfáar] *W*, 'dreyrfar' *R C*, 'dreurfar' *Tˣ* | dróttir] *W R Tˣ*, dottur *C* **26** Rósta] *W R Tˣ*, róstu *C* | varð] *W R Tˣ*, vann *C* **27** Randvies] *W R Tˣ*, Randvérs *C*

21 Ská*l*m *og* hjalt vann hilmi reiðan hoddbeiðöndum.

entities, and it is governed by the conjoining of loose entities and the loosening of joined entities, as here:

(21) Point and hilt made the ruler angry with the gold-requesters [MEN].

Here an indivisible entity, the sword, is signified by point and hilt, separate entities. And further it says:

(22) My wife gave in to the clothed man and his desire; I saw man and clothes come in at the [same] time.

Here a clothed man is mentioned instead of himself and the clothes which he gave to the woman in order to obtain his desire, and in the second place it is said that each of the two, man and clothes, came in when a clothed man came in, and that *hendiadys* is called 'separate' where joined entities are used instead of loose entities. But that *hendiadys* is called 'conjoined' where loose entities are used instead of joined entities, such as one can observe in the examples that are written above.

8 EBASIS is a departure from the subject matter, when the poet drifts off course, as Bragi the poet did in the *drápa* he composed about King Ragnarr when he inserted those stanzas that tell about the fall of Sǫrli and Hamðir, the sons of King Jónakr and Guðrún Gjúkadóttir, when they fell before the men of King Erminrekr, and this stanza is one of those:

(23) Erminrekr then awakened with an evil dream among the blood-stained troops in the eddy of swords [BATTLE]. There was tumult in the hall of the chief kinsmen of Randvér [= the dynasty of the Goths], when the raven-

---

22 Kona mín þýddiz inn klædda karl og þörf sína; eg sá karl og klæði koma inn í því sinni.
23 Erminrekr knátti eðr að vakna við illan draum með dreyrfáar dróttir í sverða flaumi. Rósta varð í ranni höfuðniðja Randvies, þá er hrafnbláir of barmar Erps hefndu harma.

þá er hrafnbláir hefndu
harma Erps of barmar.

Stundum verðr ebasis þá er skáldið tekr stef af öðru efni en kvæðið er,
sem *í* Nikulásdrápu er stefið er af guðligri þrenningu, sem hier:

5   Öll þing boða eingla (24)
    eining í þrenningu,
    órofnuðu jafnan
    alls grams l*o*fi framda.

    Stundum verðr ebasis af því að skáldið tekr dæmi þeim hlutum sem
10 hann vill frægja eða ófrægja af öðrum frásögnum, svá er og í sama
    kvæði Nicholao dæmi tekin | af inum sæla Johanne baptista að auka   p. 11
    hans virðing, sem í þessi vísu:

    Jón laut í höll hreinum (25)
    hjarta sals ins bjarta
15 meyjar mannvitsfrægrar
    mildingi bragninga.

Og leiðir skáldið *þar lof* Johannis svá til enda að þaðan af aukiz lof
heilags Nicholai. Slíkt ið sama má og þessi fígúra *verða í* lastmælum
að illr maðr er kallaðr annarr Júdás eða dæmi tekin til nökkurs ills
20 manns að auka hans níð.
    Eru þessir hlutir eða hættir ebasis—sá er Bragi lofaði frændr Áslaug-
ar í Ragnarsdrápu að hans virðing sýndiz meiri en áðr var hon, og hin*n*
að setja stef í jarteignakvæði heilagra manna af sjálfum Guði til þess
að sýna vinnara allra tákna og samvinnara sinna vina, svá og að birta
25 annan helgan mann með annars dæmum, eða lasta annan illan mann
    með annars illri endrminning—fyrir nauðsyn eða skynsemi skrauss

---

W R T^x C **1** hrafnbláir] *T^x C*, hrafnblám *W*, 'hrafnblarir' *R*   **2** of] *R T^x*, og *W*,
um *C* | barmar] *R T^x C*, barma *W* | *R T^x C end*   **4** í] *add.*   **8** lofi] 'l[. . .]fi' *W*
17 þar lof] 'þ[. . .]' *W*   **18** verða í] '[. . .]' *W*   **22** hinn] hin *W*
24 Öll þing eingla boða eining í þrenningu, jafnan framda órofnuðu l*o*fi grams

black brothers of Erpr [= Hamðir and Sǫrli] avenged [their] injuries.

At times *ebasis* occurs when the poet takes a refrain from another subject matter than the poem deals with, as in *Nikulásdrápa* where the refrain deals with the Holy Trinity, as here:

(24) All the assemblies of angels proclaim unity in Trinity, always worshipped with unbroken praise of the ruler of all [= God].

At times *ebasis* occurs when the poet takes examples illustrative of the things he wants to praise or blame from other narratives. Thus it also happens in the same poem to Nicholas that examples are drawn from [the life of] the blessed John the Baptist in order to increase his [Nicholas's] reputation, as in this stanza:

(25) John bowed to the pure generous prince of princes [= God (= Christ)] in the hall of the bright chamber of the heart [BREAST > WOMB] of the maiden famous of understanding.

And the poet there concludes the praise of John in such a way that the honour of the holy Nicholas is increased thereby. In a similar manner this figure can also occur in defamations so that an evil man is called another Judas, or examples are taken from some evil man in order to increase his disgrace.

These parts or forms of *ebasis*—the one in which Bragi praised the relatives of Áslaug in *Ragnarsdrápa* so that his [Ragnarr's] honour should appear greater than before, and the other one, the use of a refrain about God himself in a poem about the miracles of holy men in order to show the maker of all signs and the helper of his friends, and in the same manner to throw light on one holy man through the examples of another, or to criticise one evil man through the unsavoury recollection of another—are surely allowed for reasons of

alls.
25 Jón laut hreinum mildingi bragna í höll ins bjarta sals hjarta mannvitsfrægrar meyjar.

eða lastmælis vel leyfilig*ir*, en ónýt*ar efnisafgaungur eru með öllu flýjandi.

9 EMPHASIS setr undirstaðligan hlut fyrir hræriligum hlut sem þá er vier merkjum nökkuð tilfelli mannsins fyrir sjálfum honum, sem að nefna glæpinn fyrir glæpamanninum eða vizkuna fyrir vitringinum, og geingr þessi fígúra um alla þessa vísu:

> Píndr er stuldr, þar er standa (26)
> stafnreiðar hímleið*ir*
> víða vingameið*i*,
> viðir hjá torgi miðju.
> Morð eru hjólum hörðum
> hegnd, þau er illa giegndu,
> þar er riett vísar ræsir
> rómsæl*l* skipun dóma.

Hier er stuldrinn kallaðr píndr og morðin hegnd, þar sem morðinginn er hegndr og þjófrinn.

Sumir menn kalla emphasen það er vápn*ið* er kallað með því verki sem af því gieriz, sem Þorleifr kvað:

> Hef eg í hendi, (27)
> til höfuðs gierva,
> beinbrot Búa,
> böl Sigvalda,
> vá víkinga,
> vörn Hákonar;
> sjá skal verða,
> ef vier lifum,
> eikikylfa
> óþörf Dönum.

Hier er kylfan kiend eða merkt með þeim tilfellum sem af henni máttu gieraz, og hefir ymsar líkingar í einni vísu, og kallar Óláfr það

W **1** leyfiligir] leyfiligra *W* | ónýtar] ónýtrar *W* **8** hímleiðir] hímleiða *W*
9 vingameiði] vingameiðar *W* **14** rómsæll] rómsæl *W* **17** vapnið] 'vapn*in*'
W **19** Hef] *291 7 Flat 510 FskB^x FskA^x begin* | Hef eg] *all others,* hefir *W*
25 verða] *W Flat 510,* vera *291 FskB^x FskA^x* **26** ef] *all others,* er *FskB^x*
27 eikikylfa] *291 7 Flat,* eikikylfan *W 510,* eikiklubba *FskB^x,* alriklubba *FskA^x*
28 Dönum] *291 7 Flat 510 FskB^x FskA^x end*

necessity or of ornament or blame, but useless departures from the subject matter are to be avoided at all costs.

9 EMPHASIS uses a substantive entity instead of a moveable entity, as when we signify some accidental quality of a man instead of the man himself, such as mentioning the crime instead of the criminal, or wisdom instead of the wise man, and this figure is seen throughout this stanza:

(26) Theft is punished by the windswept tree, where universally loathed trees of the prow-chariot [SHIP > SEAFARERS] stand in many places near the middle of the market-place. Murders, which were bad, are chastised by hard wheels, where the praised [lit. applause-fortunate] ruler carries out correctly the order of the courts.

Here the theft is said to be punished and the murders chastised, whereas the murderer is chastised and the thief.

Some men call it *emphasis* when the weapon is referred to by the deed which is carried out by it, as Þorleifr said:

(27) He has in his hand, ready for a head, the bone-breaker of Búi, the ruin of Sigvaldi, the woe of vikings, the defence of Hákon; this oaken club shall prove unhelpful to the Danes, if we [I] live.

Here the club is designated or signified by the occurrences which might be effected by it, and it has various comparisons in one stanza, and Óláfr calls it *finngalknað* when comparisons of one entity are

---

26 Stuldr er píndr vingameiði, þar er hímleiðir viðir stafnreiðar standa víða hjá miðju torgi. Morð, þau er giegndu illa, eru hegnd hörðum hjólum, þar er rómsæll ræsir vísar riett skipun dóma.
27 Eg hef í hendi, gierva til höfuðs, beinbrot Búa, böl Sigvalda, vá víkinga, vörn Hákonar; sjá eikikylfa skal verða óþörf Dönum, ef vier lifum.

finngalknað er líkum er skift á einum hlut í inni sömu vísu, og berr bezt að inn sami háttr sie haldinn um alla vísu, allra helzt *í* einstaka vísum, en eigi hæfir sá háttr í stórkvæðum.

10 EXFLEXIGESIS er skýring eða glöggvari greining fyrirfarandi hluta, sem Eilífr kvað:

Báru mæta móti (28)
málmþings viðir pálma
(sveit hrauð) seggja bæti
(sorg), er hann kom til borgar.
Svá laðar siklingr skýja
síns hjarta til bjart*a*,
þá er fyrða gram færa
fögr verk með trú sterkri.

Er þessi fígúra kölluð af alþýðu GLÓSA, og er sú grein þar í millum að þessi fígúra exflexigesis glósar eða skýrir sanna frásögn, svá sem inn ágæti Salomon merkir Várn Herra, en musterið heilaga kristni.
En ICONA setr fram tvá hluti af líku efni.
En PARABOLA setr fram ólíka hluti svá sem það að kalla þenna heim akr, þyrn auðæfin, fuglana djöfla með líking, en ei með sannleik.
PARADIGMA dregr saman lík dæmi og skýrir hon sjálf það er hon talar áðr með fígúru og eiginligri undirstöðu.
Exflexigesis hefir fleiri kynkvíslir í látínu, þvíað hon skýrir eigi að eins um liðna hluti, heldr og eftirkomandi hluti, sem í bók Boetii, en eigi finn eg það í norrænuskáldskap.

11 EUPHONIA er gagnstaðlig CATENPHATON, og verðr hon á margar leiðir, þvíað hvervetna þar sem catenphaton er | flýið fyrir skynsemi að p. 11 forðaz ljótt atkvæði, þá geingr þar inn euphonia, og standa þær greinir full*gierla fr*ammi þar sem fyrrnefnd fígúra er fram sett. Óláfr segir og: Euphonia verðr þar sem *ófagrir lí*mingarstafir eru skiftir í þá stafi sem fegra hljóða, sem í þessum nöfnum: lækr og ægr, þvíað 'æ' þykkir

---

W   2 í] add.   6 mæta] mæt á W   11 bjarta] bjartir W   12 þá] 'þeir' W
28   fullgierla frammi] 'full[. . .]a*mm*i' W   29 ófagrir límingarstafir] '[. . .]min*g*ar stafìr' W

changed in the same stanza, and it is most appropriate that the same comparison is kept throughout the stanza, especially in single stanzas, but this way of doing it is unfitting for grand poems.

10 EFFLEXEGESIS is the explanation or clearer exposition of previous things, as Eilífr said:

(28) Trees of the weapon-meeting [BATTLE > WARRIORS] carried glorious palms to meet the curer of men [= God (= Christ)], when he came to the city; the company banished sorrow. Thus the prince of the clouds [= God (= Christ)] invites pure [men] to his heart, those who bring the ruler of men [= God (= Christ)] beautiful deeds with strong faith.

This figure is commonly called GLÓSA, and the distinction between them is that this figure, *efflexegesis*, glosses or explains a true account, just as the illustrious Solomon signifies Our Lord, and the temple [signifies] holy Christianity.

And ICON puts forward two entities of the same material.

And PARABOLA puts forward dissimilar entities, such as calling this world a field, richness a thorn, devils birds in a simile, but not in truth.

PARADIGMA collects similar examples and explains itself what it says previously with a figure and with its true meaning.

Efflexegesis has more branches in Latin because it explains not only past things, but also future things, like in the book of Boethius, but I do not find this in Norse poetry.

11 EUPHONIA is the opposite of CACENPHATON, and it occurs in many ways, because wherever *cacenphaton* is avoided in order to steer clear of an impleasing pronunciation, *euphonia* enters, and these distinctions are described clearly above where the aforementioned figure is described. Óláfr also says: *Euphonia* occurs wherever unpleasing conjoined characters are changed into those letters that sound more beautiful, as in these nouns: 'lækr' [*løkr*] and 'ægr' [*ǿgr*], because 'æ'

---

28 Viðir málmþings báru mæta pálma móti bæti seggja, er hann kom til borgar; sveit hrauð sorg. Svá laðar siklingr skýja bjart*a* til hjarta síns, þá er færa gram fyrða fögr verk með sterkri trú.

hvervetna lýta mál, nema þar sem skynsemi má fyrir gjalda að þau orð sem það stendr í, dreifaz af þeim orðum sem 'á' stendr í, sem hier segir:

  Því veldr ár, að ærir (29)
  akr búmanna spakra;
  æra verðr með árum
  undan dólga fundi;
  ræða geingr af ráða
  runa syst*i*r ólystug;
  órar dregr að ærum
  ýtum skiemda flýtir.

Og enn segir svá:

  Æli telz, það er ólu (30)
  ósnotran mann gotnar;
  ælir vatn, þ*ar* er álar
  allstrangir fram hallaz;
  heitir †lær† á †læru†,
  læringar kienningar;
  kallaz mærr á Mæri,
  mæring, ef gjöf tæriz.

  Hætta verðr á hættu, (31)
  hæting ef böl rætir;
  ást er nær að næra,
  nú er vær konan færi;
  skeind tekr æðrin æðaz,
  æðr deyr, þá er br[. . .]

12 Lepos er það ef rík persóna er merkt með margfaldri tölu, og er það þá kurteisi ef sá hefir ráðuneyti er til er talað, sem Arnórr kvað:

W **2** það] þar *W* | á] 'áá' *W* **9** systir] systur *W* **13** Æli] 'Øli' *W* **15** þar] '*þat*' *W* **19** mærr] 'męr' *W* **25** æðrin] æðr enn *W* **26** br. . .] *hole in W*

29 Ár veldr því, að akr spakra búmanna ærir; verðr æra með árum undan fundi dólga; ræða syst*i*r runa geingr ólystug af ráða; flýtir skiemda dregr órar að ærum ýtum.

is thought everywhere to blemish speech, except where reason may explain that those words in which that sound is found are derived from those words which contain 'á', as it says here:

(29) [Year's] abundance is the reason that the field of wise farmers gives a good crop; one has to row with oars to avoid [lit. away from] a meeting with enemies; the sister of the boar [SOW] on heat goes unwilling from the hog; the breeder of shameful deeds [DEVIL] causes fits of madness to crazy men.

And further it says:

(30) He is considered a wretch, whom men brought up as an unwise man; water causes dredging, where very strong channels incline forwards; †lær† is named from †læra†, lessons [are called] instructions, it is called *mærr* in Møre, a prestation if a gift is given.

(31) To take risks leads to danger, if threatening plants misfortune; it is better to nourish love, now placid women are [lit. is] fewer; the scratched vein begins to become angry, the eider duck dies when . . .

12 LEPOS is when a powerful person is signified with the plural number, and this is courteous if the one who is addressed has a body of counsellors, as Arnórr said:

30 Telz æli, það er gotnar ólu ósnotran mann; ælir vatn, þar er allstrangir álar hallaz fram; †lær† heitir á †læru†, kienningar læringar, kallaz mærr á Mæri, mæring, ef gjöf tæriz.
31 Hætta verðr á hættu, ef hæting rætir böl; nær er að næra ást, nú er vær konan færi; skeind æðrin tekr æðaz, æðr deyr þá er br ...

Yppa ráðumz yðru kappi, (32)
Jóta gramr, í kvæði fljótu.

Hier er konungsins persóna margfölduð, en ekki heyrir það að tala svá til óbreyttra manna, og ef öðruvís er giert, þá verðr það soluecismus, sem fyrr segir.

13 ANTITOSIS er umskifti talna eða falla og tíma með settu endimarki. Um fallaskifti sem hier:

'Þá, er eg leyfi mey mjóva, (33)
mær er þín, fyr vild sína:'
Hörn mælti það horna
hjörþings við bör kringinn.

Hier er rægiligt fall sett fyrir nefniligu falli.
Um talnaskifti verðr antitosis sem hier:

Sveit fylla ein alla (34)
alls framm jóa Glamma.

Hier stendr þetta nafn 'sveit' sem margfalt nafn stýrt af margföldu orði 'fylla'.

Um tímaskifti standa nóg dæmi í Soluecismo, en ekki er nýjum skáldum fallið að líkja eftir slíkum hlutum, er til þess eru að eins sett að skilja fornskálda verka.

14 ANTITETON verðr ef in síðustu orð svara inum fyrstum, og verðr hon á svá margar leiðir sem orðum fær skift í vísu svá að regla sie haldin undir riettri kveðandi, og standa þessir hættir mest í því sem stælt er kveðið eða langlokum, sem hier:

W **1** Yppa] C W(103) Mork Flat H Hr begin | ráðumz] A W(103) Mork H Hr, ráðum W, 'raduzt' Flat **2** fljótu] all others, fljóta Flat | C W(103) Mork Flat H Hr end

32 Ráðumz yppa kappi yðru, gramr Jóta, í fljótu kvæði.
33 'Þá mjóva mey, er eg leyfi fyr vild sína, mær er þín:' Hörn horna mælti það

(32)   I mean to raise up your prowess, prince of the Jótar
[DANISH KING = Magnús], in a swift poem.

The person of the king is here pluralised, but it is unfitting to speak in this way to undistinguished men, and *solecismus* occurs if this is done, as is said above.

13 ANTITOSIS is the exchange of numbers or cases and tenses for a definite purpose.
Concerning the change of cases as here:

(33)   'That slim girl whom I praise for her good will, the girl is yours:' the Hǫrn ‹= Freyja› of drinking horns [WOMAN] said that to the smart tree of the sword assembly [BATTLE > WARRIOR].

Here the accusative case is used instead of the nominative case.
Concerning the change of numbers, *antitosis* occurs as here:

(34)   One detachment fills all the steeds of Glammi ‹sea-king› [SHIPS] all [the way] forwards.

Here this noun *sveit* [detachment] is used as a plural noun, governed by the plural verb *fylla* [fill].
Concerning the change of tenses, sufficient examples are found in *Soloecismus*, but it is not appropriate for new poets to imitate such things, which have only been explained so that one can understand the works of the ancient poets.

14 ANTITHETON occurs if the last words agree with the first, and it occurs in as many ways as it is possible to divide words in a stanza while the rules of metrical arrangement are observed. These variants are mainly found when the poem is equipped with inlay [*stál*] or late closures [*langlokur*], as here:

við kringinn bör hjörþings.
34 Ein sveit fylla alla jóa Glamma alls framm.

Hákon ræðr með heiðan (35)
(hefir dreingja vinr feingið)
—lönd verr buðlungr brandi
breiðfeld—(mikið veldi)
rógleiks náir ríki
remmi-Týr að stýra
—öld fagnar því—eignu;
orðróm konungdómi.

Hier giegnir þessi orð saman: 'Hákon ræðr konungdómi' er fyrst standa og síðast, og er þessi regla liettust af fyrrsagðri fígúru, er antiteton heitir. Sú er önnur hennar species ef máli lýkr á þenna hátt í vísuhelmingi, og sie tvau mál í vísu*helming*i, sem hier:

Hákon veldr og hauldum (36)
—harðráðum Guð jarðar
tiggja lier með tíri—
teitr þjóðkonungs heiti.
Vald á víðrar foldar
—vindræfrs jöfurr gæfu
öðlingi skóp ungum—
örlyndr skati görla.

Þetta heitir stælt, og er það inn fegrsti háttr.
Sú er in þriðja species er fleiri mál ganga um eina vísu en tvau, og lýkz mál í síðustum orðum, sem hier er kveðið:

Óláfr kunni blóthús brenna (37)
Bráðan hitti | Magnús váða, p. 11

W 1 Hákon] R T^x W(140) U(47r) U(50r) begin | heiðan] U(47r) ends
3 lönd] *all others*, land U(50r)   5 náir] *all others*, 'siair' U(50r)
6 remmi-Týr] *all others*, renni-Týr W(140)   7 eignu] *all others*, eignum W
8 konungdómi] R T^x W(140) U(50r) end   13 vísuhelmingi] vísuorði W
14 Hákon] R T^x W(140) U(47r) U(50r) begin | og] W T^x W(140) U(50r), ok *corrected from* en R | hauldum] U(47r) ends   16 tiggja lier] W R T^x W(140), 'ti[. . .]r' U(50r)   17 þjóðkonungs] W T^x W(140), þjóðkonungi R, þjóðkonungs U(50r)   18 Vald] W R W(140) U(50r), 'vauld' T^x 21 görla] W T^x W(140) U(50r), '[. . .]' R | R T^x W(140) U(50r) end

35 Hákon ræðr konungdómi með heiðan orðróm; vinr dreingja hefir feingið

(35)   Hákon rules the kingdom with radiant reputation; the friend of warriors [RULER] has obtained great power; the prince protects the wide lands with the sword; the strengthening-Týr ‹god› of strife-play [BATTLE > WARRIOR] is able to control his own realm; mankind welcomes that.

Here these words which are positioned first and last belong together: '*Hákon rœðr konungdómi*' [Hákon rules the kingdom], and this version of the aforementioned figure, which is called *antitheton*, is the easiest.

It is another variant of this figure if it concludes the sentence of the half-stanza in this manner, and there are two sentences in the half-stanza, as here:

(36)   Happy Hákon commands the name 'mighty king' and the freeholders; God grants the firm-ruling prince the earth with glory. The liberal-minded monarch has complete control of the wide land; the ruler of the wind-roof [SKY/HEAVEN > = God] created good luck for the young lord.

This is called *stælt* [equipped with inlay], and that is the most elegant metre.

This is the third variant when more than two sentences are found in a stanza, and the sentence ends with the last lines, as it is said here:

(37)   Óláfr, who got a famous fall to the ground [death], was able to burn [heathen] sacrificial buildings. Magnús

---

mikið veldi; buðlungr verr breiðfeld lönd brandi; remmi-Týr rógleiks náir að stýra eignu ríki; öld fagnar því.
36 Teitr Hákon veldr heiti þjóðkonungs og hauldum; Guð lier harðráðum tiggja jarðar með tíri. Örlyndr skati á görla vald víðrar foldar; jöfurr vindræfrs skóp ungum öðlingi gæfu.
37 Óláfr, sá hlaut ágætt fall til vallar, kunni brenna blóthús. Magnús hitti bráðan váða, píndr sóttum, þá er örl*ö*g *end*uz. Vier frágum Harald, mildan hjörleiks, hníga riett á enskri sliettu; arfi hans tók nú við starfa, vinr dróttar fekk hættan helverk.

Harald frágum vier hjörleiks mildan,
hans arfi tók nú við starfa,
dróttar vinr fekk helverk hættan.
hníga riett á enskri sliettu.
sóttum píndr, þá er örl*ög* end*uz.*
ágætt fall sá hlaut til vallar.

Hier er ið fjórða og ið fimta vísuorð *saman um* mál. Ið þriðja og ið sietta vísuorð er sier um mál, og eru fjögur heil mál í þessi vísu sem nú var talt.
    Sú er in fjórða species innar sömu fígúru ef tvau mál ganga jafnfram um vísu og lýkz mál í helmingi, en þó eitt efni um alla með inum sömum tveim málum, sem hier:

Haki Kraki (38)
hoddum broddum
særði mærði
seggi leggi;
veitir neitir
vella pella
báli stáli
beittiz heittiz.

Hier er ið fyrsta og ið síðasta orð í fjórðungi saman og annað og ið þriðja, en mál öll lúkaz í helmingum.
    Þessa vísu má og kalla anatecor e*r* fjögur mál ganga um alla vísu, og *eru um* mál saman in fyrstu vísuorð í báðum helmingum, og önnur slík og in þriðju, og með einum hætti in fjórðu:

Mætr Hákon vann (39)
en Magnús fann
hjörr Eiríks hiekk
hans bróðir giekk
langfeðra láð,
lögvizku ráð;

W 5 örlög enduz] 'örl[...]uz' *W* 7 saman um] '[...]' *W* 23 er] 'en*n*' *W* 24 eru um] '[...]' *W* 28 hjörr Eiríks hiekk hans bróðir giekk] 'h. e. h. ha*n*s bro. g.' *W*
38 Haki særði leggi broddum; Kraki mærði seggi hoddum; veitir pella heittiz

encountered sudden danger, tormented by illness, when his fortunes came to an end. We [I] have heard [that] Haraldr, generous with sword-play [BATTLE], certainly fell on an English field; his heir now took on the business [of government], the friend of the people [RULER = Magnús or Óláfr Haraldssynir] contracted a dangerous mortal illness.

Here the fourth line in conjunction with the fifth make up a sentence. The third and the sixth line constitute a sentence, and there are four complete sentences in the stanza which has now been quoted.

This is the fourth kind of the same figure if two sentences run parallel throughout a stanza, and the sentence ends within the half-stanza, yet one subject matter [is kept] throughout the complete stanza with the same two sentences, as here:

(38) Haki wounded legs with pikes; Kraki ('Pole-ladder') honoured men with treasures; the giver of costly materials [GENEROUS MAN = Haki] was burnt [lit. heated] on a pyre; the squanderer of gold [GENEROUS MAN = Kraki] was killed by a steel weapon.

Here the first and the last word in the couplet go together, and the second and the third, and all sentences end within the half-stanzas.

One may also term this stanza in which four sentences run through the complete stanza *antitheton*—and the first lines of both half-stanzas constitute one sentence, and thus the second [lines] and the third, and in the same way the fourth [lines]:

(39) Excellent Hákon won his paternal ancestors' land, but Magnús gained counsel of legal learning; Eiríkr's sword

báli; neitir vella beittiz stáli.
39 Mætr Hákon vann láð langfeðra, en Magnús fann ráð lögvizku; hjörr Eiríks hiekk á slóð rítar; bróðir hans giekk að refsa þjóð.

á rítar slóð;
að refsa þjóð.

Þessa vísu þarf skamt að færa til ins fyrra háttar:

  Mætr Hákon vann (40)
  en Magnús fann
  hjörr Eiríks hiekk
  hans bróðir giekk
  að refsa þjóð;
  á rítar slóð;
  lögvizku lund;
  langfeðra grund.

  Haki Kraki (41)
  hamdi framdi
  geirum eirum
  gotna flotna;
  hreytir neytir
  hodda brodda
  brendiz endiz
  báli stáli.

15 ANTIPOSORA er það ef maðr svarar þeim hlutum sem maðr býz að kæra á hann á þingi, og stendr upp búinn að segja fram sökina, en segir eigi:

  Þier giet eg, karl, ef þú kærir, (42)
  kraunk orð búin—forðum
  fat eg várkunnar vinnur—
  —verðu kyrr og sit—fyrri!
  Sakir áttu á mier miklar;
  munu nær vera hæri
  þær, sem þína aura
  —það er hættiligt!—fætta.

W **10** lögvizku] 'lǫgvizlv' *W*

40 Mætr Hákon vann grund langfeðra, en Magnús fann lund lögvizku; hjörr Eiríks hiekk á slóð rítar, bróðir hans giekk að refsa þjóð.
41 Haki hamdi gotna geirum; Kraki framdi flotna eirum; hreytir hodda brendiz

hung upon the shield's track [ARM], his brother was busied with punishing people.

This stanza is closely related to the previous verse-form:

(40) Excellent Hákon won his paternal ancestors' land, but Magnús gained a disposition of legal learning; Eiríkr's sword hung upon the shield's track [ARM], his brother was busied with punishing people.

(41) Haki restricted [killed] men with spears; Kraki ('Pole-ladder') promoted men with tranquillity; the scatterer of hoards [GENEROUS MAN = Haki] was burnt on a pyre; the user of points [WARRIOR = Kraki] was killed by a steel weapon.

15 ANTHYPOPHORA comes about if one responds to those things that someone else has prepared to charge him with at an assembly, and gets up ready to declare the case, but does not speak:

(42) Fellow, if you bring a charge first, I think hurtful words will be ready for you; formerly I followed the practices of compassion; be quiet and stay sitting! You have great offences to charge me with; those which will diminish your fortune, will become still greater. That's risky!

báli; neytir brodda endiz stáli.
42 Karl, ef þú kærir fyrri, eg giet kraunk orð búin þier; eg fat forðum vinnur várkunnar; verðu kyrr og sit! Áttu miklar sakir á mier; þær, sem fætta þína aura, munu nær vera hæri; það er hættiligt!

16 ACLACASSIS er það ef maðr setr tvenna skilninga gagnstaðliga með einum orðum, sem hier:

> Mætum stend eg að móti (43)
> mensveigjanda eigi;
> rís eg við Ránar eisu
> runni flærðarkunnum;
> því heit eg víst að veita
> vígs dreingiligt geingi;
> þier heit eg mest að móti
> meginstrangliga að ganga.

Hier er þessi fígúra tvítekin og sýnd í báðum vísuhelmingum.

17 ANSIMEHISA verðr ef maðr snýr svá sem með orðum myrkrar skilningar, sem hier er ritað:

> Sveit lifir ill til átu (44)
> annlaust þokumanna,
> en klaustrs búi kristinn
> kalds, að lífið haldiz.

Þokumenn eru þeir kallaðir er alla penninga sína neyta upp í ofáti og ofdrykkju, og bera þeir það nafn sakir snápskapar síns, þvíað þeir sjá eigi satt ljós riettrar framferðar og lifa að eins til þess að eta sem í sitjandi myrkvastofuþoku. En siðlátir menn eta eigi meira en svá mikið að þeir láti eigi af að lifa, og þykkir þessi fígúra mjög skaðsamlig.

18 APOSIOPESIS er viljanlig þrotnan máls sakir hryggðar eða óþykkju, sem hier er kveðið:

> Eigi er ván, að eg vága (45)
> viljag hyrjar þilju
> eiga orðagnóga
> —em eg reiðr—konu leiðaz,
> þá er mier, en frá færumz,

W **4** mensveigjanda] mansveigjanda *W* **29** þá] þar *W* | færumz] færum *W*

43 Eg stend eigi að móti mætum mensveigjanda; eg rís við flærðarkunnum runni eisu Ránar; eg heit því víst að veita dreingiligt geingi vígs; eg heit mest að ganga meginstrangliga að móti þier.

16 ANTICLASIS comes about if one devices two opposing meanings with the same words, as here:

(43) I do not stand opposed to the excellent necklace-distributor [GENEROUS MAN]; I oppose the blatantly deceitful tree of the fire of Rán ‹goddess› [GOLD > MAN]; I certainly promise to give valiant support in [lit. of] a fight; I promise most to oppose you very strongly.

Here this figure is repeated and shown in both halves of the stanza.

17 ANTIMETABOLA occurs when one changes, as it were, [the meaning] with words of obscure signification, as it is written here:

(44) The evil company of fog-men lives trouble-free for eating, but the Christian inhabitant of the cold cloister [eats] to stay alive.

Those are called fog-men who spend all their money indulging in food and drink, and they bear that name because of their folly, since they do not see the true light of proper behaviour, and live only for eating as if they sat in the fog of the prison cell. But virtuous men eat no more than such that they do not cease to live, and this figure is considered very detrimental.

18 APOSIOPASIS is a deliberate interruption of an utterance on account of grief or disapproval, as it is said here:

(45) It is not to be expected that I will want to marry the loquacious plank of the fire of the waves [GOLD > WOMAN]—I am angry—[I want to] avoid that woman who formerly [rejected] me, and get out of the courtship

44 Ill sveit þokumanna lifir annlaust til átu, en kristinn búi kalds klaustrs [etr], að lífið haldiz.
45 Eigi er ván, að viljag eiga orðagnóga þilju hyrjar vága—eg em reiðr—[eg vil] leiðaz konu, þá er [kastaði] mier forðum, en færumz frá bænarorðum; in óprúða brúðr verðr sitja og sýta sig.

forðum, bænarorðum;
sitja verðr og sýta
sig brúðr in óprúða.'

Hier eru viljanliga ór vísunni þessur orð 'sakir reiðiþokka', 'eg vil', og í öðrum stað: 'kastaði'. Og skal svá upp taka: 'Eigi | er ván að eg vilja, þvíað ek em reiðr, eiga þá konu orðmarga er mier kastaði þá er eg bað hennar. Leiðaz vil eg hana þó að nú vili hon eiga mig. Siti hon og sýti að skilja sína heimsku.'
Þessi fígúra stendr í Guðs orðum þeim er hann talar til júða fyrir fígúru undir nafni Hierusalem borgar.

p. 117

19 EUPHEMISMOS er gott umskifti stafa í orðinu sem Dávíð setti 'exultat' fyrir 'exaltat', sem stendr í þessi vísu:

Það saung og í gröf geinginn (46)
grundu huldr til stundar
enn með iðran sannri
öðlingr til refsingar:
'hugþekka mun hlakka
hróðrslung*in* loftunga
mána vald*r* inn mildi
mín riettvísi þína.'

Hier er sagt að tungan hlakki yfir riettvísi Guðs þar sem hitt væri alþýðligra að segja að hann hæfi upp Guðs orð með tungunni. En þetta umskifti var giert til þess að setja það orð er meira þótti vert í stað ins minna.

20 SINEPTESIS er óskapligt umskifti talna eða skilninga, sem hier er kveðið:

Víngarðr hafði öl-Giefn orðið (47)
(unda vargs), sú er nú eru margar,
(neytir skili þann krók), með kæti

W **18** hróðrslungin] hróðrslung W **19** valdr] vald W **27** öl-Giefn] '[. . .]lgefn' W [lit. wooing words]; let the inelegant woman sit and commiserate with herself.

Here these words are deliberately left out of the stanza: *sakir reiði-þokka* [on account of anger], *eg vil* [I want] and in another place: *kastaði* [she rejected]. And the stanza should be construed thus: 'It is not to be expected that I would want—because I am angry—to marry that woman of many words, who rejected me when I wooed her. I will loathe her, although now she wants to marry me. She can sit and lament so that she can understand her stupidity'.

This figure is found in those words of God which he speaks to the Jews figuratively under the name of the city of Jerusalem.

19 EUPHEMISMOS is a good exchange of letters in the word, as [when] David replaced '*exaltat*' [exalts] with '*exultat*' [exults], as it is found in this stanza:

(46) The king, covered with earth for a time as punishment and gone into the grave, yet sang that with true repentance: 'my eulogy-encircled tongue of praise will exult your righteousness, the merciful ruler of the moon [= God].'

Here it is said that the tongue exults over the justice of God when it would be more common to say that he exalts the words of God with his tongue. But this exchange was made in order to use the word that was esteemed higher rather than the one [esteemed] lower.

20 SYNEPTHESIS is an inappropriate exchange of numbers or persons, as it is said here:

(47) Ale-Gefn ‹= Freyja› [WOMAN], she who now are many, had become a vineyard with cheerfulness and abandoned her preserved chastity; let the user of the wolf of

46 Öðlingr, huldr grundu til stundar til refsingar og geinginn í gröf, saung það enn með sannri iðran: 'hróðrslung*in* loftunga mín mun hlakka hugþekka riettvísi þína, inn mildi vald*r* mána.'

kvensku h*e*ft og láti*ð* eftir;
fyrðum dugir, að ósíðr orða
—oss vægðu, Guð, jafnan—lægðiz;
vára þó hann í vatni skíru
5   verka sekt og píslarmerki.

Hier er bæði skift tölum og skilningum, og er þessi figúra með öllu ekki í vana dragandi, þó að persónum finniz skift í Saltara og öðrum heilugum bókum.

   21 ONOPOMENON segir eða h*e*fir stórar sögur með fám orðum, sem
10 hier:

   Beraz liet frá mey mætri   (48)
   mætr foldsala gætir;
   umsnið*n*ing tók auðnu
   einn veitandi hreinnar,
15 áðr skatna van*n* vatni
   vatnskírn jöfurs batnað;
   fastandi bar freistni
   friðar kiennari þrenna.

   Píndr reis upp með anda   (49)
20 angrleystu herfangi;
   hlýrna gramr til himna
   heim sótti Guð dróttin*;
   sendi ástaranda
   alls hirðandi virðum;
25 sá kiemr drótt að dæma
   dauða lífs á hauðri.

Hier er ávarp theologie fært í tvær dróttkvæðar vísur. Þessi sama figúra kallaz öðru nafni BRACHILOGIA og hefir *sömu* upprás nafns og in

---

W **1** heft] 'h[. . .]ft' *W* | látið] láti *W*   **9** hefir] 'h[. . .]f*ir*' *W*   **13** umsniðning] 'u*m*snið*n*[. . .]g' *W*   **15** vann] vanr *W*   **22** dróttin] dróttinn *W*   **28** sömu] *add.*

47 Öl-Giefn, sú er nú eru margar, hafði orðið víngarðr með kæti og láti*ð* eftir kvensku h*e*ft; neytir vargs unda skili þann krók; dugir fyrðum, að ósiðr orða lægðiz; Guð, vægðu oss jafnan; hann þó sekt verka vára í skíru vatni og píslarmerki.
48 Mætr gætir foldsala liet beraz frá mætri mey; einn veitandi hreinnar auðnu

wounds [AXE > WARRIOR] understand that ambiguity; it helps men that a bad habit of words should be diminished; God, spare us always; he washed the guilt of our sins in pure water and [in] the sign of his passion.

Here numbers as well as persons have been exchanged, and this figure should certainly not be used habitually, even though exchanged persons can be found in the Psalter and other holy books.

21 OLIOPOMENON tells or covers great stories with few words, as here:

(48)　The excellent keeper of the earth-halls [SKY/HEAVEN > = God (= Christ)] allowed himself to be born from an excellent maiden; the one granter of pure destiny [= God (= Christ)] underwent circumcision, before the baptism of the prince of men [= God (= Christ)] improved the water [lit. gained improvement for the water]; the teacher of peace [= God (= Christ)] fasting bore a threefold temptation.

(49)　Tortured, he rose up with the sorrow-liberated booty of souls; the prince of heavenly bodies [= God (= Christ)] came home to the Lord God in the heavens; the carer of everything [= God] sent the spirit of love to men; he will come to judge the host of the dead on the land of life.

Here a summary of the Bible is reworked into two *dróttkvætt* stanzas. This same figure is called BRACHILOGIA by another name, and this

---

tók umsnið*n*i*ng*, áðr vatnskírn jöfurs skatna van*n* vatni batnað; kiennari friðar bar fastandi þrenna freistni.
49 Píndr reis upp með angrleystu herfangi anda; gramr hlýrna sótti Guð dróttin* heim til himna; hirðandi alls sendi virðum ástaranda; sá kiemr að dæma drótt dauða á hauðri lífs.

fyrri. Sumir meistarar segja að CLIMAX sie hennar species, sú er um
jafnar gráður leiðir hverja málsgrein af annarri, sem hier:

    Hugsan flýtir lysting ljóta, (50)
    lysting fæðir samþykt skæða,
5   samþykt fæðir synd og nauðir,
    synd spenr á sig illa venju,
    ill venja dregr nauðsyn nóga,
    nauðsyn leiðir sál í dauða,
    dauði spillir æði öllu
10   andar lífs með beisku grandi.

22 EMOPHASIS glósar myrkan hlut með öðrum jafnmyrkum hlut eða
myrkara, sem hier:

    Sæll er sienn í milli (51)
    siðvendis kvikvenda
15   mána ranns af mönnum
    mildingr, *þá* er barz hingað,
    eða þá er djúp að djúpi
    dorgtúns niða borgar
    um hljóðraufar hávar
20   hátt samþykkið vátta.

Hier eru orð Abbacuch spámanns þau er hann segir Guð dróttin sienn
milli siðvendis kvikenda og í þenna heim komanda, sett í inn fyrra
vísuhelming, en glósa yfir sett sú er Dávíð segir undirdjúp vatnanna
kalla á annað undirdjúp um þær himinborur sem cataracte kallaz og
25 opnuðuz er Nóaflóð drekti öllum heimi útan þeim mönnum sem í
örkinni váru.

En til þess að þenna myrkleik megi skilja segir Augustinus að
spámaðrinn sá fyrir | að Guð mundi holdgaz og var sienn milli tveggja   p. 11
kvikenda uxa og asna, er merkja júða og heiðingja, í milli Moysi og
30 Helie í myndskiftingu Várs Herra á fjallinu, og milli tveggja latróna
með sier krossfestum, og að lyktum millum tveggja lögmála.

W **1** climax] 'dvnax' W **3** Hugsan] W(120) begins **4** fæðir] W, flýtir W(120)
9 æði] W, eðli W(120) **10** grandi] W(120) ends **16** þá] sá W **24** cataracte]
'katarakte' W **30** myndskiftingu] myndskiftingar W
50 Hugsan flýtir ljóta lysting, lysting fæðir skæða samþykt, samþykt fæðir

name has the same origin as the [name of the] previous one. Some masters say that CLIMAX, which by equal steps leads each sentence from another, belongs to this group, as here:

(50) Thought hastens ugly desire, desire feeds noxious consent, consent feeds sin and sufferings, sin attracts to itself a bad habit, a bad habit brings with it compulsion aplenty, compulsion leads the soul to death, death destroys the whole nature of the life of the soul with bitter injury.

22 HOMOPHESIS glosses something obscure by something equally or more obscure, as here:

(51) The blessed prince of the house of the moon [SKY/ HEAVEN > = God (= Christ)] was [lit. is] seen by men between animals of uprightness, when he was born into this world [lit. hither], or when the deep of the trolling line-field [SEA] loudly bore witness [lit. bears witness] of concord to the deep across the high sound-crevices of the stronghold of the phases of the moon [SKY/HEAVEN].

Here are those words of the prophet Habakkuk in which he says that the Lord God coming into this world is seen between beings of good conduct, placed in the first half-stanza, and the explanation is added where David says that the abyss of the waters calls to the other abyss through those openings in the sky which are called cataracts and which were opened when Noah's flood drowned the whole world except those people who were in the ark.

In order that one might understand this obscurity, Augustine says that the prophet foretold that God would take flesh and was seen between two beings, an ox and an ass, which symbolise the Jews and the Gentiles, between Moses and Elijah in the transfiguration of Our

synd og nauðir, synd spenr á sig illa venju, ill venja dregr nóga nauðsyn, nauðsyn leiðir sál í dauða, dauði spillir öllu æði lífs andar með beisku grandi.
51 Sæll mildingr ranns mána er sienn í milli kvikvenda siðvendis, þá er barz hingað, eða þá er djúp dorgtúns vátta hátt samþykkið að djúpi um hávar hljóðraufar borgar niða.

Og þessi tvau lögmál, ið forna og ið nýja, kallar Leo páfi inn málsnjalli tvenn vatnadjúp, þau er annað er yfir himnum en annað undir himnum, og Dávíð segir að á kallaz með röddum cataractarum, það er himinraufanna þeirra sem vötnin sendu til jarðar í flóðinu Nóa, og merkja þær höfuðfeðr og spámenn, postula og predikara, þá er himnesk vötn heilagrar predikanar senda á jörðina til þess að fyrirkoma Guðs óvinum, það er löstum og lýtum, og að döggva hjörtu riettrúaðra manna með regni heilsamrar kienningar. Og er þá að sönnu sienn sjálfr sannleikrinn, það er sjálfr Guð, milli kvikenda siðvendis, er ið forna lögmál—fram sagt forðum af þeim feðrum sem váru fyrir hingaðburð Guðs sonar svá sem af himni runnin vötn, er fram eru borin milli manna þeirra, sem siðvönd kvikendi ætti að vera í heilagri kirkju, og samþykkjanda nýju lögmáli—fagrliga fram flutt og útskýrt með guðspjalligri kienning og af postuligum röksemdum fyrir predikara nýs lögmáls. Birtiz þá fullkomið samþykki lögmálanna, það er þau hafa sín á milli, ef fram eru bornar spásögur heilagra feðra um gietnað og hingaðburð, predikan, pínsl og dauða, upprisu, uppstigning Várs Herra og ástgjöf Heilags Anda og inn efsta dóm og eilíft líf, er í móti beraz vitni af nýju lögmáli, að nær öll þessi stórmerki eru fram komin, en þau sem óorðin eru munu án efa fram koma.

23 Epimenon er sú fígúra er ið sama orð er oftar en um sinn sett, annað tveggja til þess að öruggligar megi skiljaz það sem flutt er, sem víða má finna í theologia, ella er ið sama orð fyrir fegrðar sakir oftar sett, sem í dunhendu eða iðurmæltum hætti. Verðr það stundum í upphafi sem í greppaminni, en stundum í miðju eða í enda, og má það kalla háttaföll eftir fornum skáldskaparhætti, en sá má nýta er vill, og *eftir* líkja, en hinn ónýta er það vill. En í upphafi, sem hier:

W   13 útskýrt] útskýrd W   26 sá má] sama W | eftir²] add.

Lord on the mountain, and between two thieves crucified with him, and finally between two laws.

And Pope Leo the eloquent calls these two laws, the old and the new, two abysses, of which one is above the sky and the other below the sky, and David says that they call upon one another with the voices of the cataracts, that is of the openings in the sky which sent the waters to the earth during Noah's flood, and they symbolise the patriarchs and prophets, the apostles and preachers who send the heavenly waters of holy preaching to the earth in order to destroy the enemies of God, that is vices and flaws, and in order to bedew the hearts of the orthodox with the rain of salutary preaching. And then indeed Truth itself is seen, that is God himself, between two beings of good conduct, when the old law—pronounced in olden times by those fathers who lived before the birth of the son of God into this world, just like the waters that have streamed from heaven, which are carried forth between those men, who ought to be beings of good conduct in the holy church, and agreeing with the new law—is beautifully presented and explained by the evangelical teaching and apostolic authority through the preachers of the new law. The complete agreement of the laws, that which is between them, is revealed if the prophesies of the holy fathers about the conception and birth, preaching, torture and death, Resurrection, Ascension of Our Lord and the gift of grace of the Holy Spirit and the Last Judgement and eternal life are presented and the testimonies of the new law are held up against them, [then one will see] that almost all these great wonders have occurred while those that have not yet occurred will occur without doubt.

23 EPIMONE is that figure where the same word is used more than once, either so that that which is pronounced may be understood more certainly, as can be found widely in the Bible, or when the same word is used more often for the sake of beauty, as in *dunhenda* or the *iðurmæltr* verse-form. Sometimes it occurs at the beginning [of the line], as in *greppaminni*, but at other times in the middle or at the end, and according to the old way of composing that may be termed *háttaföll*, he who wants to can use and imitate it, and he who does not want to use it can avoid it. At the beginning [of the line], as here:

Eg em synda bót (52)
og sæmdar hót,
eg birti sál,
eg bæti mál.

Í miðju, sem hier:

Þar er ekki ilt (53)
og ekki vilt,
fæz ekki aungt
og ekki þraungt.

Í enda, sem hier:

Þar er ómælt vald (54)
og ágætt vald;
þar er algiert vald
og eilíft vald.

Þessi figúra sýniz í upphafi og í enda, sem hier:

Eg blessa þig, (55)
eg bið fyr þig,
eg fæ fyr þig,
eg frelsa þig.

24 ANTOPAZIA er sú figúra ef tveir hlutir eru svá bundnir og samþykkir að það megi segjaz annarr giera sem annarr gierir; á þá lund sem tunga er kölluð samþykk hjarta:

Máni skínn af mæ*ni* (56)
moldar hofs um foldir
alla stund, meðan endiz
ævi lands og sævar.
Veit eg fielaga fljótum
fróns prýði vel þjóna;

W **23** Máni] *2368ˣ 743ˣ begin* | mæni] mæðu *W 2368ˣ 743ˣ*

52 Eg em bót synda og hót sæmdar, eg birti sál, eg bæti mál.
53 Þar ekki er ilt og ekki vilt, fæz ekki aungt og ekki þraungt.
54 Þar er ómælt vald og ágætt vald; þar er algiert vald og eilíft vald.

Translation 43

(52) I am the remedy of sins and the mark of honour, I illuminate the soul, I improve speech.

In the middle, as here:

(53) There is nothing evil and nothing false, there will be nothing cramped and nothing constricted.

At the end, as here:

(54) There is unmeasured power and excellent power; there is complete power and eternal power.

This figure appears at the beginning and at the end, as here:

(55) I bless you, I pray for you, I obtain for you, I save you.

24 HOMOPATHION is that figure in which two things are joined together and agree in such a way that it can be said that the one does what the other does; in that way in which the tongue is said to agree with the heart:

(56) The moon shines from the roof-ridge of the temple of the ground [SKY > ZENITH] throughout countries all the time while the life of land and sea endures. I know that the adorner of the earth [SUN] serves its swift

---

55 Eg blessa þig, eg bið fyr þig, eg fæ fyr þig, eg frelsa þig.
56 Máni skínn af mæ*ni* hofs moldar um foldir alla stund, meðan ævi lands og sævar endiz. Veit eg prýði fróns þjóna fljótum fielaga vel; ýtar vitu eigi þeim auðið lífs nie dauða.

þeim vitu eigi ýtar
auðið lífs nie dauða.

Hier er tunglinu kient embætti sólarinnar að skína jafnliga á jörðina fyrir því er það hefir ekki ljós af sier heldr af sólinni, og er dökkt þeim megin sem frá henni horfir. En albjart það er að henni horfir. En þá sýniz það hálft bjart er það hefir svá langt geingið frá sólinni, eða á svá langt til hennar að það sie þá í suðri eða norðri, er hon er í austri eða vestri. |

25 ANTROPUSPATOS er sú fígúra er það er kient guðdóminum sem manndómsins er, sem það að hann standi, siti, gangi, reiðiz, gleðiz, elski, sýti, sem hier er kveðið:

> Ádám sá, þann alt í heimi (57)
> orði skóp í gaungu forðum;
> þenna kiendi Stephánus standa
> stórumvitr og spámenn sitja;
> reiði tala hans bækr sem blíðu
> brögnum jafnt sem hryggð og fögnuð
> ástargnótt með öðrum háttum
> ýta kyns, þeim er guðdóm lýta.

En staðligar hræringar og líkamligt tilfelli megu með fígúru, en eigi með sannleik, til Guðs talaz. Og er þá sem Guð gangi frá oss er vier gaungum frá honum fyrir afbrigð hans boðorða, en til vár þá er vier krjúpum til hans með iðran undir hans miskunn. Staða hans er vár staða í góðu eða búið fullting í nauðsynjum. Seta hans er dæming um fólksins verðleika þvíað dómarans er að sitja. Reiði hans er refsing sú er hann leggr á illvirki mannfólksins. Gleði hans er gæzka vár. Svefn hans er kallaðr það er vier sofum með svefni dauðligra synda. Og vaknan hans er það er vier vöknum við sjálfa oss. Sýting hans er það ef hann giefr oss að sýta ill verk vár. Ást hans er það er hann giefr oss

W 2368^x 743^x **1** vitu] W 743^x, vita 2368^x **2** dauða] 2368^x 743^x end **28** sjálfa] 'salfa' W companion well; people do not know that that one has been allotted neither life nor death.

Here the office of the sun, to shine continuously on the earth, has been assigned to the moon, because it does not have light from itself, but from the sun, and it is dark on the side which faces away from it. But the side which faces the sun is fully shining. And half the moon appears shining when it has passed so far away from the sun, or is at such a distance from the sun, that it is in the south or the north, when the sun is in the east or the west.

25 ANTHROPOSPATHOS is that figure in which that which belongs to mankind is attributed to the Godhead, such as that he stands, sits, walks, gets angry, rejoices, loves, feels sorrow, as it is said here:

(57) Adam once saw walking along that one who created everything in the world by means of a word; greatly wise Stephen recognised him standing and prophets [saw him] sit; books speak to men of his anger as well as his kindness, an abundance of love equally with sorrow and joy along with other characteristics of the race of men that demean the Godhead.

Local movements and physical properties can be attributed to God in a figurative sense, but not literally. And it is as if God departs from us when we depart from him on account of breaches of his commands, but [comes] to us when we, under his grace, crawl to him with contrition. His standing is our standing in good or [our] ready support in need. His sitting is the judgement of the worthiness of the people, because it befits the judge to sit. His anger is the punishment he places upon the misdeeds of mankind. His rejoicing is our goodness. It is called his sleep when we sleep the sleep of deadly sins. And it is his awakening when we wake to ourselves. His lamenting is when he gives us the ability to lament our own misdeeds. His love is when he gives us the ability to love him, so that, on account of this love, he

---

57 Ádám sá forðum í gaungu þann skóp alt í heimi orði; stórumvitr Stephánus kiendi þenna standa og spámenn sitja; bækr tala brögnum reiði hans sem blíðu, ástargnótt jafnt sem hryggð og fögnuð með öðrum háttum kyns ýta, þeim er lýta guðdóm.

að elska sig svá að þar fyrir giefi hann oss þá giftu að vier hjálpimz fyrir hans miskunn.

Hefir sjá fígúra nafn tekið af antropos girzku nafni því sem maðr er á vára tungu, og pasis, það er setning svá sem vier setjum Guði mannliga reglu um hræring og aðra hluti, svá sem þeir villumenn er antroposormite heita, er Guði ætla mannliga limu sakir einfeldi eða fátækleiks eiginligs skilnings, og skilja eigi að Guð er óskiftiligr og óbrugðligr, hvervetna nálægr, eigi með staðligri nálægð heldr með almætti einum saman.

26 SIMATRISMOS er sú fígúra er lof eða lestir eru saman lesnir í einum capitulo og klausu eða versi í látínu, en með einni vísu eða með fleirum í norrænu, sem hier:

Ábiels lofar ævi (58)
ómeinsemi hreina;
öld lofar Ienóch mildan
einkiend siðavendni;
Nóe lofaz öflugs ævi
ágætu hreinlæti;
Siem lofar fært til fremdar
fórnarhald um aldir.

Trúa lofar Ábráms ævi, (59)
Ísách lofar vísan
ván; lofar Jácób* einum
ástsemd hugarfremdum;
skýrr lofar Jóséphs ævi
órskurðr fyrirburða;
Guðs lofar ætt og ævi
Áróns göfug þjónan.

W **11** capitulo] 'kapitło' *W* **23** Jácób] Jácóbs *W*

58 Ómeinsemi lofar hreina ævi Ábiels; siðavendni, einkiend öld, lofar mildan Ienóch; ævi öflugs Nóe lofaz ágætu hreinlæti; fórnarhald, fært til fremdar, lofar Siem um aldir.
59 Trúa lofar ævi Ábráms, ván lofar vísan Ísách; ástsemd lofar *Jácób einum hugarfremdum; skýrr órskurðr fyrirburða lofar ævi Jóséphs; göfug þjónan Guðs lofar ætt og ævi Áróns.

may give us that good fortune that we might be saved because of his grace.

This figure has taken its name from *anthropos*, the Greek noun for that which is 'man' in our tongue, and *pasis*, that is 'placement', as when we impose human constraints concerning movements and other things upon God, like those heretics who are called 'anthropomorphites' who assign human limbs to God because of their simplicity and the poverty of their own understanding, and they do not understand that God is unchanging and unvarying, omnipresent, not because of a physical presence but solely because of his omnipotence.

26 SYNACRISMOS is the figure where praise or vices are collected in one chapter, [one] clause or [one] verse in Latin, but in one or more stanzas in Norse, as here:

(58) Innocence extols the pure life of Abel; integrity of morals, specific to mankind, commends gentle Enoch; the life of powerful Noah is praised on account of extraordinary purity; the observance of sacrifice, performed in honour [of God], will celebrate Shem forever.

(59) Faith extols Abraham's life, hope celebrates wise Isaac; love praises Jacob for singular excellences of mind; a clear interpretation of omens lauds the life of Joseph; the worthy service of God commends the kin and the life of Aaron.

Moysen lofar ljósan (60)
lagamál ið brennfagra;
þig lofar all*t* með öllu
alls heims, jöfurr beima.

5   Slíkt sama er þessi fígúra saman lestr lasta.

27 Therethema er sú fígúra er oft er spurt af inum sama hlut og andsvarað eftir sama hætti, sem hier:

Hverr deyr? Hjarðar stýrir. (61)
Hví? Fyr sauða lífi.
10   Hvessu? Hiekk á krossi.
Hvar? Þar er Lassarus jarðaz.
Hvienær? Helzt að nóni
Hverir knúðu að? Júðar.
Hverr nýtr? Heiðni bötnuð.
15   Hvað gieldr? Djöfuls veldi.

Hier eru sextán mál í vísu og er jafnan spurt og svarað í vísuorði. Má og þessi sama fígúra vera með minnr þraungdum spurningum:

Hverr fell? Hörða stillir. (62)
Hvar? Þar er karlfólk barðiz.
20   Hvienær? Hneig að nóni.
Hver* var sök? Öfund vöknuð.
Hverr vá? Kálfr hielt darri.
Hverir bændu slíks? Þrændir.
Hvað nýtr? Heilsa bötnuð.
25   Hvað sýtir? Fira lýti.

W   3 allt] allr *W*   12 Helzt] 'helldz' *W*   21 Hver] hverr *W*   23 bændu] bendu *W*

60 Ið brennfagra lagamál lofar ljósan Moysen; all*t* alls heims lofar þig með öllu, jöfurr beima.
61 Hverr deyr? Stýrir hjarðar. Hví? Fyr lífi sauða. Hvessu? Hiekk á krossi. Hvar? Þar er Lassarus jarðaz. Hvienær? Helzt að nóni. Hverir knúðu að? Júðar.

(60) The burning fair law-giving extols bright Moses; everything of all the world praises you absolutely, lord of men [= God].

In the same manner, this figure is a compilation of vices.

27 TERETEMA is the figure where questions are often asked about the same thing and answered in the same manner, as here:

(61) Who dies? The leader of the flock. Why? For the life of the sheep. How? He hung on a cross. Where? Where Lazarus is buried. When? About the ninth hour. Who instigated it? The Jews. Who gets the benefit? Heathendom is reformed. What suffers? The devil's power.

Here there are sixteen sentences in the stanza and questions are repeatedly asked and answered in the stanza. This same figure might also occur with less compressed questions:

(62) Who fell? The ruler of the Hörðar [NORWEGIAN KING = Óláfr Haraldsson]. Where? Where men were fighting. When? He fell at the ninth hour. What was the cause? Awakened ill-will. Who struck? Kálfr held the spear. Who requested such a thing? The Þrændir. What benefit is there? Health restored. What laments? Men's sin.

Hverr nýtr? Bötnuð heiðni. Hvað gieldr? Veldi djöfuls.
62 Hverr fell? Stillir Hörða. Hvar? Þar er karlfólk barðiz. Hvienær? Hneig að nóni. Hver* var sök? Vöknuð öfund. Hverr vá? Kálfr hielt darri. Hverir bændu slíks? Þrændir. Hvað nýtr? Bötnuð heilsa. Hvað sýtir? Lýti fira.

COMMENTARY

Chapter 1: Protheseos paralange

The initial part of the definition closely parallels *D* (ll. 2573–74). *D* does not present any examples of the use of the figure but three examples can be found in *Dg* (82r). The first of these is *'multa super Priamo' id est 'de Priamo'* [*Aen*, I 750] '"many things over Priamus," i.e. "about Priamus"'.

2,1 Protheseos The scribe has left space for a two-line initial and a rubric at the point where *FoGT* begins in W. The general tendency of the scribe in this part of W is to mark chapter divisions with two-line initials (on the significance of this, see p. xiii).

2,1 prepositio 'preposition': This is the only occurrence of this Latin word in W. Elsewhere the Old Norse term *fyrirsetning* is used (at pp. 99 ll. 21, 31; 103 l. 7; 110 l. 3).

2,2 viðkæmiliga 'appropriate': *Viðkæmiliga* is an adverb, but it has been rendered by an adjective in the English translation.

2,2 Þorleifr Þorleifr jarlsskáld 'Jarl's poet' Rauðfeldarson, born at Brekka in Svarfaðardalur, northern Iceland, some time in the second half of the tenth century. Many sources, including *Landnámabók* (ÍF 1, 254), both versions of *Skáldatal* (*SnE* 1848–87, III 256, 266), *Sneglu-Halla þáttr* (ÍF 9, 285–86), the Icelandic version of Oddr Snorrason's life of Óláfr Tryggvason (ÍF 25, 191), and Haukr Valdísarson's *Íslendingadrápa* (st. 18) mention Þorleifr as a skald. Most of the poetry attributed to him and almost all the biographical information about him is found in *Þorleifs þáttr jarlsskálds* (ÍF 9, 213–29), first preserved in the late fourteenth-century manuscript Flateyjarbók. The *þáttr* describes Þorleifr's antagonistic relationship with Hákon jarl Sigurðarson of Hlaðir (ruled Norway 970–95), which reaches its climax when Þorleifr, disguised as an old man, recites the poem *Jarlsníð* 'Jarl's libel' in the jarl's presence. The context of the stanza cited here is unknown, though it is addressed to Hákon, and may possibly be from the first, laudatory part of *Jarlsníð* (so Almqvist 1965–74, I 197), or from another poem in the jarl's honour.

Stanza 1

A variant version of this half-stanza is also cited in *TGT* (mss A, 4v and W, p. 103). In *TGT* the same half-stanza is quoted as an example

Commentary 51

of a solecism (a syntactic error): *Stundum verðr soloecismus þá er sami partr er óviðkæmiliga settr, sem jarlsskáld kvað* [st. 1]. *Hér er 'í' fyrirsetning fyrir 'af' sett* (*TGT* 1884, 17) 'At times a solecism occurs when [another word belonging to] the same part of speech is inappropriately used, as the earl's poet said [st. 1]. Here the preposition "in" is used instead of "of"'. The example of *TGT* in W is garbled and does not contain the preposition *í* (see critical apparatus to 2,3). *FoGT* thus provides a figure that was defined but faultily exemplified in the W text of *TGT* with a name and a correct example. *FoGT* occasionally refers back to *TGT* (18,30–20,1, 20,28 and 24,18), but not at this point. In *TGT* the stanza is ascribed to *Þorleifr jarlsskáld* (A) and simply *jarlsskáld* (W).

2,3 Höfðu...Hákon 'We ... Hákon': The line is metrically defective in all mss and has no internal rhyme.

2,4 gingum 'went': The form from infinitive *ginga* is indicated by the rhyme with *-þingi* (cf. *ANG* §504 and Anm. 1, 5).

2,6 forvistu 'leadership': The manuscript form 'forostu' is unmetrical, because it is not possible to have a short first syllable *for-* followed by a vowel in this metrical position. It has therefore been normalised to the earlier *forvistu*.

2,7 óviðkæmiliga 'inappropriately': An emendation first made in *SnE* 1818, 335 that has been adopted by all subsequent editors.

Chapter 2: Liptota

D defines *liptota* in two ways: 1) when words signify more than they imply (l. 2575)—this corresponds to the definition accompanying st. 2; and 2) when a double negation is used instead of one affirmation (l. 2576)—corresponding to the definition accompanying st. 5. No examples are given in *D*, but *Dg* (82r–v) gives three: 1) Saying less but meaning more: *mihi iussa capessere fas est* [*Aen*, I 77] 'it is fitting that I obey orders'. *D* does not explain how this example, which is drawn from Servius's commentary to the *Aeneid* (ed. Thilo and Hagen 1881–1902, I 77), should be understood as 'saying less but meaning more'. 2) Two negations equal one affirmation: *'nonnumquam legi' id est 'multotiens legi'* '"I have not never read" i.e. "I have often read"'. 3) A negation equals an emphatic affirmation: *non mediocriter conturbatur animus meus .i. valde conturbatur* 'my soul is not moderately disturbed, that is, it is very disturbed'.

2,10 þrjár 'three': Written '.iij.' in W. *FoGT* gives four definitions and four examples of the figure. Therefore the reading *þrjár* should perhaps be changed to *fjórar* 'four' ('.iiij.' in the orthography of W, e.g. p. 116 l. 5), but this chapter's general lack of congruence between the definitions and their illustrations suggests that the textual problems are to be sought at a deeper level.

2,10 Stundum...11 til 'at times ... implies': This definition corresponds to the first definition of this figure given in *D* (l. 2575).

2,11 Eiríkr viðsjá The Icelander Eiríkr viðsjá 'the Circumspect' fought on the side of the Northerners in the battle on the heath, thought to have taken place in 1014, and described in *Heiðarvíga saga* (ÍF 3, cxxiv–cxxvii, 301–23). In this saga seven *lausavísur* are attributed to Eiríkr and st. 2 is the last of these to be cited there and the only one witnessed outside the saga. Holm perg 18 4° (Holm18) of c. 1300–50 is the main manuscript for *Heiðarvíga saga*. There st. 2 is preceded by two other sts by Eiríkr, and they are cited to support the prose text's claim that very heavy losses of men resulted from the battle.

Stanza 2

FoGT records only the first six lines of this stanza, whereas Holm18 has two additional lines, which were probably original to it. They are (7–8): *fell geysla lið Gísla | gunnǫrunga sunnan*. If the additional lines are added, the second *helmingr* can be construed thus, following Holm18 (except for *ættskarð* l. 6 (2,17)): *Enn varð eigi in minna | ættskarð, þat er hjó Barði |—fell geysla lið Gísla—| gunnǫrunga sunnan*. Prose order: *Enn ættskarð gunnǫrunga sunnan, þat er Barði hjó, varð eigi in minna; lið Gísla fell geysla*. Translation: 'Yet the notch in the family of the battle-nourishers [WARRIORS] from the south, which Barði cut, was not the smaller; Gísli's band fell in great numbers'. For other ways of construing ll. 7–8, see *Skj* B, I 201, *Skald*, I 105 and *NN* §2310.

2,12 Styrr...Snorri According to *Eyrbyggja saga* (ÍF 4, 21), Styrr's given name was Arngrímr and he was the son of Þorgrímr, but he was nicknamed Víga-Styrr 'Killer-Stir(rer)' because of his bellicose nature. Snorri is Snorri goði 'the Priest' Þorsteinsson.

2,12 snart 'swift': Understood as a neuter adjective qualifying *sverðþing* 'sword-assembly', though it could also be the adverb *snart* 'swiftly'. Holm18's *snarr* must be taken as a masculine adjective qualifying *Styrr*.

Commentary 53

2,14 geir-Nirðir 'spear-Nirðir ‹gods› [WARRIORS]': An emendation first indicated by Árni Magnússon in AM 761 b 4°ˣ, f. 65r, and adopted in *SnE* 1848–87, II 192 and by Ólsen (*FoGT* 1884, 238–39). It provides *skothending* with *gierðu*. The compound *geir-Njǫrðr* 'spear-Njǫrðr ‹god› [WARRIOR]' is attested from *Guðrúnarhvǫt* 8,5 and the plural *-Nirðir* from Eskál *Vell* 26,7[I] (*hlym-Njǫrðum* 'din-Nirðir') and Anon *Pl* 52,3[VII] (*óski-Nirðir* 'wishing-Nirðir', the last three letters by emendation). Njǫrðr, name of one of the Old Norse gods of the Vanir group, often appears in man- or warrior-kennings (Meissner 1921, 273–75). The second element in W's *geirníðir* is probably a scribal error. It could possibly be construed without emendation as an unattested agent noun, masc. pl., -*níðir* 'mockers', from *níða* 'to compose níð "insult, mockery, libel"', though a warrior-kenning of this type is not recorded and there would be no *hending*. The misreading *geirviðir* 'spear-trees' [WARRIORS] of W's *geirníðir* was first printed by Rask in *SnE* 1818, 335 (see *SnE* 1848–87, II 193, n. 4). The same misreading occurs in *Skj* A, I 210 and is reproduced in *Skj* B, I 201 and *Skald*, I 105, as well as by Poole (1991, 185). *Geirviðir* is attested in the singular as a personal name in *Stjǫrnu-Odda draumr* (StjOdd *Geirfl* 2,8[V]) and as a warrior-kenning in Bjbp *Jóms* 25,5[I]. Holm18's variant is *gnýverðir* 'noise-guardians', in which the second element is the nominative plural of *vǫrðr* 'guardian, protector', a common element in kennings for men or warriors (cf. *LP*: *vǫrðr*).

2,15 Gíslungum 'of the Gíslungar': Literally, 'for the Gíslungar'. Name of a family from Borgarfjörður, within which the personal name Gísli was common (cf. ÍF 3, 255 n. 1). These people are the southern opponents of Barði Guðmundarson. Holm18 has the genitive plural form *Gíslunga*.

2,17 ættskarð 'the notch in the family': *Hap. leg.*, but W's reading must be correct; Holm18's *eitt* 'one' makes no sense in context. The image is of cutting a notch in a piece of timber.

2,17 Barði Barði Guðmundarson, a man from the north of Iceland, who seeks vengeance from the Gíslungar on account of the death of his brother.

2,18 er áðr er greint 'which is mentioned earlier': This is a reference to the first *helmingr* of the stanza (2,12–15).

2,20 Stundum…21 talið 'Sometimes … mentioned': This definition seems to be a variant of the one given in 2,10–11.

2,20 útþanning 'a stretching out': *Hap. leg.*, cf. *þenja* vb. 'stretch'. One would perhaps expect the form *útþaning*.

2,21 sem hier 'as here': In the incompletely transmitted st. 3 'not none' means 'very many'. Therefore the stanza does not really illustrate the definition it is said to exemplify.

Stanza 3

Stanza 3 is the first of the 47 anonymous stanzas or part-stanzas cited in *FoGT*, a proportion of the total number of 62 stanzas quoted in the treatise much higher than what is found in earlier Icelandic vernacular grammatical treatises. There are good grounds to infer that these anonymous stanzas were the work of the author of the prose text; for a discussion, see Introduction, § 5.

2,22 Sprungu 'ran': *Springa* in the sense 'run' was uncommon in Icelandic before the fourteenth century. The verb's more common earlier meaning was 'to burst, break asunder' (cf. *LP: springa*). Kock (*NN* §1442) understands *sútir* 'sorrows' as the subject of *springa* in its earlier sense, but the prose gloss makes it clear that it is here equivalent to *renna* 'run'.

2,22 eingir 'no': The ms.'s *eingar* (fem. nom. pl.) is emended here to the masc. form of the adjective to give the sense 'no [men]'. The fem. *eingar* could agree with either *sútir* 'sorrows' in l. 2 (2,23) or *sveitir* 'groups' in l. 4 (2,25), most likely in the configuration *Eigi sprungu eingar sútir ór ... bæjum* 'No sorrows ran from the ... farmsteads'. However, this interpretation does not accord with the prose gloss.

2,23 . . . The scribe of W left a gap, enough for a word of two syllables, between *ór* 'from' and *sútir* 'sorrows', and this has caused problems of interpretation for the whole stanza. In this edition, the missing part of ... *sútir* has been understood as a disyllabic verb, forming an independent clause with *sútir*. However, the missing verb cannot be the *greru* 'grew' suggested by Ólsen (*FoGT* 1884, 240), because this verb has a short stem, and a long stem is required by the metre, which is *dróttkvætt* 'court metre'. Finnur Jónsson's proposed reading *fengusk* 'struck' (*Skj* B, II 231) would be possible here.

2,24 hávar 'distinguished': Literally 'high'. This is an emendation (so *Skj* B, II 231, *Skald*, II 120 and *FoGT* 2004, 54) of W's 'havvi' (possibly an inflected form of *hár* adj. 'high') which is difficult to accommodate to the syntax of any of the proposed interpretations of this *helmingr*. It is here construed with *sveitir* 'groups' in l. 4 (2,25), itself an emendation from W's *sveiti*. Sveinbjörn Egilsson (*SnE*

1848–87, III 153) understood 'havvi' as a form of the noun hǫfuð 'head', while FoGT 1884, 240 emends 'havvi' to heima 'homes', giving the clause því heitr hyrr giekk á heima 'because hot fire attacked homes', but this is far from the manuscript form.

4,1 runnu 'were running': The emendation of W's rynni (3rd pers. pl. pret. subj. of the verb renna) to runnu (3rd pers. pl. pret. indic. of the same verb) was introduced in FoGT 1818, 336 and has been followed by all subsequent editors. Indicative is the expected mood for a causal subordinate clause in Old Norse (cf. Nygaard 1906 §298).

4,2 Sumstaðar...mikinn 'In some places ...'great': This definition is illustrated by st. 4, but it also fits st. 3 better than the one given above (2,20–21).

Stanza 4

Stanza 4 is a helmingr about the power of the Holy Spirit over men. Its likely reference is to the feast of Pentecost or Whitsunday (Old Icelandic hvítasunnudagr), which commemorates the descent of the Holy Spirit from heaven to Christ's Apostles (Acts II), after which they were able to begin their mission of baptising people into the Christian faith. The reference in the helmingr to 'pure water' in l. 2 (4,4) most likely alludes to the Christian rite of baptism. It was customary in the Middle Ages for many catechumens to be baptised at Pentecost in imitation of the events described in Acts.

4,3 Fingr...5 Guðs 'The finger of the one God' [fingr eins Guðs]: A kenning-like phrase for the Holy Spirit, paralleled in Anon Heilags anda drápa 'Drápa' of the Holy Spirit' (Anon Heildr 13,1, 3, 4[VII] hreinn fingr hægri handar salkonungs sólar 'pure finger of the right hand of the king of the hall of the sun [(literally 'of the hall-king of the sun') SKY/HEAVEN > = God]', where it is a direct imitation of dextrae Dei tu digitus 'you, finger of the right hand of God', st. 3,2 of the Latin Pentecost hymn Veni Creator Spiritus. The Latin hymn, usually ascribed to Hrabanus Maurus (d. 856), was normally sung during the office of Pentecost at Terce, because the Holy Spirit was thought to have descended upon the Apostles at the third hour (cf. Acts II.15).

4,6 að því sinni 'at that time': That is, at the time of the visitation of the Holy Spirit to the Apostles.

4,8 Stundum...játan 'At times ... affirmation': This definition parallels the second definition of Liptota given in D (l. 2576).

Stanza 5

An ingenious, but cryptic *helmingr*, doubtless composed for the purpose of exemplifying *liptota* involving the use of a double negative, here *neitar ní* 'does not deny' in l. 1 (4,9). The negative particle *ní* is a form of *nei* 'no', attested only here and in *Am* 48,8 in Old Icelandic poetry.

4,10 Nytju 'of Nytja ‹river›': The name of a mythical river; cf. *Nyt* in *Grímnismál* 28,4, Anon Þul *Á* 6,1^{III} and *Gylfaginning* (*SnE* 2005, 33), here forming the determinant of a regular gold-kenning.

4,11 ... There is nothing missing in W between the words *geirþings* 'of the spear-assembly' and *Gunnr*, a valkyrie name, but this line is too short, so it is clear that a word has been left out, presumably by the scribe. It must begin with *g* for purposes of alliteration and have two syllables. Earlier editors have conjectured *góðir* 'good' or *glaðir* 'cheerful', both qualifying *meiðar* 'trees'.

4,13 játaðiz 'consented': The reflexive form of the verb *játa* is usually constructed with the preposition *undir* 'under': *játask undir e-u* 'consent to [i.e. under] something'. Often in the context of marriage proposals. Occasionally, as in *FoGT*, it occurs with a direct object in the dative: *Þat er minn vili ok bœnastaðr, at þér játiz junkera Rémundi* (*Rémundar saga*, ed. Broberg 1909–12, 209–10) 'it is my wish and desire that you consent to *junkeri* Rémundr'.

Chapter 3: Topographia and related figures

This chapter presents four related figures whose names all have *graphia* '-graphy' as their second element. In W the names of three of the figures (*topographia*, *cosmographia* and *chronographia*) are written with initials in the form of *litterae notabiliores*, while the name of the last figure (*bethgraphia*) does not stand out in any way. The four figures are so closely related that all previous editors have treated them in a single chapter. Their lead has been followed here as well. *D* only defines two of the figures: *topographia* (l. 2577) and *chronographia* (l. 2578). *G* defines three: *topographia*, *chronographia* and *cosmographia* (I 72–73). *Bethgraphia* has no known parallels. *G*'s definitions of *chronographia* and *topographia* (quoted below in commentary to 6,1–2) cannot be said to be better parallels to *FoGT* than those of *D*. Neither *D* nor *G* gives any examples of the use of these figures, but a number of examples are given in *Dg* and *Gg*. None of these examples resembles the examples given in *FoGT*.

4,15 Tophographia...16 segja 'Topographia ... describe': *D*'s definition of *topographia* (l. 2577) agrees with the definition in *FoGT*.
4,15 tíðendin...16 segja 'the events ... describe': The same phrasing recurs below (6,5–6).

Stanza 6
Stanza 6 is the first of three anonymous *helmingar* in *dróttkvætt* metre in honour of St Nicholas, bishop of Myra near Patara in Lycia, present-day Turkey, to be cited by the writer of *FoGT*. The two later citations (sts 24 and 25) are said by the writer to be from a *Nikulásdrápa*, while the present *helmingr* is probably from the same poem, to judge by its subject-matter. No other parts of this poem survive, though there is plentiful evidence of the popularity of the saint and his cult in medieval Norway and Iceland from at least the twelfth century, possibly earlier, and a good deal of both prose and poetry in his honour (Blöndal 1949; Widding 1961; Widding *et al.* 1963, 326–27; Cormack 1994, 136–38; Sverrir Tómasson 1982). Bari, in South Italy, to where Nicholas' relics were removed in 1087, Myra and Patara are mentioned in the *Leiðarvísir* 'Itinerary' of Abbot Nikulás (*AÍ*, I 20), generally identified with Nikulás Bergsson (d. 1159), and St Nicholas is associated with these places there. Aside from the present fragments, there are several fifteenth-century or later Icelandic poems about Nicholas, including a *Nikulásdiktur* and the *hrynhent Nikulásdrápa* of the priest Hallur (Jón Þorkelsson 1888, 80–82, 315–19; *ÍM*, II 413–33). *Skj* B, II 174 dates the poem in the later thirteenth century, and places it alongside Anon *Heildr*[VII], though it is possible that it may be slightly younger. Stanza 6 bears some resemblance to chapter 12 of Bergr Sokkason's fourteenth-century *Nikulás saga erkibiskups*. The relevant passages are quoted in *FoGT* 1884, 243–44 n. 3. *SnE* 1848–87, II 194–95 cites sts 7–10 from the priest Hallur's *Nikulásdrápa* on the same subject. The background story is that the sinful and depraved people of the important and wealthy city of Patara were harrassed by a basilisk, sent by God on account of their sins, an episode that forms a prelude to the legend's account of the birth of the saintly Nicholas. Thus this stanza is likely to have come from an early part of the *drápa*.
4,16 þau...segja 'the events ... to describe': The same phrasing is found below (6,5–6).

4,17 Firð 'removed': An emendation of W's 'Frið', presuming a scribal metathesis, first suggested by Sveinbjörn Egilsson in *LP* (1860): *sorg* and accepted by all subsequent editors. *Firð* 'removed', pret. part. of *firra* 'deprive, keep away from' (cf. *LP*: *firra* 4), goes well with *sorgum* 'from sorrows' in l. 2 (4,18), and stands in apposition to *borg Pátera* 'the city of Patara'. *Frið* (from *friðr* 'peace') does not fit the context. The reading *fríð* 'beautiful' while agreeing with *borg* 'city' in l. 2 (4,18), requires the construal *fríð borg Pátera stóð sorgum í bygð breiðri* 'the beautiful city of Patara endured sorrows in the broad settlement [the world]'. The verb *standa e-u* 'endure something' is attested, though rarely, in Old Norse (cf. Fritzner: *standa* 15).

4,18 borg Pátera 'the city of Patara': Situated in Lycia, in the southwestern part of the Mediterreanean coast of Turkey. It was the birthplace of St Nicholas, possibly born c. 300 CE. He later became bishop of the neighbouring city of Myra. Patara was a major trading port in antiquity and the early Christian period.

4,20 lítt 'not at all': Literally 'little'. W reads 'lut', which could be construed as *hlut* 'lot, part, number', a reading accepted in *SnE* 1848–87, II 194–95. This, however, requires the *sorgum* (4,18) to be understood as *saurgum* from *saurigr* 'dirty, filthy'. See discussion in *FoGT* 1884, 243–44.

4,21 fóstsystir 'foster-sister': The text of W is damaged at this point. The emendation of *SnE* 1818, 336 has been followed by all subsequent editors.

4,21 bethgraphia No other occurrences of this word have been found in Old Norse or Latin texts. The term itself differs from its 'foster-sisters' in chapter 3 by having a Hebrew word (*beth* 'house') as the first element, rather than a Greek one. That *beth* means house in Hebrew was well known in the Middle Ages, even among people with no knowledge of Hebrew. Another reflection of this knowledge in Old Norse manuscripts can be found in the homily on the Epiphany in the Norwegian Book of Homilies: *Bethleem þýðir brauðs hús* (ed. Indrebø 1931, 61, see also p. 41) 'Bethlehem means house of bread' (see also the sermon on the Eucharist in AM 671 4°, c. 1320–40, ed. Þorvaldur Bjarnarson 1878, 186–87). The fourteenth-century miscellany AM 732 b 4° contains an enumeration and explanation of the names of the letters of the Hebrew alphabet on f. 6v. It begins: *Notandum est quod aleph interpretatur doctrina, beth domus, gimel* ... (ed. I. McDougall

Commentary

1986–89, 199) 'Note that *aleph* means "doctrine", *beth* "house", *gimel* …'. The *bethgraphia* above all must have been the description of the house of the Lord (*domus Domini*), Solomon's temple in Jerusalem (Mal. VI ff.). An elaborate description in Old Norse of the temple in Jerusalem can be found in *Stjórn* III (ed. Astås 2009, 1021–25).

Stanza 7
An amusing *helmingr* about men entering and leaving a 'many-raftered' house, making use of conventional house-kennings, whose base-words refer to animals, often wild ones, as here (cf. Meissner 1921, 430). This stanza appears in the Y version of *LaufE* among kennings for a house (*LaufE* 1979, 358), and in a similar environment in Resen's *Edda Islandorum* (*RE* 1665, Gg 1v).
4,23 íugtanni 'the bear': A compound noun often used as a nickname for a bear, or for men with the personal names Bjǫrn and Bjarni (cf. RKet Lv 1,6[IV], Anon Þul *Bjarna* 1,11[III]). The word *íugtanni* 'bear' is correctly spelled in *RE* 1665, but in some mss of *LaufE* the word is given as 'jngtanne'. On the etymology, see *AEW*: *íugtanni*.
4,24 menn ór munni 'men … from the mouth': Both nouns have missing letters in W, the *e* and associated common mark of abbreviation of *menn* have been obliterated by a hole and the last two letters of *munni* are covered by a blot; nevertheless, the restoration of these words is uncontroversial.

6,1 Cosmographia…2 setningu 'Cosmographia … design': Not defined in *D*. *G* defines it along with *chronographia* and *topographia*: *Temporis esse solet descriptio chronographia, | topographia loci, sed mundi cosmographia* (I 72–73) 'The description of time is usually *chronographia*, [the description] of a place [is usually] *topographia*, but [the description of] the world [is usually] *cosmographia*'. *FoGT* is much more specific than the Latin parallel in that it states that the figure speaks *frá heimsins skipan, skapan, stöðu eða hætti eða setningu* 'about the order of the world, its creation, state or nature or design'.
6,1 Cosmographia The name implies a description of *cosmos* 'the ordered universe', but *FoGT* follows *G* in restricting the extent of *cosmos* to this world (*heimsins*).
6,1 skipan…2 setningu 'order … design': Of the five terms *skipan*, *háttr* and *setning* seem to be nearly synonymous, and they are used as synonyms elsewhere in Old Norse literature as well, e.g. *Rómverja*

[...] *telja ok halda Januarium af skipan ok setningu Pompilii* [...] *fyrstan* (*Stjórn* I, ed. Astås 2009, 419) 'the Romans [...] reckon and count January as the first [month] because of the ordering and design of [Numa] Pompilius' and *vissi hon eigi með hverjum hætti eða skipan hon kennir sik ór komna þeim píslum* (*Duggals leizla*, ed. Cahill 1983, 52 middle text) 'she [the soul] did not know how or by what means or fashion she feels herself released from those torments'.

6,1 skipan skapan 'order ... creation': These two alliterative words are occasionally paired, but usually in the more logical order where creation is followed by ordering, e.g.: *hafði hann nú framit ok algert þessi vii daga verk með fyrrsagðri skapan ok skipan ok skýringu* (*Stjórn* I, ed. Astås 2009, 38) 'he had now done and completed those deeds in the course of seven days in the aforementioned creation and ordering and explanation'. Another example can be found in *Stjórn* I, ed. Astås 2009, 10.

Stanza 8
Stanza 8 is a couplet illustrating the figure of *cosmographia* in the terms laid down in *FoGT*. Ólsen (*FoGT* 1884, 245) thought it might be older than the treatise itself, as he did not consider it a very convincing illustration of the figure, but it seems perfectly acceptable as an example of God's order and design for the world.

6,4 friðar 'of salvation': *Friðr*, which may also mean 'peace', is here given its specifically Christian sense of 'salvation' (cf. *LP: friðr* 5).

6,5 Cronographia...6 segja 'Chronographia ... to describe': As was the case with *cosmographia* (6,1), the definition of *FoGT* is narrower than the one given in *D* (l. 2578).

6,5 tíðendin...6 segja 'the events ... to describe': Notice how the same phrasing is used above (4,15–16).

6,6 sem hier 'as here': At this point W has only *sem* '(such) as'. *FoGT* generally introduces anonymous examples with *sem hier*, but occasionally fuller forms are used: *sem hier er kveðit* (26,24; 32,24; 34,25–26; 44,11) or *sem hier er ritat* (32,13) 'as is said/written here'. Since this is the only instance in *FoGT* where a *sem* is used without an accompanying *hier* to introduce an example, it seems right to follow *SnE* 1848, 201 and subsequent editions in adding *hier*.

Stanza 9

Stanza 9 is appropriate to the figure of *chronographia*, for it specifies the exact time of Christ's death on the Cross, as mentioned in three of the four gospels (Matt. XXVII.45–46; Mark XV.33–34; Luke XXIII.44–45), where it is said that darkness fell upon the earth at the sixth hour and lasted until the ninth, at which time Christ died. The office of the ninth canonical hour, nones, is named in l. 2 (6,8). This stanza appears among terms for Christ in the Y version of *LaufE* (*LaufE* 1979, 364) and in a similar environment in *RE* 1665, Hh 2r.

Stanza 10

The opening line of this *dróttkvætt* stanza is very similar to Snorri Sturluson's *Háttatal* 14 (SnSt *Ht* 14,1[III] *Hákun rœðr með heiðan*), and the writer may well have had it in mind, as Snorri's stanza appears later in the treatise as *FoGT* st. 35. Sveinbjörn Egilsson (*SnE* 1848–87, II 190 n. 1) first suggested that the main event mentioned in this stanza might be a reference to the burning of the cathedral at Skálholt by a lightning strike in 1309, mentioned in many of the Icelandic annals. Cf. *Lárentíus saga biskups* (ÍF 17, 304), *Skálholts-Annaler* (ed. Storm 1888, 202). This took place in the reign of King Hákon háleggr 'Long-leg' Magnússon of Norway (r. 1299–1319). As the stanza represents the event as having taken place in the past, it has been presumed to date from after Hákon's death in 1319, thus providing a *terminus post quem* for the stanza and possibly for the treatise as a whole (cf. *FoGT* 1884, xliii). The stanza presents the cathedral fire as God's punishment of the sinful Icelanders. It is an open question as to whether the writer of *FoGT* considered this an example of contemporaneous events or of a named ruler of the land, or both. The stanza's syntax is difficult if W's *af* 'from, out of' l. 4 (6,16) and *ok* 'and' l. 7 (6,19) are retained; they have been emended to *að* in both instances, following suggestions of Sveinbjörn Egilsson in the first instance and Jón Þorkelsson in the second (cf. *FoGT* 1884, 246 nn. 4 and 6).

6,14 handsterkr 'strong-handed': This adjective could be construed either with *Hákon*, as here, or with *Guð* 'God'.

Chapter 4: Hypallage

The definition of *FoGT* follows that of *D* (l. 2579). The same definition is provided by *Gg* (p. 56) while *G* gives one example without an accompanying definition: *'Trade rati uentos' dicas, hypallage fiet* (I 39) 'If you say "give the ship to the winds", *hypallage* will occur'. The example given in *G* is the standard example of the figure, and can be found e.g. in Isidore of Seville's *Etymologiae* (I 36.22) and in Servius's commentary to *Aen*, I 9: ... *hypallage, quae fit quotienscumque per contrarium verba intelleguntur. sic alibi 'dare classibus austros'* [*Aen*, III 61], *cum ventis naves demus, non navibus ventos* (ed. Thilo and Hagen 1881–1902, I 15) '... hypallage, which occurs whenever words are understood by means of the contrary. Thus [he says] elsewhere 'to give the winds to the fleet', when we should give the ships to the winds, not the winds to the ships'. Servius defines the figure in a more general way than *D* and *FoGT*.

6,21 verðr það er 'occurs when': The phrasing is unusual in the grammatical literature. The more common phrase *X verðr* (or *verðr X*) *þá er* 'X occurs when' can be found e.g. in chapter 1 (2,1), in *TGT* (1884, 75 l. 10) and in *FGT* (ed. Hreinn Benediktsson 1972, 222).

6,21 þolandi 'passive': This present participle is a literal translation of the Latin term *patiens* 'passive' (lit. 'suffering'). *FoGT* is the only Old Norse grammatical text which uses *þolandi* in this technical sense. *TGT* uses *píning* 'suffering', e.g.: *í því skilsk hon* [sc. *hluttekning*] *frá nafni at hon merkir gerð eða píning ok hefir ymsar stundir sem orð* (*TGT* 1884, 11) 'the participle is distinguished from the noun in that it signifies action or suffering and has various tenses as verbs'.

6,22 gierandi[1] 'active': This present participle is a literal translation of the Latin term *agens* 'active' (lit. 'doing'). *FoGT* is the only Old Norse grammatical text which uses *gerandi* in this technical sense. *TGT* uses *gerð* 'active', cf. commentary to *þolandi* above (6,21).

6,22 sem hier 'as here': Stanza 11 cannot be said to illustrate the definition given in 6,21–22. The point of the verse is that the adjective is transferred from the word to which it logically belongs to another word: The slain man's inheritance > the man's slain inheritance. However, in st. 11 the word from which the adjective has been transferred (i.e. 'man') has been left out.

Stanza 11

This *dróttkvætt* stanza is in the variant form called *alhent* 'fully rhymed' by Snorri Sturluson in *Háttatal* (cf. SnSt *Ht* 44[III], SnE 2007, 21 and 83), and consists of several short, moralising statements about the parlous state of the world. There are two pairs of full rhymes in each line. Ólsen (*FoGT* 1884, 250–52) thought that the stanza, and ll. 3–4 (6,25–26) and 7–8 (8,1–2) in particular, might be an allusion to the situation in Denmark in the interregnum of 1332–40, when the kingdom was divided into four parts. He suggested that the reference to Jutlanders (*Jótar*) in l. 3 (6,25) might allude to the uprising in Northern Jutland against the German count Gert (Gerhard III of Holstein), which resulted in his death at the hands of Niels Ebbesen and his brothers and ultimately in the ascent of Valdimar IV to the throne in June 1340.

6,24 grafins...meiðar 'The trees of the †*seiðs grafins*† [GOLD(?) > MEN]' [*Meiðar* †*grafins seiðs*†]: The noun *meiðar* appears to be the base-word of a man-kenning, but the phrase *seiðs grafins*, of which the most obvious translation would be 'of the engraved (or "buried") coalfish', does not provide a satisfactory determinant. Several interpretations of the two untranslated words, which probably form a kenning for gold, have been proposed, but none of them is entirely satisfactory. The emendation *eiðs gramnis* 'of the isthmus of the snake' [GOLD] was adopted by *FoGT* 1884, 247–48, *Skj* B, II 232 and *FoGT* 2004, 34, but *gramnis* is unmetrical, as a short disyllabic word is expected here. The emendation of 'grafins' to *gramnis* was first proposed by Jón Ólafsson of Svefneyjar (1786, 61), and has been followed by all subsequent editors except Kock (*Skald*, II 120 and *NN* §2354), who retains *grafins*. This unattested manuscript form may be a variant of the snake-*heiti grafningr* (cf. Þul *Orma* 2,3[III]). W's *seiðs* 'of the saithe/coalfish' could also form the base-word of a snake-kenning, but would be otiose in this sense if *grafins* also denotes a snake. Hence editors have emended *seiðs* to *eiðs* 'of the isthmus' to provide a base-word that will produce a gold-kenning following the pattern 'land of the snake'.

8,3 Hier...kallaðr 'Here ... slain': On the notion of a 'slain inheritance', cf. *Jónsbók*: *Ef maðr verðr fyrir þeiri villu, at hann vegr mann til arfs eða ræðr bana fram kominn, þá hefir hann fyrirvegit þeim arfi* (ed. Ólafur Halldórsson 1904, 88 cp. 10) 'If a man errs so that he slays a man in order to obtain the inheritance or has him slain, then he has forfeited the inheritance by manslaughter'.

8,4 í...fígúra 'the same ... another place': This is a reference to *Aen*, III 61, whence the example is drawn. The same example is given in *Dg* (82v): *'Date classibus austros' pro 'classes austris'* [*Aen*, III 61] '"give the winds to the ships" instead of "the ships to the wind"'. A modified form of the same Virgilian example is used as an illustration of *hypallage* in *G* (I 39). The Old Norse example in st. 12 is clearly based on the Virgilian line.

Stanza 12
Stanza 12 uses two conventional kennings to provide an indigenous couplet imitating its Latin model. Góinn l. 2 (8,6) is the name of a mythical serpent in *Grímnismál* 34,4 and *Gylfaginning* (*SnE* 2005, 19); see also Anon Þul *Orma* 2,2[III].

8,9 í öðrum stað segiz svá 'in another place it is said thus': Again, *stað* 'place' refers to a passus in a particular text, namely *perflavit fistula buccas* 'the flute blew through the jaws' in Theodulus's *Ecloga*, l. 6 (ed. Mosetti Casaretto 1997). These words are quoted in *D* (l. 2581) and can also be found in *Gg* (p. 56). The Old Norse example is clearly modelled on the Latin example.

Stanza 13
Like st. 12, this couplet was probably invented by the writer of *FoGT* to imitate the Latin example *perflavit fistula buccas* (see note to 8,9 above). Nevertheless, the couplet succinctly conveys a common medieval Scandinavian disdain for the musical performances of minstrels, which are usually represented as grotesque, both in sound and in the physical movements required to produce the sound. Cf. Máni Lv 2[II] and 3[II], where very similar vocabulary is used.
8,11 höfuðskrípamanns 'the lead minstrel's': The compound is *hap. leg.* but cf. *skrípalǫt* 'strange gestures' (Máni Lv 2,4[II]), used of a minstrel who plays both a fiddle and a flute. In Máni's stanza *skríp*- rhymes with *píp*-, as here. Old Icelandic *skrípi* means something monstrous or grotesque.
8,12 blása 'to blow': *ONP* takes *blása* to be the only attestation of a feminine noun meaning 'wind instrument, flute'. This is the most natural interpretation and many parallel examples with the structure 'X is called Y' can be found in the Old Norse corpus. But this interpretation is at odds with st. 13, which shows that *blása* must be understood as the infinitive of the verb *blása* 'blow'. *SnE* 1848–87, II 199 and *FoGT* 2004, 62 also take *blása* to be an infinitive.
8,14 nauðsynja 'necessities': Comparing with Latin parallels, such as *ornatus necessitatisue causa* (*Barbarismus*, ed. Holtz 1981, 667) 'for the sake of ornament or necessity', one would expect the singular *nauðsynjar*. *TGT* uses the plural in one instance: *fyrir nauðsynja sakir eða fegrðar* (1884, 86) 'for the sake of necessities or beauty' and the

singular in another: *fyrir fegrðar sakir eða nauðsynjar* (1884, 100) 'for the sake of ornament or beauty'—only in ms. A, W has *nauðsynja*.

Chapter 5: Prosopopoeia
FoGT defines *prosopopoeia* as the insertion [in a poem/text] of a new person. The definition deviates from the one given in *D* (l. 2582), *Dg* (82v) and *Gg* (p. 118), where the figure is defined as the formation (*D*) or fashioning (*Dg* and *Gg*) of a new person. *G*'s definition stands on its own: *Si bene quis recitet, tunc prosopopoeïa fiet* 'if one recites well, then prosopopoeïa will occur'. *FoGT* divides the figure into three subgroups: 1) when something living addresses something lifeless (st. 14), 2) when something lifeless addresses something living (st. 15) and 3) when something lifeless addresses another lifeless thing (sts 16 and 17). *Gg* divides the figure into five subgroups and the first three correspond exactly to those of *FoGT*: *Quando animata res loquitur ad inanimatam, ut Ouidius in* Tristibus *loquitur ad librum suum dicens* '[...]'. *Vel quando res inanimata loquitur ad animatam rem, ut in* Metamorphosi *tellus ad Iouem* '[...]'. *Vel quando res inanimata loquitur ad rem inanimatam, ut libri Ouidii adinuicem* '[...]' (p. 118) 'When something animate speaks to something inanimate, as Ovid speaks to his book in *Tristia*, saying '[...]'. Or when something inanimate speaks to something animate, as the earth speaks to Jupiter in *Metamorphoses* '[...]'. Or when something inanimate speaks to something inanimate, as the books of Ovid speak to one another '[...]''. *Gg* adds two further subgroups: one where a rational being speaks to an irrational being (a man to a beast) and where an irrational being speaks to another irrational being. Ólsen quotes a condensed and corrupt version of *Gg* at this point (*FoGT* 1884, 124–25n.). *Dg*'s explanation is somewhere between *FoGT* and *Gg*: *quando res animata et rationalis loquitur ad rem inanimatam, uel econuerso, uel quando rationale loquitur ad irrationale, uel econuerso* (82v) 'when something animate and rational speaks to something inanimate or the other way around, or when a rational [being] speaks to an irrational one or the other way around'.

8,15 ísetning 'insertion': This word appears to be attested twice in the Old Norse corpus. The other attestation is found in a chapter heading in *Jónsbók*: *Um arfs ísetning ok skulda lykning* (ed. Ólafur Halldórsson 1904, 88). In this legal text *ísetning* probably means 'illegal possession of an inheritance (cf. *NGL*, 5 s. v. *íseta*). The *Jónsbók* attestation would then be semantically unrelated to the attestatin in

FoGT and translate as 'About the illegal possession of an inheritance and the payment of debts (cf. Schulman 2010, 117 for a different translation).

Stanza 14
Another moralising stanza, even stronger than sts 10 and 11, here addressed to the land of Iceland (= the Icelanders). If the writer of *FoGT* was a cleric, as seems likely, he would have identified with the views of 'those who seldom use swords' in ll. 7–8 (8,23–24).

8,20 píslir 'punishments': W's reading is obscured by a hole, but the emendation is confirmed by *aðalhending* and by sense and has been adopted by all editors.

8,22 óþýð 'rough': Feminine adjective agreeing with *fold* 'land' l. 7 (8,23); W has the masculine form *óþýðr*, which must therefore be emended.

8,23 þeim...24 neyta 'those ... swords': That is, members of the clergy. *Neyta* 'use' normally takes the genitive of what is used, but the dative *sverðum* 'swords' here may possibly (so *FoGT* 1884, 253 n. 5) have been influenced by the writer's knowledge of Latin constructions with a similar sense, like *uti gladiis* 'to use swords', though *utor* takes the ablative rather than the dative case.

8,25 talar skáldið nefndri fígúru 'the poet speaks using the above-mentioned figure': The construction *tala e-u* is unusual and the dative is perhaps best seen as a dative of manner (cf. Nygaard 1906 §110c).

8,26 nefnir...byggja 'names the land ... inhabit it': Geoffrey of Vinsauf's *Poetria nova* also uses the castigation of a land instead of its inhabitants as an example of *prosopopoeia*, beginning: *Quid, Gallia, garris?* (ed. Faral 1924, 213, l. 517) 'Why, France, do you prattle?' (trans. Kopp 1971, 52). Another example of the same figure can be found in the diary of the Bergen humanist Absalon Pedersen Beyer (d. 1575) where he writes: *Væ dig Bergen du fule Sodoma oc Gomorrhæ søster* (ed. Iversen 1963, 140) 'Woe to you, Bergen, you foul sister of Sodom and Gomorrah'.

8,26 það 'it': The emendation of *þau* to *það* was first introduced in *SnE* 1818, 338 and has been adopted in all subsequent editions.

Stanza 15
Stanza 15 illustrates the kind of *prosopopoeia* that attributes life and speech to an entity normally regarded as inanimate, in this case water,

which symbolises the act of alms-giving. The stanza's metre is a variety of *runhent* 'end-rhymed' with four-syllable lines rhyming in pairs. The opening line is reminiscent of similar stanzas (in *tøglag* 'journey metre'), enumerating the qualities of a poet and a troll-woman respectively, in Bragi *Troll*[III] and Anon (*SnE*) 9[III], where the first lines begin *Skǫld kalla mik* and *Trǫll kalla mik*.

10,1 kalla mig 'I call myself': Understood here, in conformity with the sense of the prose commentary, to mean 'I call myself', even though this sense would more usually be rendered by *kǫllumz*. *Kalla mig* could also mean 'they call me [water]' or 'call me [water]'; cf. *FoGT* 1884, 254 n. 1.

10,9 vatn Krists 'the water of Christ': The water of Christ usually signifies either the baptismal water or the water that ran with the blood from the wound in Christ's side at the Crucifixion (John XIX. 34). A specimen of the rich medieval religious water symbolism can be found in *Messuskýringar* (ed. Kolsrud 1952, 37–39).

10,10 svá... 11 syndabruna 'just as ... fire of sins': *FoGT* here paraphrases Sir. III.33: *Ignem ardentem extinguit aqua et elemosyna resistit peccatis* (ed. Weber *et al.* 1994, 1033) 'Water quencheth a flaming fire, and alms resisteth sins' (trans. *Douay-Rheims Bible*). Often quoted in the form *Sicut aqua extinguit ignem, ita eleemosyna extinguit peccatum* (see Kirby 1976–80, I 120) 'Just as water quenches fire, so alms-giving quenches sin'. The same passage is paraphrased in *Kristinn réttr Árna Biskups*: *Ǫlmusugerð er it mesta miskunnarverk. Hverr sem þetta gerir réttliga ok með góðum vilja, þá biðr hon ok þiggr af Guði miskunn sínum gjafara, ok sløkkvir svá hans syndir sem vatn sløkkvir eld* (*NGL*, V 31) 'The gift of alms is the greatest work of mercy. Whoever does this rightly and with good will, then the work of mercy asks and receives of God mercy for its giver, and it quenches his sins, just as water quenches fire'. Kirby (1976–80, I 120–21) lists three additional Old Norse quotations of this Biblical passage.

10,11 syndabruna 'the fire of sins': The compound *syndabruni* 'fire of sins' is a *hap. leg.*

10,14 Barruk 'Baruch': *FoGT* erroneously ascribes the parable of the battle between the sea and the forest to the *Book of Baruch*. Ólsen saw some similarity to Baruch VI.62 (*FoGT* 1884, 125n.), and Meissner (1932, 103–04) suggested that it referred to the Syrian apocalypse of Baruch 36–39 but the parable comes, as Paasche has shown (1928), from *2 Esdras* (IV.13–17): *Proficiscens profectus sum ad silvam* *lignorum campi, et cogitaverunt cogitationem et dixerunt: Venite et eamus et faciamus ad mare bellum, ut recedat coram nos, et faciamus nobis alias silvas. Et similiter fluctus maris et ipsi cogitaverunt cogitationem et dixerunt: Venite ascendentes debellemus silvam campi, ut et ibi consummemus nobismet ipsis aliam regionem. Et factus est cogitatus silvae in vano, venit enim ignis et consumpsit eam. Similiter et cogitatus fluctuum maris, stetit enim harena et prohibuit eam* (ed. Weber *et al.* 1994, 1936) 'I went into a forest of trees of the plain, and they made a plan and said, "Come, let us go and make war against the sea, so that it may recede before us, and so that we may make for ourselves more forests." In like manner the waves of the sea also made a plan and said, "Come, let us go up and subdue the forest of the plain so that there also we may gain more territory for ourselves." But the plan of the forest was in vain, for the fire came and consumed it; likewise also the plan of the waves of the sea was in vain, for the sand stood firm and blocked it (trans. *NRSV*, 1776–77)'.

10,15 yfirgang 'transgression': This word also carries the connotations: 'arrogance, presumption'.

Stanzas 16 and 17

The two *dróttkvætt* sts 16 and 17 form a pair and must be understood together. They provide a versified account of the passage from 2 *Esdras*, referred to in the prose text as from Baruch. The two stanzas turn the Latin text into a poetic dialogue in which the forest and the sea speak directly to one another.

10,18 varð skrjúpr í því 'in that it was weak': That is, the forest did not foresee that its plan to take over the sea's territory could lead to its own destruction by fire.

10,19 ... W has a hole here and a word is missing. *SnE* 1848–87, II 202 n. 2 conjectured *reitu* 'marked out space, territory', and this has been accepted by later editors. The word must begin with *r* to alliterate and be of two syllables.

10,23 eg upp 'I up': W has another hole, and the *eg* and the *u* of *upp* are missing.

10,31 sterkr 'strong': W has *sterk*, but the masculine adjective nominative singular is required here to qualify *bani* 'killer'.

10,31 bol 'trunk': W's 'bǫl' must be a spelling for *bol* 'trunk of a tree'.

12,1 Skógr...3 júða 'The forest ... of the Jews': 2 *Esdras* already contains a moral interpretation of the fable, namely that one should be content with what one has. *FoGT*'s allegorical interpretation, which might be based on a foreign source, supplements the moral interpretation of *2 Esdras*.

12,1 chaldeos 'Chaldeans': This ethnonym is declined according to the Latin inflection (acc. pl.).

12,1 Þjóðir...2 eldinn 'The peoples ... by the fire': Subjects and objects appear to have been transposed in this passage. One would have expected *sandr merkir þjóðir þær sem eyddu ríki chaldeorum, en eldrinn guðspjalligan kenning* 'the sand signifies the peoples who destroyed the kingdom of the Chaldeans, while the fire signifies the evangelical teaching'. Alternatively, a passive construction could have been used.

12,1 chaldeorum 'of the Chaldeans': Declined in accordance with the Latin declension (gen. pl.).

12,2 kienning 'teaching': Not in W. This word was first added in *SnE* 1848, 202, and it has been adopted in all subsequent editions. The collocation *guðspjallig kenning* is also found below (at 40,14) and in *Pétrs saga postola* I (ed. Unger 1874, 9).

Chapter 6: Apostropha

The initial part of the definition corresponds to the one given in *D* (ll. 2583–84).

12,4 ef 'in which': *Ef* is not uncommonly used to introduce a dependent relative clause (see *ONP*: ³*ef* B). The same usage is found below (42,20).

12,5 setr...6 til 'rightly uses ... in the second': This second part of the definition differs from both *Dg* and *Gg* (p. 101). *Dg* explains: *Apostrophe est sermonis a persona ad personam directio. Et fit ut si factus fuerit sermo de aliquo in tertia persona, et postea dirigatur ad eundem in secunda, ut: 'Nec te tua plurima Panthu labentem pietas, nec Apollinis infula* [< *insula*] *texit'* [*Aen*, II 429–30] (82v) '*Apostropha* is the direction of speech from a person to a person, and it occurs if speech has been made about someone in the third person, and afterwards is directed to the same in the second, such as "Neither your great piety, Panthus, nor the headband of Apollo protected you, when you fell"'. The point here is probably that Aeneas, who has just mentioned two fallen Trojans, suddenly apostrophises the dead Panthus. If this is right, *ad eundem* 'to the same' makes little sense here.

12,5 nafn "name": *Nafn*, like Latin *nomen*, has the double meaning of 'name, appellation' and 'noun'. The context apparently requires *fornafn* 'pronoun' since neither names nor nouns have person as an inflectional category (cf. the comment below on *í fyrstu skilningu* 12,5). The Old Norse definition differs from the Latin definitions and no examples are provided.

12,5 í fyrstu skilningu 'in the first person': Instances of *skilning* in the sense of '(grammatical) person' have not been found outside *FoGT*, but the Icelandic Book of Homilies uses *skilning* in the sense 'division, person (of the Trinity)': *Ek trúi enn ok á anda inn helga sem á fǫður ok á son, því at þær þrjár skilningar eru aljafnar ok eitt* (ed. de Leeuw van Weenen 1993, 68v) 'Furthermore, I believe in the Holy Ghost as in the Father and the Son, because those three divisions are equal and one'. The Old Norse Latin primer, fragmentarily preserved in AM 921 III 4°, uses *grein* fem. for 'grammatical person' (ed. Ólsen 1884, 156). On the Latin primer, see most recently Gade (2007b).

12,6 En þó finnz öðruvís giert 'Yet it can also be found in a different way': It is not explained how the following three examples differ from the initial definition.

12,6 Snorri Snorri Sturluson (1179–1241) was a wealthy Icelandic chieftain and an important political figure in the turbulent dealings between the Icelanders and the Norwegian crown in the first half of the thirteenth century. He visited Norway twice and was twice lawspeaker of Iceland. The *Edda* (c. 1225), a treatise on poetics and mythology, is securely attributed to him, and his authorship of *Heimskringla*, a series of biographies of the kings of Norway, is probable. Snorri was also a poet. Aside from his *Háttatal* 'List of Metres', a *clavis metrica* comprising 102 stanzas, which forms, together with a prose commentary, the fourth part of his *Edda* and was composed for his Norwegian patrons, Jarl Skúli Bárðarson and King Hákon Hákonarson, only fragments remain of his poetic oeuvre. These include seven *lausavísur*, one scrap of a poem addressed to a bishop and another about Skúli.

Stanza 18

Stanza 18 is one of Snorri Sturluson's seven extant *lausavísur* and is recorded in no other source, although it was copied by Árni Magnússon, presumably from W, in AM 761 b 4°ˣ on f. 351r. It is a charming, light-hearted address to an unnamed seafarer, probably a merchant or ship's captain, about to put to sea from Norway to Iceland, to carry the speaker's, Snorri's, greetings to a certain Eyjólfr. Snorri was in Norway 1218–20 and again 1237–39, so this stanza is likely to date from one or other of those two periods.

12,8 Eyjólfi 'to Eyjólfr': Identified in the prose text as Eyjólfr Brúnason (see note to 12,16 on the significance of this identification). It is not known where in Iceland he came from. Only one *helmingr* by this poet has survived (Ebrún Lv 1[III]), and it was recorded in the X version of *LaufE*, possibly from lost leaves of W (cf. *LaufE* 1979, 176–77, 269–70, 345n.). It is a rather amusing half-stanza about a Norwegian merchant who buys a pair of shoes, designated by the kenning *snekkjur ilja* 'warships of the footsoles', which is included in *LaufE* to illustrate poetic synonyms for the leg. It is not dissimilar in tone to Snorri's stanza.

12,8 elfar … 9 úlfseðjandi 'feeder of the wolf of the river [(literally 'wolf-feeder of the river') SHIP > SEAFARER]': A playful, inverted kenning, imagining the master of the ship 'feeding', i. e. loading cargo onto, his ship. Kock (*NN* §2825) considers the imagery refers to the behaviour of wolves preying on corpses in the water after a naval battle, but this context does not seem appropriate here.

12,10 heim 'home': That is, to Iceland, revealing Snorri's orientation towards his native land, as observed by Ólsen (*FoGT* 1884, 256 n. 1).

12,15 sannauðigra manna 'of truly rich men': If the prose commentary is to be believed, Eyjólfr's riches must have comprised his skill as a poet and his generosity with knowledge rather than material wealth.

12,16 Þessi … gott 'This … poet': Eyjólfr Brúnason is the only poet whose patronymic is mentioned in *FoGT* and the only poet whose poetic abilities are characterised. Perhaps this is an indication that the writer did not presume that the audience of *FoGT* would be familiar with Eyjólfr and his poetry.

12,17 Óláfr It has usually been presumed, though it cannot be confirmed, that this Óláfr, named here without a patronymic, is Óláfr hvítaskáld 'White poet' Þórðarson (c. 1210–59), Snorri Sturluson's nephew and the author of *TGT*. Stanzas 19 and 20, two *dróttkvætt* couplets, are all that remain of a poem, possibly a *drápa*, in honour of one Thomas, generally considered to be St Thomas Becket (c. 1120–70), Archbishop of Canterbury, who was canonised in 1173. No medieval title of the poem from which these extracts come is known to exist, but the name 'Thomas drapa' appears in Árni Magnússon's copy of the two couplets in AM 761 a 4°x, f. 84r, where he speculates on whether the composer was Óláfr svartaskáld 'Black poet' Leggsson or some other Óláfr. The text of this poem is extant only in W.

Stanza 19
Stanza 19 is a couplet addressed to a saint, presumed to be St Thomas from the stanza following.

Stanza 20
It is presumed, from the prose text's *í öðrum stað* 'in another place' (12,21), that st. 20 comes from the same poem as st. 19, and that both couplets are about Thomas. Thomas Becket is also the subject of the first four stanzas of the fourteenth-century fragment *Heilagra manna drápa* (Anon *Heil* 1–4[VII]) and there is a late *Thómas diktur erkibyskups* in the sixteenth-century manuscript AM 713 4° (*ÍM*, II 459–62). This charismatic medieval saint, who came to symbolise the independence of the Church in the face of secular powers, was the subject of several Latin and Old Norse prose lives. The two most complete Old Norse texts are *Thómas saga* I (second half of the thirteenth century) and *Thómas saga* II (first half of the fourteenth century). *Thómas saga* II was written by Abbot Arngrímr Brandsson, who was also the author of a saga about Guðmundr Arason. This version of the saga, together with two fourteenth-century fragments, appears to draw on an Icelandic translation of the now lost Latin life of Thomas by Robert of Cricklade (Duggan 2004), probably by the priest Bergr Gunnsteinsson, active in the late twelfth-early thirteenth century (Widding *et al.* 1963, 334; Stefán Karlsson 1973; Jakobsen 1993). Thomas Becket was very popular in Iceland, especially among churchmen seeking independence from secular chieftains, and his shrine at Canterbury very early became the goal of pilgrimage by pious Icelanders such as Hrafn Sveinbjarnarson (Cormack 1994, 156–57).

12,24 Er...26 framburðar 'This figure ... by someone': *D* (l. 2584) mentions letters, but not prologues. Cf. also *Dg*: *Huius etiam exempla multa reperies in auctoribus et in litteris missiuis* (82v) 'You will find many examples of this figure in the *auctores* and in sent letters'.
12,24 jafnan 'always': All editors have removed the superfluous *er* between *fígúra* and *jafnan*.
12,25 þeim prologis bóka er einhverjum eru ætlaðar 'in those prologues of books which are destined [for correction or publication]

by someone': The most logical antecedent of *ætlaðar* 'intended' (fem. nom. pl.) is *prologis* (masc. dat./abl. pl.), which is a Latin word and inflected accordingly, but the two do not agree in gender. The antecedent of *ætlaðar* must therefore be *bóka* (fem. gen. pl.), but this makes the use of the demonstrative *þeim* before *prologis* slightly awkward. Therefore, Ólsen suggested an emendation of *í þeim prologis bóka* to *í prologis þeirra bóka* 'in prologues of those books' or *í prologis bóka* 'in prologues of books' (*FoGT* 1884, 127n.).

Chapter 7: Hendiadys
The initial part of the definition does not correspond well with the one given in *D* which speaks of transforming an adjective into a noun or the other way around (ll. 2585–86). The examples below (sts 21 and 22) make it clear that *FoGT* by *sundrlauss hlutr* 'separate entity' means a distinct entity while *óskiftiligr hlutr* 'indivisible entity' means a unified whole.

12,27 er[2] **'where'**: The emendation of W's 'en*n*' to *er* was introduced in *SnE* 1818, 339 and has been adopted in all subsequent editions. Ólsen (*FoGT* 1884, 128) was the first to flag it as an emendation.

12,27 eru merktir fyrir 'signify': The collocation *vera merkt fyrir* can have two opposite meanings. Both occur on p. 18 of *Pétrs saga postula* I (ed. Unger 1874). The first meaning is 'being signified by': *Eru þessi líf merkt fyrir .ii. systr, veraldligt fyrir Martham, en upp- litningarlíf fyrir Mariam* (ll. 9–10) 'These ways of life are signified by the two sisters, the worldly by Martha and the contemplative life by Mary'. The other meaning of *vera merkt fyrir* is 'signify': *Þat er hugsanda, at engi maðr misjafni með þessum inum ágætum Guðs postolum, þó at annarr sé merktr fyrir upplitningarlíf, þat sem á sér berr líking himnesks lífs, en annarr beri líking þessa heims lífs, sá sem merktr er fyrir verkligt líf. Því at í því lífi sem Petrus merkir váru þá báðir, en í því sem Johannes merkir váru ókomnir báðir ...* (ll. 19–25) 'Note that no one should make these two outstanding apostles of God [Peter and John] unequal, even though the one signifies the contemplative life, which carries in itself a likeness to the heavenly life, and the other, he who signifies the worldly life, carries the likeness of the life of this world. For they were both in the life which Peter represents, but neither of them had yet come to the life which John represents...' (Cf. Fritzner: *merkja* 5). *FoGT* requires the second meaning of *vera merkt fyrir* in this context, but in 14,5, immediately following st. 21, the first sense is required.

14,1 er...2 hluta 'it is governed ... joined entities': It is difficult to make sense of this part of the definition. In this edition *hon* (i.e. the figure *hendiadys*) is taken as the subject of a passive clause (*patiens*) while *samfesting* and *leysing* are interpreted as agents in the accusative. The sentence can also be construed *er hon underdregin samfesting laussa hluta ...*, taking *samfesting* as a nominative and *undirdregin* as an attributive adjective. *SnE* 1848–87, II 207 reads as in this edition, but translates: *Endiadis* [...] *est figura, qua duæ res disjunctæ pro una indivisa significantur, aut una res indivisa pro duabus divisis; cui figuræ subjecta est compactio rerum solutarum et solutio rerum compactarum* 'Endiadis is the figure by which two separate entities are signified instead of one undivided, or one undivided instead of two separate; subsumed under this figure is the joining together of loose entities and the loosening of joined entities'. *SnE* 1848–87 thus sees *samfesting* and *leysing* as subjects in the nominative. Since the main verb of the sentence (*er*) is placed in the first position, the plural is not required even though there are two subjects (cf. Nygaard 1906 §70a). The interpretation of *SnE* 1848–87 seems to require an oblique form of the pronoun while W has the nominative 'hº' *hon*.

Stanza 21
The couplet illustrates *hendiadys* in the way this figure is explained by the prose text, but the scribe of W makes two transcription errors in l. 1 (14,3) of words which are correct in the prose text immediately below, viz. *skálm* 'point', which he renders as *skamm* in the verse line, and *og* 'and', which he gives as *ef* 'if'. These mistakes suggest that the scribe is very unlikely to have been either the writer of *FoGT* or the redactor of W.

14,5 merkt fyrir 'signified by': See commentary to 12,27 above.

Stanza 22
Stanza 22 is a somewhat contrived *helmingr* illustrating the occurrence of 'joined' and 'loose' entities, probably influenced by the standard Latin examples *armatum virum* 'armed man' and *arma virumque* 'arms and the man', the first two words of Virgil's *Aeneid*. It imagines a scenario in which the speaker views (presumably with jealousy in mind) the efforts of another man, *karl inn klædda* 'the clothed man' (14,7), to entice the speaker's wife to have sexual relations with him

by offering her presents of fine clothes. So *karl inn klædda* must be taken here to refer to the man and the clothes he was carrying, not wearing, as one might normally expect of such a phrase.

14,7 Þýddiz...8 sína 'My wife ... his desire': The prose gloss appears to understand the phrase *þörf sína* to refer to the man's desire for the woman, whom he hopes to attract with a present of clothing, although *sína*, being reflexive, should properly refer back to the grammatical subject of the sentence, *kona mín* 'my wife' and denote her desire, not the man's.

14,9 karl 'man': Ólsen (*FoGT* 1884, 258) emends this second instance of the noun *karl* in the *helmingr* to *kauða* 'wretch' to obtain *skothending* and to avoid repetition, but there is no manuscript support for such a change.

14,13 heitir...15 hluta 'that hendiadys ... joined entities': Compare the designations *sundrlaus endiadis* 'separate hendiadys' and *samföst endiadis* 'conjoined hendiadys' with *Dg*: *Endiadis est adiectiui in substantiuum uel substantiui in adiectiuum permutatio siue resolutio, ut in Virgilio: 'Arma uirumque cano', et in littera: 'Armatumque uirum'* etc. *Et fit duobus modis, siue coniunctim et disiunctim. Coniunctim fit quando adiectiuum et substantiuum ponitur in littera ut 'armatum uirum'. Disiunctim fit quando solum adiectiuum ponitur uel solum substantiuum* (82v) '*Endiadis* is the permutation or transformation of an adjective into a noun or of a noun into an adjective, as in Virgil "Of arms and a man I sing" [*Aen*, I 1] and in the text [of *D*]: "an armed man" etc. And it occurs in two ways, viz. conjoined or separate. The conjoined [*hendiadys*] occurs when an adjective and a noun is given in the text, such as "an armed man". The separate [*hendiadys*] occurs when only an adjective is given [in the text] or only a noun'.

Chapter 8: Ebasis
The initial definition agrees with *D* (ll. 2589–90). *G* does not contain a figure by the name of *ebasis* (or something similar, a common variant of the name is *ecbasis*) and the figure is not commonly found in rhetorical tracts. Quintilian mentions that some call arguments derived from causes or efficients *ecbasis* (*Institutiones oratoriae*, V 10.86). This agrees well with the literal meaning of the Greek term (i.e. 'outcome'). However, *D* and *FoGT* clearly had a different understanding of the figure and they are closer to the figure Quintilian calls

parekbasis (*Institutiones oratoriae*, IV 3.14) 'digression'. *Dg* explains *ecbasis* as follows: *Ecbasis est quedam euagatio materie, vel est digressio quedam a principali materia, ut apud Georgica Virgilii in tempestatis descriptione apparet. Sed nota quod hec figura nihil ualet nisi reuertatur ad propositum. Quod si fiat pulchra est* (82v) 'Ecbasis is a departure from the matter or it is a digression from the principal matter, as can be seen in Virgil's *Georgics* in the description of the storm. But note that this figure is of no use unless it is brought back to the main subject. If that happens, it is beautiful'. *Dg*'s source at this point is probably Servius's commentary to *Georgics*, I 322: *Est autem hoc loco ecbasis poetica ad describendam tempestatem* (ed. Thilo and Hagen 1881–1902, III 200) 'A poetic *ecbasis* is here used to describe the storm'.

14,17 sem...20 konungs 'as ... Erminrekr': The writer evidently sees the section on Hamðir and Sǫrli in *Ragnarsdrápa* as a departure from the actual subject matter of the poem, i.e. King Ragnarr. According to the commonly accepted modern interpretation, *Ragnarsdrápa* is an ekphrastic shield poem that primarily consists of descriptions of mythological and legendary scenes. The shield was a gift of the king to the poet, and the poem about the shield is the poet's counter-gift (Clunies Ross 1993). The king is first and foremost extolled indirectly through the praise of his magnificent gift to the poet. The writer sees the mythological and legendary sections (i.e. the bulk of the preserved parts of the poem) as excursuses, and *FoGT* therefore challenges our interpretation of the poem. It is possible that the writer knew more about *Ragnarsdrápa* than we believe we do, but it is equally possible that he knew less. In fact, most of his comments on the contents of *Ragnarsdrápa* and the story about Hamðir and Sǫrli can be extracted from *Snorra Edda*. *FoGT* provides only one piece of information about *Ragnarsdrápa* that cannot be derived directly from *Snorra Edda* as it is preserved in mss R, T^x and C (the section on Hamðir and Sǫrli is not found in W), namely that Hamðir and Sǫrli are the relatives of Áslaug (on this see commentary to 16,21–22 below).

14,17 Bragi...18 skáld 'Bragi the poet': Bragi inn gamli 'the Old' Boddason. This skald was a Norwegian who probably lived in the second half of the ninth century. *Landnámabók* (ÍF 1 vol. 1, 82) mentions him as being associated by marriage with the family of Arinbjǫrn *hersir* from Firðir (Fjordane) in Western Norway, and *Egils saga* (ÍF 2, 182 and n. 2) places him in the same context. Bragi seems to have been active as a poet in Norway not long before the settlement of

Iceland (c. 850−70). In *Skáldatal*'s list of poets (*SnE* 1848−87, III 251−69), Bragi is the first named skald whose works have survived, although they are probably incomplete. In *Skáldatal* he is associated with three patrons, Bjǫrn at Haugi, probably a Norwegian ruler, though some sources consider him Swedish (Jón Jóhannesson 1940), Eysteinn beli and Ragnarr loðbrók 'Shaggy breeches', there said to be a Danish king who himself composed poetry. Snorri Sturluson (*SnE* 1998, I 72−73) associates Bragi's poem *Ragnarsdrápa* with the legendary Viking Ragnarr loðbrók. Several legendary narratives attach to the figure of Bragi, and it is also possible that he was considered a god, as Icelandic traditions mention a supernatural being of this same name, often associated with the art of poetry (cf. *Grímnismál* 44,7, *Lokasenna*, *Sigrdrífumál* 16,2 and *Snorra Edda*, especially the introduction to *Skáldskaparmál*).

14,19 þær...21 þeim 'those stanzas ... one of those': A passage in *Vm Erp Sorla og Hamder* of *LaufE* (*LaufE* 1979, 250–51) seems to have been inspired by knowledge of these lines, while the Y^2 version of *LaufE* also introduces st. 23 (Bragi *Rdr* 3) as well as the introductory line *og er þessi visa ejn af þeim er þar eru um ortar* which almost certainly draws on *FoGT* (see *LaufE* 1979, 160–61, 251n.).

14,19 Sörla og Hamdis 'Sǫrli and Hamðir': *FoGT*, like *Snorra Edda*, names Sǫrli first, while *Hamðismál* gives Hamðir pride of place.

14,19 Hamdis 'Hamðir': The correction of 'hanðis' to *Hamdis* was introduced in *SnE* 1848, 203 and has been accepted by all subsequent editors.

14,20 Erminreks 'Erminrekr': On the form of the name, see commentary to 14,23 below.

Stanza 23

Stanza 23 is preserved in two sources, the *Skáldskaparmál* section of *SnE* (in mss R, T^x and C) and in *FoGT*. In *Skáldskaparmál* (cf. *SnE* 1998, I 50−51) the stanza is the first of a sequence of four stanzas and a *stef* 'refrain' specifically ascribed to *Ragnarsdrápa*, and these stanzas are cited at the end of a long passage recounting various narratives about the legendary Niflungar and their descendants, among whom were the brothers Hamðir and Sǫrli. The *Ragnarsdrápa* stanzas are introduced thus: *Eptir þessum sǫgum hafa flest skáld ort ok tekit ymsa þáttu. Bragi hinn gamli orti um fall Sǫrla ok Hamðis í drápu þeiri er hann orti um Ragnar loðbrók* 'Most poets have composed [poetry] based on these stories, and have used various parts [of them].

Bragi the old composed [poetry] about the death of Sǫrli and Hamðir in that *drápa* that he composed about Ragnarr loðbrók'. In the four stanzas cited in *Skáldskaparmál* Bragi depicts the vengeance carried out by the brothers Hamðir and Sǫrli, sons of Guðrún Gjúkadóttir and King Jónakr, upon the Gothic king Erminrekr, because he had their sister, his wife Svanhildr, put to death for supposed adultery with his own son Randvér. The brothers attack Erminrekr in his hall and maim him, but fail to kill him, whereupon the Goths turn upon Hamðir and Sǫrli, and kill them by pelting them with stones. This legend is also the subject of the eddic poem *Hamðismál* (see Dronke 1969, 159–242 for a comparison of this and other sources), which tells that Svanhildr was torn apart by wild horses and Randvér was hanged (*Hamðismál* 2–3 and 17).

14,22 Knátti…25 draum 'awakened with an evil dream' [*knátti að vakna við illan draum*]: An Icelandic idiom used of someone who awakes from sleep to a nightmarish reality over which he has no control (cf. Wood 1960). Some scholars (e.g. Vogt 1930, 3–5) maintain that Erminrekr was asleep and woke *from* a bad dream. In *Skáldskaparmál* Guðrún advises the brothers to attack Erminrekr at night while he is asleep.

14,23 Erminrekr A legendary Gothic king, whose image in Germanic legend may have been based upon some attenuated knowledge of the historical Ostrogothic ruler Ermanaric (d. c. 375 CE). For the historical record, see Ammianus Marcellinus, *Rerum gestarum libri qui supersunt* XXXI, ch. 3 (Rolfe 1948–52, III 394–96) and Jordanes, *Getica* (Mommsen 1882, 91–92). 'Erminrekr', the variant recorded in W and C, more frequently given in Old Icelandic as 'Jǫrmunrekr' ('-rekkr'), is the older of the two forms (so *FoGT* 1884, 259 n. 1), and closer to the Germanic Latinised original '(H)ermanaricus'; cf. *AEW*: *Jǫrmunr, Jǫrmunrekr*.

14,24 dreyrfáar 'blood-stained': W's bisyllabic *-fáar* is required to produce a six-syllable *dróttkvætt* line here.

14,26 Rósta varð í ranni 'There was tumult in the hall': A formulaic introduction to the topic of a hall-fight; cf. *Hamðismál* 23,1 *Styrr varð í ranni* 'There was uproar in the hall' and the Old English *Beowulf* 1302a *Hrēam wearð in Heorote* (*Beowulf* 2008, 45) 'There was uproar in Heorot'.

14,27 Randvies höfuðniðja 'of the chief kinsmen of Randvier [= the dynasty of the Goths]': Some scholars (so Finnur Jónsson in *Skj* B, I 1) consider this kenning to refer to Erminrekr himself, the father of Randvér, believing that the plural *hǫfuðniðjar* is intended to have a singular referent. But there is no reason to abandon the plural sense, which then denotes the Gothic royal house as a whole.

16,1 hrafnbláir 'raven-black': The brothers Hamðir and Sǫrli were linked in Old Norse legend with the Niflungar, traditionally supposed to have been dark in colour; cf. Old Norse *nifl-*, 'mist', 'darkness' (only in compounds like *Niflhel*, part of the underworld), Old High German *nebul*, Old English *nifol*, Latin *nebula* 'fog, mist, cloud'.

16,2 Erps of barmar 'the brothers of Erpr [= Hamðir and Sǫrli]': This kenning for Hamðir and Sǫrli depends upon a knowledge of the role played by a third brother, Erpr, in the lead-up to their attack on Erminrekr. Erpr 'the Dark Brown One', the son of Jónakr by a different mother, possibly a slave (*inn sundrmœðri*, *Hamðismál* 13,1), offers to help his brothers kill Erminrekr, as an arm helps a leg, as he says in *Hamðismál*, but his cryptically phrased offer is scornfully refused, Hamðir and Sǫrli killing him on the road. According to both *Hamðismál* and *Skáldskaparmál*, this fratricidal act means that they cannot succeed in killing Erminrekr outright. Bragi's use in this kenning of the poetic noun *barmi*, meaning a child fed at the same breast as another, is deeply ironic. The pleonastic particle *of*, attached to *barmar*, is untranslatable (cf. Kuhn 1929).

16,3 Stundum...er[2] 'At ... with': This variant of *ebasis* has no parallel in *D* and appears to be an original contribution by the writer to the doctrine of his treatise.

16,4 í 'in': The preposition was first added in *SnE* 1848, 203. All subsequent editors have accepted this emendation.

Stanza 24

As the prose text makes clear, st. 24 is a refrain *helmingr* (*stef*) from the anonymous poem here identified as *Nikulásdrápa*, from which the writer of *FoGT* has already quoted, without naming it, as st. 6. Such a *drápa* is likely to have had more than one *stef*.

16,8 alls grams 'of the ruler of all [= God]': Finnur Jónsson (*Skj* B, II 174), followed by *FoGT* 2004, 66 and 109, takes this kenning with the first two lines, *Ǫll þing engla boða eining alls grams í þrenningu*, which he renders as *Alle engleskarer forkynder alkongens enhed i treenigheden* 'All the hosts of angels proclaim the king of all's unity in

Commentary

Trinity'. However, it seems less disturbing of word order to take the kenning with the final two lines.

16,8 lofi 'with praise': The present condition of W has obscured the second letter of this word, but all earlier editors have read *lofi* without difficulty.

16,8 framda 'worshipped': Preterite participle of *fremja* 'further, promote, practise, worship', inflected as a feminine accusative adjective to agree with *einning* 'unity'.

16,9 Stundum...10 frásögnum 'At ... narratives': The writer here continues his line of thought from 16,3-4 above, but now adds that one can praise or blame the subject of a poem by introducing other praiseworthy or blameworthy subjects into it for the sake of comparison. The comparison remains implicit in his example (st. 25), but other (now lost) parts of *Nikulásdrápa* may well have made the comparison explicit.

16,11 Nicholao 'to Nicholas': The name of the saint is given in the dative according to the Latin declension.

16,11 af inum sæla Johanne baptista 'from the blessed John the Baptist': Two cases appear to be mixed in the prepositional phrase: *inum sæla* is in the dative, while *Johanne baptista* is in the ablative and inflected as in Latin.

16,12 hans 'his': The explanation in 16,17-18 below shows that the antecedent of the pronoun *hans* 'his' is Nicholas.

Stanza 25

Stanza 25 is another *helmingr* from *Nikulásdrápa*. It requires an understanding of the narrative recounted in the gospel of Luke (I.41), in which John the Baptist, still in his mother Elizabeth's womb, leaps in recognition of the infant Jesus in the womb of his mother Mary, who is visiting Elizabeth. According to Luke I.36, the two women were cousins. Exactly how the poet used this incident as a *dæmi* in his poem about St Nicholas is uncertain, but the evidence of the priest Hallur's later poem (sts 14 and 16 are cited for comparison in *SnE* 1848-87, II 210-11 n. 1) suggests that the circumstances surrounding the birth of both saints was the point of comparison. If so, this *helmingr* must have come not very long after the stanza numbered 6 in *FoGT*.

16,13 í...14 bjarta 'in the hall of the bright chamber of the heart [BREAST > WOMB]' [*í höll ins bjarta sals hjarta*]: Following the suggestion of Sveinbjörn Egilsson and Ólsen (*SnE* 1848-87, III 157; *FoGT*

1884, 260 n. 3), this kenning has been interpreted as having two elements, although it is possible to understand it as having only one, with the sole referent being WOMB.

16,15 meyjar mannvitsfrægrar 'of the maiden famous of understanding': This is a reference to John the Baptist's mother Elizabeth, who conceived him late in life following a visit from the angel Gabriel (Luke I.5–25). It is also possible to understand the phrase to refer to the Virgin Mary rather than Elizabeth, in which case the kenning *í höll ins bjarta sals hjarta* 'in the hall of the bright chamber of the heart [BREAST > WOMB]' (ll. 1–2) refers to the Virgin's womb and to Christ within it.

16,17 þar lof 'there ... the praise': W is damaged at this point. All editors have accepted the restoration of *SnE* 1818, 340.

16,17 Johannis 'of John': The name of the saint is given in the genitive according to the Latin declension.

16,18 Nicholai 'Nicholas': The name of the saint is given in the genitive according to the Latin declension.

16,18 Slíkt...20 níð 'In ... disgrace': Compare this sentence to Snorri's description of kennings for despicable men in *Skáldskaparmál*: *Kent er ok við jǫtna heiti, ok er þat flest háð eða lastmæli* (*SnE* 1998, I 40) 'Names of giants are also used, and this is mostly as satire or criticism' (trans. Faulkes 1987, 94).

16,18 verða í lastmælum 'occur in defamations': W is damaged at this point. *SnE* 1848–87, II 210; *FoGT* 1884, 130 and *FoGT* 2004, 39 restore *verða í* while the earlier editions suggest *vera í* 'be in' (*SnE* 1818, 314; *SnE* 1848, 204).

16,21 Eru...18,2 flýjandi 'These parts ... at all costs': The final sentence of chapter 8 has an unusually long insertion that recapitulates the substance of the chapter. When the main clause is picked up again in 16,26 it has been broken apart and two emendations are necessary (see the commentaries to *leyfiligir* (18,1) and *ónýtar* (18,1).

16,21 ebasis 'of ebasis': The context requires that this word be interpreted as a genitive. Since it is written as 'ebasis' in W, the word must either be uninflected or a genitive where the genitival ending (-*s*) has been shortened (*ebasiss > ebasis*). Alternatively, one can see *ebasis* as the Latin genitival form (nom. sg. and gen. sg. of this Greek loanword into Latin are identical).

16,21 sá...22 hon 'the one in which Bragi ... greater than before': These words indicate that the writer of *FoGT* considered the stanza he had cited about Hamðir and Sǫrli's revenge on Erminrekr (st. 23) to constitute indirect praise of Ragnarr loðbrók because of Ragnarr's supposed connection with the Niflungar, among whom Hamðir and Sǫrli were sometimes counted (cf. Finch 1993). According to the tradition represented in *Vǫlsunga saga* and apparently known to Snorri Sturluson in *Skáldskaparmál* (*SnE* 1998, I 50), this connection was through his wife Áslaug. The phrase *frændr Áslaugar* 'the relatives of Áslaug' (16,21–22) then refers to the two brothers and their act of vengeance. According to *Vǫlsunga saga*, Áslaug was the daughter of Sigurðr Fáfnisbani and Brynhildr, and was fostered by Brynhildr's maternal uncle Heimir after her parents' deaths.

16,22 hinn 'the other one': W writes 'hin' which has been interpreted as *hinn* (masc. nom. sg.) so that it agrees with *hlutr* masc. or *háttr* masc. in 16,21 above. The scribe usually writes the masculine form of the determiner *hinn* as 'hiñ'. *SnE* 1848, 204 was the first edition to make this emendation. It has been adopted in all subsequent editions.

18,1 leyfiligir 'allowed': At this point W has *leyfiligra*, genitive plural of the adjective *leyfiligr*. This word follows two other genitives (*skrauss eða lastmælis* 'of ornament or blame'), but it does not fit into the sentence syntactically. *SnE* 1848, 204 emended *leyfiligra* to *leyfiligir* (masc. nom. pl.) so that it agrees with *hlutir* 'parts' and *hættir* 'forms' in 16,21 above. All subsequent editors have adopted this reading.

18,1 ónýtar 'useless': W has *ǫnytrar*, fem. gen. sg. of the adjective *ónýtr*. This does not work syntactically and *SnE* 1818, 341 therefore emended to *ónýtar*, fem. nom. pl., so it agrees with *efnisafgaungur* 'departures from the subject matter'. All subsequent editors have adopted this reading.

18,2 flýjandi 'to be avoided': Literally 'fleeing'. This Latinate passive use of the present participle is described by Nygaard (1906 §§238–39).

Chapter 9: Emphasis
This chapter presents two varieties of the figure *emphasis*: 1) when a quality of a man is mentioned instead of the man himself and 2) when the effect of an object is mentioned instead of the object itself. The second variant, mentioning the crime instead of the criminal (as in st. 26) or the effect of the weapon instead of the weapon itself (as in st. 27), seems to be quite close to the definition of *metonomia* given in *TGT* (1884, 106) where among other things it is defined as when *gerr*

hlutr setisk fyrir efni sínu 'the resulting entity is mentioned instead of its material' (e.g. flour instead of grain).

18,3 Emphasis...5 vitringinum 'Emphasis ... man': Although this definition clearly is related to the one given in *D* (ll. 2591–92) and *Dg* (82v) (*G* does not mention this figure), it is difficult to make sense of. It appears that the order of the phrases *undirstaðligr hlutr* 'substantive entity' and *hræriligr hlutr* 'moveable entity' needs to be reversed for the Old Icelandic sentence to cohere logically. To mention wisdom instead of the wise man or the crime instead of the criminal is to mention some accidental quality (*nökkuð tilfelli*) of a man rather than the man himself. At the abstract level the accidental quality must correspond to the 'moveable entity' (*hræriligr hlutr*) while the man himself must correspond to the 'substantive entity' (*undirstaðligr hlutr*). However, *FoGT* states that *emphasis* mentions a 'substantive entity' (e.g. the wise man) instead of a 'moveable entity' (e.g. the man's wisdom), i.e. the opposite of what one would expect. On this account, it would be reasonable to emend 18,3 from *Emphasis setr undirstaðligan hlut fyrir hræriligum hlut* to *Emphasis setr *hræriligan hlut fyrir *undirstaðligum hlut* 'Emphasis uses a moveable entity instead of a substantive entity'. However, no emendation has been made because *FoGT*'s explanation seems to mirror (at least partly) the definition in *D* and the following explanation given in *Dg*: *Emphasis est expressiua locutio. Et fit cum uolentes exprimere aliquod accidens utimur nomine substantiuo pro adiectiuo significante illud accidens ad maiorem expressionem, ut si ponatur 'scelus' pro 'scelerato', ut 'Dauus est ipsum scelus'. Id est 'ipse Dauus est sceleratus et non alius ita sicut ipse'* (82v) '*Emphasis* is a stressed utterance, and it occurs when we, wanting to express some attribute, for greater stress use a noun instead of the adjective that signifies that attribute, as when "impiety" [or "the crime"] is mentioned instead of "impious" [or the "criminal"], like "Davus is impiety itself", i.e. "this Davus is impious, and there [is] no other just like him"'. Davus was a stock name for the scheming slave in New Comedy (such as Terence's *Andria* 'The woman from Andros') and Horace often uses the name for a similar character (e.g. in *Sermones*, II 7 ll. 2, 46, 100 and in *Ars poetica* l. 237). From these and other texts, the name Davus entered medieval tradition as the name of a proverbial scoundrel. One good example of this can be found in Matthew of Vendôme's *Ars versificatoria* which contains a 96-line diatribe against Davus beginning: *Scurra vagus, parasitus edax, abjectio plebis | est Davus* (ed. Faral 1924, 125–26) 'A wandering buffoon, a voracious parasite, an outcast of the common people is Davus'. It seems likely that the writer of *FoGT* was working with a commentary similar to *Dg* but that he understood *ut si ponatur 'scelus' pro 'scelerato'* 'if "impiety" [or "crime"] is mentioned instead of "impious" [or "criminal"]' as *ut si ponatur scelus pro scelerato* 'if the crime is mentioned instead of the criminal'.

18,3 undirstaðligan hlut 'substantive entity': This collocation is presumably roughly equivalent to 'essential quality'. *Undirstaðligr* is a calque on Latin *substantiuus*. The adjective *undirstaðligr* is also used in *TGT*: *Viðrorð fegrir ok endimarkar orðit í þá líking sem viðrleggjanlig nǫfn gera við undirstæðileg* (*undirstǫðlig* W, *undirstaðlig* B) *nǫfn, svá sem hér: Sterkr maðr bersk hraustliga* (1884, 11) 'an adverb graces and delimits verbs in a similar manner as adjectives do nouns, as here: "A strong man fights valiantly"'.

18,3 hræriligum hlut 'moveable entity': This collocation is presumably roughly equivalent to 'accidental quality'. *Hræriligum* 'moveable' is mirrored by *mobile* 'mobile' in *D* (l. 2592) and *hlut* 'entity' by *proprietatem* 'quality' (l. 2591, and implicitly by *mobile* in l. 2592).

18,4 tilfelli 'accidental quality': *Tilfelli* neut. is a calque on Latin *accidens*, used in *Dg* (quoted above in the comment to 18,3–5).

Stanza 26
Several emendations are required to make grammatical and syntactic sense of st. 26. The modes of punishment mentioned here seem to capture fourteenth-century penal codes very accurately; this is one of several places in the treatise that reveal an interest in the law. Theft was punished by hanging in a public place, here a market place, while murderers were punished by being broken on a wheel (Gade 1985).

18,7 Píndr 'punished': An unusual sense of the verb *pína* 'torture, torment' (somebody), doubtless required to fulfil the conditions established in the preceding prose.

18,8 hímleiðir 'universally loathed': The meaning of this otherwise unattested compound adjective is uncertain. W reads *hímleiða* which *SnE* 1848–87, II 212, *LP* (1860) and Ólsen (*FoGT* 1884, 261) adopt unemended as an indeclinable compound adjective with the sense 'tired of waiting' [to be strung up on the gallows]. It is questionable whether such an adjective could be seen as appropriate to the description of criminals waiting to be hanged, unless it is used ironically. The same sense is assumed by Finnur Jónsson (*Skj* B, II

233), though he emends the adjective to the masc. pl. form *hímleiðir*. These editors, implicitly or explicitly, have connected the first element of the adjective, *hím-*, with the Old Icelandic verb *híma* 'loiter, hang around' and the noun *hímaldi* 'laggard, dreamer, good-for-nothing'. Ólsen (*FoGT* 1884, 261 n. 2) tentatively suggested the first element could perhaps be written *hvím-*, and this spelling was adopted by Kock (*Skald*, II 121), though without explanation. The second element of the adjective seems to be formed from *leiðr* 'loathed, disliked, hateful'. An alternative sense of *hímleiðir* was proposed by Finnur Jónsson in *LP*. He interprets the compound (*LP*: *hímleiðr*) as = *hveimleiðr*, understood as composed of the elements *hveim* 'by each' and *leiðr* 'loathed', to give the sense 'loathed by each, universally loathed', and this interpretation has been adopted here. It is supported by the occurrence of *hvimleiðr* in the sense 'hated, loathed' in some late medieval texts, including *Grettis saga* and *Gríms saga loðinkinna* (see *ONP hvimleiðr*), as well as in at least one early *ríma* (Finnur Jónsson 1926–28, 193).

18,9 víða 'in many places': Here construed as an adverb 'in many places, widely'. So also *SnE* 1848–87, II 212–13, III 157 and *FoGT* 1884, 261. Kock (*Skald*, II 121 and *NN* §2355) emends to the adjective *víðum* 'wide, broad' to agree with *vingameiði* 'windswept tree' in the same line, while Finnur Jónsson (*Skj* B, II 233) and *FoGT* 2004, 40 emend to the neuter form of the adjective, *víðu*, to agree with *torgi* 'market place' (18,10). Neither emendation is necessary to make sense of the *helmingr*.

18,9 vingameiði 'by the windswept tree': W has *vinga meiðar*, regarded by all editors (except *SnE* 1848–87, 212–13) as a compound noun for the gallows, following the reference in *Hávamál* 138,2 where the god Óðinn claims that he hung for nine nights *vindgameiði á*. The first element of the compound is a contraction of *vindga-* (from *vindugr* 'windy'); cf. *LP: vingameiðr*.

18,10 hjá torgi miðju 'near the middle of the market-place': Or possibly 'in the middle of the market-place', though *hjá* is not to be expected, if so (cf. *FoGT* 1884, 261–62 n. 4). Some editors (e.g. *Skj* B, II 233, *FoGT* 2004, 110–12) take this phrase with the first clause, viz. *Stuldr er píndr hjá miðju torgi víðu/víðum vingameiði* 'Theft is punished in the middle of the [wide] market-place by the wide windswept tree'.

18,14 rómsæll 'praised' (lit. 'applause-fortunate'): Sveinbjörn Egilsson's emendation (*SnE* 1848–87, II 212) for W's *rómsæl* has been adopted by all subsequent editors. This compound adjective is *hap. leg.*

18,15 þar sem morðinginn er hegndr og þjófrinn 'whereas the murderer is chastised and the thief': The logic of this sentence would be improved if the word *píndr* 'tormented' was appended to the end, so that it reads: *Hier er stuldrinn kallaðr píndr og morðin hegnd, þar sem morðinginn er hegndr og þjófrinn píndr* 'Here the theft is said to be tormented and the murders chastised, whereas the murderer is chastised and the thief tormented'.

18,17 Sumir ... 20,3 stórkvæðum 'Some ... poems': This part of the definition has no parallel in *D* or *Dg*.

18,17 Sumir menn 'some men': A reference to *sumir meistarar* is found below at 38,1. *TGT* refers to unnamed authorities in a similar way (1884, 45, 69 n. 129).

18,17 emphasen 'Emphasis': This Greek accusative form of *emphasis* was normally used in Latin.

18,18 Þorleifr Þorleifr skúma 'Dusky' Þorkelsson, a tenth-century Icelander, mentioned in accounts in both *Jómsvíkinga saga* and *Fagrskinna* of the battle at Hjǫrungavágr, c. 986, in which a group of Icelanders fought on the side of the Norwegians against the Jómsvíkingar. Þorleifr is reported to have been killed in this battle. In *Jómsvíkinga saga* (ed. Petersens 1879, 73) he is said to have been the son of Þorkell inn auðgi 'the Wealthy' from Mýrar in Dýrafjörður, north-west Iceland, while in *Fagrskinna* (ÍF 29, 131) Skúmr is given as his personal name.

Stanza 27

Stanza 27 in *fornyrðislag* metre is the only surviving piece of poetry in Old Norse attributed to Þorleifr skúma. It is said to be by him both here and in *Jómsvíkinga saga*, but is attributed to Vígfúss Víga-Glúmsson in *Fagrskinna*. A version of this stanza clearly lies behind a short poem recorded by Saxo Grammaticus (VII 2, 10, ed. Friis-Jensen 2005, I 450) and put into the mouth of Haldanus, who uses a club against his Swedish opponents Sivaldus and his seven sons, in order to counteract their supposed sorcery, which he thought might affect weapons made of iron. In the Old Norse historical sources the speaker of the stanza (Þorleifr or Vígfúss) swings a club and responds to an observer (either Eiríkr jarl Hákonarson or Hákon jarl Sigurðarson) who asks what this action means. Previous editors have suspected that either the third and fourth or the fifth and sixth lines of this ten-line stanza have been inserted into it after the original composition, both on grounds of its length (eight lines would be normal) and its loose syntax, and because the fifth and sixth lines are absent from the *Fagrskinna* manuscripts. Magnús Ólafsson included this stanza in the longer, Y version of his *LaufE* (*LaufE* 1979, 380), together with a somewhat garbled version of *FoGT*'s following prose commentary. Resen's *Edda Islandorum* also has this stanza and a slightly more correct prose text (*RE* 1665, Ji 3v; Faulkes 1977, 30).

18,21 Búa 'of Búi': Búi digri 'the Stout' Vésetason, one of the leaders of the Jómsvíkingar at Hjǫrungavágr.

18,22 Sigvalda 'of Sigvaldi': Sigvaldi jarl Strút-Haraldsson, another of the leaders of the Jómsvíkingar.

18,24 Hákonar 'of Hákon': Hákon jarl Sigurðarson (ruled Norway 970–95), leader of the Norwegians at Hjǫrungavágr.

18,27 eikikylfa 'oaken club': The club described by Saxo is also of oak; Haldanus is said to have torn an oak tree up from its roots and fashioned a cudgel from it *in solidam clauę speciem* (VII 2, 10, ed. Friis-Jensen 2005, I 450).

18,28 Dönum 'to the Danes': The Danes were allies of the Jómsvíkingar at Hjǫrungavágr.

18,29 kiend eða merkt 'designated or signified': The participles *kiend* 'designated [by a kenning]' and *merkt* 'signified' are synonymous here, and they show that the writer understood the circumlocutions in st. 27 as kennings. *Skáldskaparmál* does not use the verb *merkja* in connection with kennings, but one often finds *kenna*, e.g. *Kona er ok kend við allar Ásynjur* (*SnE* 1998, I 40) 'Woman is also referred to in terms of all Asyniur' (trans. Faulkes 1987, 94).

18,30 ymsar líkingar 'various comparisons': *TGT* uses the word *líking* as well, but generally it means 'similarity' rather than 'comparison'. One example is *þá er metaphora aptrbeiðilig, ef hvern hlut má fœra til annars, þat er líking er á milli, sem at kalla sjóinn jǫrð skipa eðr fiska eðr sækonunga* (1884, 28) '*Metaphora* is reciprocal if the objects between which there is similarity [*líking*] are mutually transferrable, as when the sea is called the land of ships or fishes or sea-kings' (trans. Collings 1967, 104).

18,30 og kallar Óláfr það finngalknað 'and Óláfr calls it *finngalknað*': *FoGT* refers here to a passage in *TGT* (1884, 80) in which Óláfr Þórðarson uses this term as an equivalent to Old Icelandic *nykrat* when discussing a form of the figure *cacenphaton*, in which the attributes of a living creature are ascribed to something inanimate. The poetic example given (Anon (*TGT*) 11,1[III]) is of the use of the verb *gekk* 'went' with the subject *skíð flóðs* 'ski of the sea [SHIP]'. This is a different kind of so-called fault from that complained of by the writer of *FoGT*, who is concerned about a variety of images being used in one stanza for a single referent, in this case a series of diverse kenning-like phrases for a club. Whereas in *Háttatal* (*SnE* 2007, 7) Snorri Sturluson also uses the adjectival substantive *nykrat* 'monstrous, monstrosity' (from the preterite participle of an unrecorded verb based on the noun *nykr* 'water monster' or 'hippopotamus'; see *ONP*: *nykr*) to describe frequent changes in the kenning types used to refer to a single referent in a stanza, he nowhere uses the term *finngalknað*. The *TGT* usage indicates that the two terms were synonymous for Óláfr. Both have the underlying sense of 'monstrosity', denoting a fabulous creature imagined to have disparate parts, part animal and part human. In the case of the *nykr*, the creature was an indigenous water-horse (cf. Old English *nicor* 'water monster') or, in exotic texts, a hippopotamus, an animal whose name in Greek means literally 'horse of the river'. A *finngalkn* (the commonest nominal form) or *finngalkan* (on these forms, see *ONP*: *finngalkan*, *finngalkn*) seems to have been a similarly hybrid monstrosity, in one instance, a fragment of an Old Icelandic *Physiologus* (see *ONP*: *finngalkan*), denoting a centaur. The adjectival substantive *finngalknat* is found only in *TGT* and *FoGT*, and the spellings of the second part differ; in *TGT* ms. A has 'finngalgknat', while W has 'finngalkat'; in *FoGT* W spells the word 'finngaalknat'. The etymology of both parts of the compound noun *finngalkn* (or *finngálkn*) is uncertain. The first element *finn-* probably derives from the name of the Saami people, Finnar, and denotes magic or sorcery (an art frequently associated with them in Old Norse sources), while the second probably has the basic sense 'monster, monstrosity' (cf. *hreingalkn* in *Hymiskviða* 24,1, where the compound is generally thought to refer to wolves; see *Kommentar*, I 329–30), though its derivation is uncertain (cf. *AEW*: *finngálkn*, *-gálpn*). The simplex *galkn* occurs several times as the base-word of kennings for battle-axe (the connection presumably being with the axe-kenning type with troll-woman as base word); so Hókr *Eirfl* 7,4[I], Hfr *ErfÓl* 8,4[I]. In these cases the stem vowel *a* is short and this seems likely to be correct.

20,1 berr...3 stórkvæðum 'it ... poems': Nothing comparable to this statement is found in *TGT* or elsewhere, but *TGT* rejects the use of the

Commentary

figure implicitly by treating it as a subgroup of the figure *cacenphaton* 'ill-sounding'.

20,2 í 'in': This preposition is not found in W. It was added by Ólsen (*FoGT* 1884, 131) and has been adopted by later editors.

Chapter 10: Efflexegesis

The initial part of the definition agrees well with *D* (l. 2594) and *Dg*. The latter explains: *Ephexegesis est succincta expositio precedentium* (82v) 'Ephexegesis is a succinct exposition of the preceding [words/ things]'. *G* defines *efflexegesis* as the name of a figure which is similar to *periphrasis*: *Periphrasim praemissorum dic expositiuam, | Eflexegesis est eadem similisque figura* (I 88–89) 'Call a *periphrasis* of the aforementioned expositive, *efflexegesis* is the same and a similar figure'. The prose section that concludes this chapter, in which the figure is subdivided into three variants, contains material that has been transposed from another part of *D* (see commentary to 20,14 below).

20,4 skýring eða glöggvari greining 'explanation or clearer exposition': The two nouns, *skýring* and *greining* appear to be used as synonyms in this context, but *greining* has the additional meaning of 'distinction'. The initial definition of this figure is followed by st. 28, in which the second *helmingr* can indeed be said to be an 'explanation or clearer exposition' of the first *helmingr*.

20,5 Eilífr It is not certain which Eilífr is intended here. Three poets named Eilífr are known: Eilífr Goðrúnarson (c. 1000), author of *Þórsdrápa*, Eilífr Snorrason, an early thirteenth-century Icelander from whom three humorous, secular *lausavísur* have been preserved (on his biography and poetry, see Nordal 2001, 160–61), and Eilífr kúlnasveinn 'Fellow with lumps' (?) (Lind 1920–21, col. 225). In *Skáldskaparmál* four part-stanzas by the last-named Eilífr (Ekúl Kristdr[III]) are quoted in succession in illustration of kennings for Christ (*SnE* 1998, I 77–78). Most scholars have considered the present stanza, 28, in *FoGT* is probably by him, because of the similarity between its style and subject-matter and those of the four *Skáldskaparmál* verses. We do not know anything about this Eilífr, but the style and subject of the stanza suggests a date for it in the late twelfth century.

Stanza 28

This stanza is extant only in *FoGT*, but Árni Magnússon copied it in AM 761 a 4°[x] on f. 85v. There is no known external context for it. The first *helmingr* refers to Christ's entry into Jerusalem on Palm Sunday, a subject also treated in Anon *Leið* 30[VII], where similar vocabulary is used. The second *helmingr* draws a parallel between Christ's entry into Jerusalem, when crowds of people came to meet him, strewing his path with palm fronds, and the risen Christ's invitation to good Christians, who have performed good deeds, to come to him in heaven, arguably to be interpreted as the New Jerusalem.

20,6 Báru mæta móti 'carried glorious [...] to meet': The scribe of W has obviously understood this line as *Báru mæt á móti* because he has divided the text in this way. However, reading *mæt* 'glorious' requires it to be taken with *sveit* 'company' as part of an unusually fragmented intercalary clause spanning ll. 1 (20,6), 3 (20,8) and 4 (20,9) of the stanza's first *helmingr* (so *Skj* B, I 566) with the sense *mæt sveit hrauð sorg* 'the glorious company banished sorrow'. This reading is possible, though unlikely. The present edition proposes that the original ‹a› of l. 1 (20,6), which the scribe of W understood as the preposition *á*, was intended as the accusative plural ending of the previous adjective *mæta* 'glorious', which could then be construed with *pálma* 'palms'. Kock (*Skald*, I 274, *NN* §1215) emended *mæt* to *mætt* 'gloriously' (an unattested adverb) and construed it with the verb *báru* '[they] carried'.

20,9 til borgar 'to the city': The city of Jerusalem, Old Norse Jórsalaborg.

20,10 Svá...13 sterkri 'Thus ... faith': The syntax of these lines is difficult, and many editors have emended some or all of the following words, as they appear in W: *laðar* l. 5 (20,10), *siklingr* l. 5 (20,10), *síns* l. 6 (20,11), *bjartir* l. 6 (20,11) and *þeir* l. 7 (20,12). *Skj* B, I 566, *Skald*, I 274 and *FoGT* 2004, 41 do not emend, and construe thus: *svá laðar siklingr skýja til hjarta síns þeirs bjartir færa fyrða gram fǫgr verk með sterkri trú* 'thus the king of the clouds invites to his heart those who, pure, bring to the ruler of men beautiful deeds with strong faith'. The present edition follows much the same interpretation, emending only the adjective *bjartir* to *bjarta* (masc. acc. pl.), and placing it in the main rather than the subordinate clause as direct object of *laðar* 'invites'. W's *þeir* l. 7 (20,12) has also been emended to *þá* to agree with its antecedent *bjarta*; however, there are some examples of lack of agreement between antecedent and demonstrative (cf. Nygaard 1906 §260), so it might be possible to retain the unemended form *þeir*.

Commentary 91

20,14 Er...24 norrænuskáldskap 'This ... poetry': *FoGT* normally presents the various figures in the same order as *D*, but there are exceptions (the order of the figures treated in chapters 24 and 25 has been reversed, *G* forms the basis of chapters 26 and 27, and material from *G* has also been added in chapter 3). At this point, *FoGT* deviates from the order of figures in its main source, *D*. First, the writer goes into more detail on the figure of *efflexegesis* (20,14–16), and then he briefly presents the figures *icon, parabola* and *paradigma* (20,17–21), before he finally returns to *efflexegesis* once more (20,22–24). This structure implies that the writer saw the figures *icon, parabola* and *paradigma* as sub-types of *efflexegesis*. In *D* on the other hand, these three figures are considered sub-types of the figure *homozeuxis*, and they are described along with *homozeuxis* in ll. 2560–72. *Homozeuxis* is the last figure defined and exemplified in *D*'s section on tropes (ll. 2497–2572), and it comes immediately before the *colores* section, which forms the basis of *FoGT*. This means that the writer has moved a passage in *D* from its original location to the present chapter. *D*'s section on tropes is primarily based on the *Barbarismus* section of Donatus's *Ars maior* and since *Barbarismus* apparently formed the basis of *TGT*, the same three figures (*icon, parabola* and *paradigma*) are also defined and exemplified in *TGT* (1884, 116–19). In this section, therefore, we see a rare instance of overlap between *TGT* and *FoGT*. Perhaps this is why the figures have not been provided with verse examples in *FoGT*. The unusual placing of these three subtypes of *homozeuxis* in *FoGT* might have been caused by a mistake somewhere in the tradition. However, the figures do not seem out of place in *FoGT*, and one can therefore choose to regard them as testimonies to the flexibility and complexity of the classificatory system of rhetorical figures. *G* makes no distinction between *paradigma* and *parabola* (I 121–22) and does not mention *icon*.

20,14 Er...15 frásögn 'This figure ... account': The text appears to be corrupt. The writer sets out to describe the difference between *glósa* and *efflexegesis*, but we only learn that *efflexegesis* 'glosses or explains a true account', not how *glósa* differs from this. Since *glósa* is used of an account that must be considered true below (38,23), *glósa* cannot be a figure that 'glosses or explains an *un*true account'. *D* does not state that *efflexegesis* is commonly called *glósa*, but this remark might be based on l. 2565 of *D* where it is said of the figure *icon*: *haec solet ex usu quandoque parabola dici* 'In practice, this [figure] is usually called *parabola*'. This line is not translated in *FoGT*'s definition of *icon* (see commentary to 20,17 below).

20,14 glósa *Glósa* has here been rendered in the standardised Old Norse (rather than Latin) orthography since *FoGT* states that it is commonly used (*af alþýðu* 'by ordinary people'). The Latin form is *glosa*. It often occurs in Old Norse texts as a loan word (declined like the feminine *ōn*-stems). The verb *glósa* 'gloss' is also relatively common and used twice in *FoGT* (in the following sentence and below at 38,11).

20,15 inn...16 kristni 'The illustrious Solomon signifies Our Lord, and the temple holy Christianity': These allegorical interpretations of Solomon and the Temple are homiletic commonplaces.

20,17 En icona setr fram tvá hluti af líku efni 'And *icon* puts forward two entities of the same material': Where *FoGT* has *af líku efni* 'of the same material', *D* has *in simili genere* (l. 2564) 'of similar kind'. According to *D*, this figure is commonly called *parabola* (l. 2565). But this sentence has been left out of *FoGT*, or perhaps transferred to the remark above about *efflexegesis* and *glósa* (see commentary to 20,14–15 above). *Dg*'s explanation begins: *Icon est personarum inter se uel eorum que personis accidunt comparatio, ut* '*os humerosque deo similis*' [*Aen*, I 589] (81v) '*Icon* is a comparison between persons or the attributes of persons such as "his countenance and shoulders [are] like those of a god"'. *TGT* defines *icon* as follows: *Icon er samjafnan tveggja persóna eða þeirra tilfella* (1884, 116) '*Icon* is the comparison of two persons or of their abilities'. This definition is much closer to *D* than *FoGT*'s definition.

20,18 En...21 undirstöðu 'And parabola ... meaning': *D*'s description of the difference between *paradigma* and *parabola* (ll. 2566–72) is not clear, but it is evident from the more detailed description in *Gg* (pp. 135–36) that *parabola* occurs when one says 'a sower went out to sow', while the *paradigma* is the explanation of the parable: 'a preacher went out to preach'. Both *D* and *Gg* differ from *Barbarismus* (ed. Holtz 1981, 674) in their definitions of *parabola* and *paradigma*.

20,18 parabola...19 sannleik 'Parabola ... truth': *Setja fram ólika hluti* 'put forward dissimilar entities' in this context means that one entity is mentioned while the other is implied. The definition and the general tenor of the examples agree with *D* (ll. 2566–70). *TGT*'s definition is: *Parabola er samjafnan tveggja hluta í ójǫfnu kyni* (1884, 117) '*Parabola* is the comparison of two entities of a different nature'. The wording of this definition is closer to *D* than *FoGT* is.

20,18 kalla þenna heim akr þyrn auðæfin fuglana djöfla 'calling this world a field, richness a thorn, devils birds': The construction begins *kalla e-t¹ e-t²* 'to call something something (else)', but the order of the object and object predicate is changed after the first comparison so that the second and third comparisons are construed as *kalla e-t² e-t¹*. This infelicity has been evened out in the translation, but the Old Norse text has not been changed.

20,18 þenna... 19 djöfla 'this world ... devils birds': *D* and *FoGT* use examples from the parable of the sower (Mark IV.1–20; Matt. XIII.1–23; Luke VIII.4–15). The implicit nature of the reference shows that the audience is expected to recognise this immediately. Old Norse versions of the parable can be found in the Norwegian book of homilies (ed. Indrebø 1931, 69–70) and in Þorvaldur Bjarnarson 1878 (p. 188, on the basis of AM 672 4°, dated 1475–1500).

20,19 þyrn 'a thorn': *Þyrn* is here interpreted as a feminine noun in the accusative singular. *ONP* also lists it as a feminine, while Heizmann lists it as a masculine noun (1993, s. v.). Other more common forms of this noun are *þorn* masc. and *þyrnir* masc., both 'thorn, thorn bush'. The form *þyrn* is only known from two texts: *FoGT* and *Barlaams saga ok Jósaphats* in *Reykjahólabók* (ed. Loth 1969–70, I 106). Both texts use the noun in the context of the parable of the sower. The following quotation from the Norwegian book of homilies shows that the use of the singular is unproblematic in this context: *En korn þat er fell í þyrni jartegnir menn þá er auðræði hafa mikil* (ed. Indrebø 1931, 70) 'But the seed which fell in the thorns [*þyrni* is acc. sg. of *þyrnir* masc.] signifies those men who have great riches'.

20,19 djöfla 'devils': The parable of the sower only speaks of the devil in the singular, as do the Old Norse renderings of the parable mentioned in the note to *þyrn* (20,19).

20,20 Paradigma...21 undirstöðu 'Paradigma ... meaning': The precise meaning of this sentence would probably have been easier to grasp had the writer provided an example. A definition with example can be found in *TGT* (1884, 118–19), but that example appears to be corrupt and does not make sense without emendation (see Louis-Jensen 1981). If one were to imagine an exemplification of *paradigma* as defined in *FoGT*, it might consist of one stanza in which the first *helmingr* says something *með fígúru og eiginligri undirstöðu* 'with a figure and with its true meaning'. This is a reference to the typological mode of biblical interpretation where events in the Old Testament are seen as prefigurations (*með fígúru*) of events in the New Testament while historically and literally true (*með eiginligri undirstöðu*) at the same time. In his *De schematibus et tropis* Bede refers to this as *allegoria in factis* (ed. Kendall 1991, 196). In such an imagined example the second *helmingr* would then explain what was said in the first.

20,22 Exflexigesis...24 norrænuskáldskap 'Efflexegesis ... poetry': In the preceding paragraphs the writer listed three branches (*kynkvíslir*) of *efflexegesis*, and he now adds that there are more branches in Latin concerning 'future things', but that he has not found anything comparable in Norse poetry. However, since the second *helmingr* of his example of *efflexegesis* (st. 28) appears to deal with 'future things', the author's remark seems odd. It might be taken as an indication that parts of the text have been moved from their original position at one point in the history of the transmission of the text.

20,23 bók Boetii 'the book of Boethius': Ólsen suggested that this may be a reference to chapter 9 in Boethius's commentary on Aristotle's *On Interpretation* which is called *De futuris contingentibus* 'On future contingencies' (*FoGT* 1884, 132n.). However, that chapter does not deal with poetry but with the truth-value of assertoric propositions about the future, such as 'There will be a sea battle tomorrow' (see Marenbon 2003, 37–41). The context of *FoGT* hints at a poetic example rather than a logical one and the (possibly) corrupt state of the text as well as the vague nature of the reference makes it hard to identify the 'book' referred to, whether it be by Boethius or some other author. Boethius's most famous work was *The Consolation of Philosophy*, and with 42 verse sections it does include a considerable amount of poetry; however, none of the poems seem to match the character suggested by *FoGT*.

20,23 Boetii 'of Boethius': The name is declined according to its Latin declension. Anicius Manlius Severinus Boethius was imprisoned by king Theoderic the Great and executed in 525 or 526.

20,24 eg 'I': The personal pronoun in the first person appears often in the poetic examples of *FoGT*, but this is the only instance in the prose part of the treatise where the authorial 'I' is used.

Chapter 11: Euphonia

In this chapter the writer has departed rather far from the relevant section in *D* (ll. 2595–96). The text appears to be closer to *G* than to *D*, although it is not very close. *D* defines *euphonia* as a figure that occurs when one says something that sounds pleasing instead of something that does not sound pleasing. *D* gives three examples: *circuit*, *relliquiae* and *relligio*. *D* considers these forms euphonic variants of the regular forms *circuiuit* 'he walked around', *reliquiae* 'remains' and *religio* 'reverence'. The euphonic variants were used in Latin hexameter poetry for metrical reasons. The hexameter requires dactyls (–⌣⌣) or spondees (– –), but the normal (non-euphonic) forms of these words scan *cīrcŭĭuĭt*, *rĕlĭgĭo* and *rĕlĭquĭae*, and they are therefore impossible to use in the hexameter (and other dactylic metres). Because of this, classical poets used the variant forms *cīrcŭĭt*, *rēllĭgĭo* and *rēllĭquĭae*. The use of the euphonic forms was thus caused by metrical necessity, while *D* sees them as aesthetically pleasing. *G*, like *FoGT*, mentions *euphonia* in connection with its opposite *cacenphaton*: *Dictio turpe sonans cacenphaton ipsa vocatur,* | *Ut si dicatur Tydides* [< *Tytides* in *G*, cf. *Gg* (pp. 279–80)] *medidiesque.* | *Ast euphonia sit tibi dictio pulchra sonora,* | *ut si dicatur Tytides* [< *Tydides* in *G*, cf. *Gg* (pp. 279–80)] *meridiesque* (II 5–8) 'An utterance that sounds disagreeable is itself called *cacenphaton*, as when one says "Tydides" and "medidies". But let *euphonia* be a beautiful-sounding utterance, as when one says "Tytides" and "meridies"'. The point in *G* is that the forms *Tydides* 'the Tydide [i.e. Diomedes, the son of Tydeus]' and *medidies* [< *medius-dies*] 'midday' are correct from an etymological point of view, but that they do not have a pleasant sound and that one should prefer the euphonic variants. Folio 28r ll. 10–11 of AM 748 I b 4to, immediately following the text of *Skáldskaparmál*, contains a short note in Latin on *euphonia*. The note (which appears to be unrelated to *FoGT*) states: *Euphonia est bonus sonus ut 'nobiscum' et non 'cum nobis' uel quum littera scribitur et non pronunciatur ut 'circum amicta'* '*Euphonia* is a pleasant sound, like "*nobiscum*" and not "*cum nobis*" or when a letter is written and not pronounced, like "*circum amicta*"'. *FoGT* explains the figure in a very different way and this chapter of the treatise should be seen in conjunction with the thirteenth-century phonological development in Icelandic where the two vowel phonemes /æ:/ and /ø:/ merged into /æ:/ (see Raschellà 2000). This development, which is already observed in AM 645 4to (c. 1220) (Hreinn Benediktsson 1965, 67), appears to have been completed around the middle of the thirteenth century (*ANG* §120). The consequence of this development was that words such as *lǿkr* /lø:kr/ and *ǿgr* /ø:gr/ became *lækr* /læ:kr/ and *ægr* /æ:gr/. *TGT* is generally dated to the period when this process was reaching its completion—Ólsen dates it between 1242 and 1252 (1884, xxxv–xxxvii)—and the passage quoted shows that the author of *TGT*, Óláfr Þórðarson, was aware of the change, and that he considered the forms with /ø:/ more beautiful than the forms with /æ:/. His remark does not betray an awareness of the fact that the merger is a historical phonological development. In the fourteenth century when *FoGT* was written, this development had long since been completed, but the writer nevertheless betrays some theoretical knowledge of the distinction between the two sounds. Throughout this chapter, it causes complications that the scribe does not distinguish between /ø:/ and /æ:/. With only two exceptions, ‹Øli› (22,13) and ‹męr› (22,19), he uses the graph ‹æ›.

20,25 Euphonia…28 sett 'Euphonia … described': In this first part of the chapter the writer introduces *euphonia* in general terms as a figure that occurs whenever one avoids unpleasing combinations of sounds. For the various unpleasing combinations of sounds the writer refers to a previous part (of the book/work). This is a reference to *Málskrúðsfræði* (*TGT* 1884, 79 l. 15–80 l. 1) where various types of *cacenphaton* are presented. All *TGT*'s examples show words that end in the same sound(s) as those which begin the following one(s).

20,25 Euphonia…catenphaton 'Euphonia … cacenphaton': As mentioned above in the general commentary to ch. 11, *G* juxtaposes the two figures explicitly, while *D*, having treated *cacenphaton* earlier (in ll. 2380–81), only treats *euphonia* at this point. In its treatment of *cacenphaton*, *D* follows Donatus who dealt with *cacenphaton* in the chapter *De ceteris vitiis* (ed. Holtz 1981, 658). Donatus makes no mention of *euphonia*.

20,25 catenphaton 'cacenphaton': The scribe clearly wrote *catenphaton* (p. 114 l. 32 word 2). The same spelling is also used earlier on in W (p. 103 l. 25 and 31 and p. 104 l. 5 and 8–9).

20,28 Óláfr…22,2 í² 'Óláfr … "á"': Once more *FoGT* refers back to *TGT*, but this time the reference is to *Málfræðinnar grundvöllr* (*TGT* 1884, 7 ll. 24–27). The wording in *FoGT* suggests that the quotation from *TGT* is a direct one, but that is not the case. In the relevant section of *TGT* the writer states that there are three uses of a *diptongus* 'diphthong' in Latin: 1) for *hljóðfegrð* 'euphony', 2) for *sundrgrein* 'distinction', and 3) for *samansetning* 'compounding'. *TGT* then goes on to explain the uses of *diptongus* in Norse where it is said to have two purposes: *Fyrir greinar sakir er diptongus fundinn í norrǫnu sem í þessum nǫfnum 'mær'* [< mer W] *ok 'sær'* [< ser W] *at greina þau* *frá fornǫfnum 'sér'* [< ser W] *ok 'mér'* [< mer W] *ok ǫðrum þvílíkum, en fyrir hljóðsfegrð er diptongus fundinn sem hér: 'løkr'* [< løkr W] *'øgr'* [< øgr W], *þvíat fegra þykkir hljóða heldr enn 'lækr'* [< lækr W] *'ægr'* [< ægr W] (*TGT* 1884, 7) 'In Norse the *diptongus* is used for the sake of distinction, as in these nouns *mær* "maid" and *sær* "sea", in order to distinguish them from the pronouns *sér* [dative of the reflexive pronoun] and *mér* [1st pers. dat. sg. of the personal pronoun] and other similar [(pro)nouns], but for the sake of euphony *diptongus* is found as here: *løkr* "brook" *øgr* "terrible", because this is thought to have a more pleasing sound than *lækr ægr*'.

20,29 límingarstafir 'conjoined characters': The term *límingarstafr* is equated with *diptongus* 'diphthong' in *TGT* (1884, 47–48). But in *TGT diptongus* belongs to the phonological as well as the graphemic level, and the term therefore not only includes the Old Norse diphthongs (/ei/, /øy/, /au/), but also ligatures or composite characters (*TGT* mentions ‹æ› and ‹ø›) (see Raschellà 2000). In *FoGT límingarstafr* appears to refer to the graphemic aspect of ‹æ›, and possibly ‹ø›, and the translation 'conjoined characters' has therefore been favoured. *SGT* uses the related term *límingr* 'a "glueing"' to refer to the graphemic level (i.e. 'ligature').

20,30 lækr og ægr *'lækr* "brook" and *ægr* "mad"': Even though the context implies that the euphonic variants of these words are given as examples (/lø:kr/ and /ø:gr/), the ‹æ›'s written by the scribe have been retained in the text. The euphonic variants have been added in square brackets in the translation using the orthography of *ONP*. The writer of *FoGT* probably drew these examples from *TGT*. The adjective *ógr* is also found in the Codex Frisianus version of *Heimskringla* where a bull is characterised as *gamall ok ógr* (ed. Unger 1871a, 19) 'old and mad', and it appears to be a variant form of the more common *ýgr* 'mad'.

20,30 æ...22,2 á '"æ" ... "á"': The writer here states that *æ* should be avoided in all cases where it cannot reasonably be derived from a word containing *á*. In other words, *æ* is only allowed when it is the result of the i-mutation of *á*. He does not mention what one should do in the cases where *æ* does not derive from *á*. A considerable theoretical knowledge of the language is required if this is to be carried through without errors. None of the other three grammatical treatises betray a similar theoretical knowledge of the workings of *umlaut*.

22,2 dreifaz 'are derived': The verb *dreifask*, normally 'be dispersed, expelled', is not attested elsewhere in this technical sense.

Stanzas 29–31

These three stanzas, 29, 30 and 31, are all cited in support of the writer's exposition of *euphonia*, and are very likely to have been composed for the purpose. The metre of all three stanzas is *dróttkvætt*, most comparable to the subtype of *áttmælt* 'eight times uttered' that is designated in *Háttatal* (*SnE* 2007, 42, 77–78) as *fjórðungalok* 'couplets' closure' in manuscripts T[x] and U of *Snorra Edda*, where a stanza is divided into four discrete couplets. SnSt *Ht* 11[III] (*SnE* 2007, 9–10) provides a close structural parallel to sts 29–31 and may have been their model. Jón Helgason (1970) offers a close textual and phonological analysis of these stanzas, and points out that they all play on words whose root vowels are long: /a:/, /o:/, /æ:/ (the i-umlaut of /a:/) and /ø:/ (the i-umlaut of /o:/). Jón argues that this concentration indicates the writer's fascination with the mid-thirteenth century unrounding of /ø:/ to /æ:/, a change he thought the writer disapproved of, possibly because of what the prose text says about the figure of *euphonia*, though this opinion is in fact taken straight from *TGT*, hence the reference to Óláfr [Þórðarson] in 20,28. Jón goes on to suggest (1970, 208) that whoever composed these stanzas could have been born as early as 1199 or 1200, composing them in his old age. He also thought, presumably because some parts of the stanzas are semi-proverbial, that they were written down from oral tradition, although this seems very doubtful. While Jón Helgason's general conclusions do not seem particularly convincing (there is no reason why the poet's play on certain vowels should imply an old man's disapproval of the unrounding of /ø:/ to /æ:/), his analysis of individual stanzas is often enlightening, and has been referred to where relevant in the following notes. Haraldur Bernharðsson (2002, 184) gives a text of these stanzas incorporating all of Jón's conjectural emendations.

22,4 Því...11 flýtir '[Year's] abundance ... crazy men': Stanza 29 is arranged as four discrete, somewhat aphoristic couplets, and very artfully provides several examples of words containing the ligature ⟨æ⟩ and corresponding cognates with stem vowel graph ⟨á⟩. These are all found in the uneven lines 1 (22,4), 3 (22,6), 5 (22,8) and 7 (22,10) in the stanza. In l. 1 we have *ár* '[year's] abundance' and *ærir*, 3rd pers. sg. of the present tense used impersonally, from *æra* 'to give a good crop'; in l. 3 *æra* 'to row with oars' matches *árum* 'with oars', while in l. 5 *ræða* 'on heat' yields to *ráða* (from *ráði* 'hog, boar'), both phonetically and in terms of sense. In l. 7 *órar* 'fits of madness' balances *ærum* (from *ærr*, earlier *ǿrr* 'mad, crazy'). In the last case the correspondence is between /oː/ and original /øː/; cf. *AEW*: *órar* 1 and *ærr*.

22,4 ár '[Year's] abundance': Used here in the same sense as Latin *annona* 'year's yield'. A similar sense occurs on several occasions in Anon *Líkn*[VII] (see Note to *Líkn* 5/5[VII]).

22,6 æra... 7 undan 'to row with oars to avoid' [*æra undan*]: Literally 'away from'. Aside from its literal sense, this phrasal verb also means 'to give way to an enemy', 'to hesitate to fight'; cf. Jón Helgason (1970, 209–10) for examples.

22,8 af 'from': Finnur Jónsson (*Skj* B, II 233), followed by Kock (*Skald*, II 121) emends W's *af* to *at* l. 5 (22,8) and *ólystug* 'unwilling' l. 6 (22,9) to *oflystug* 'very keen, on heat', although the manuscript readings make perfect sense.

22,13 Æli... 20 tæriz 'He is considered ... a gift is given': Stanza 30 continues the strategy of st. 29, at least in the first *helmingr*, where ll. 1 (22,13) and 3 (22,15) contain pairs of words, in one of which the stem vowel is expressed by a ligature graph and in the other by a non-ligature graph for a long vowel. In l. 1 we have the pair *æli* (earlier *óli*) : *ólu* and in l. 3 *ælir* : *álar*. Although the second *helmingr* holds some serious difficulties of interpretation, it seems that the composer's strategy becomes somewhat different in that there is no opposition of ligature to non-ligature, but rather the maintenance of the same ligature in each of the two couplets. Again, as with st. 29, this stanza resolves into four couplets or *fjórðungar*.

22,13 Æli 'a wretch': W has *Øle*. Sveinbjörn Egilsson (*SnE* 1848–87, II 216–17 n. 7) argued for the spelling *auli*, but there is no problem with ⟨ø⟩ representing original /øː/, later /æː/. *Æli* occurs nowhere else as a simplex in Old Icelandic, though the compound *mannæli* 'wretched fellow' is recorded once, in *Finnboga saga ramma* (ÍF 14, 256), and in later Icelandic the form *ælingi* occurs with a similar sense. Corresponding forms are more evident in Norwegian; see Jón Helgason (1970, 212) for examples.

22,15 ælir vatn 'water causes dredging': The verb *æla* 'dredge [a deep channel]' is impersonal and *vatn* 'water' is accusative; so *FoGT* 1884, 267 n. 2 and Jón Helgason (1970, 213).

22,15 þar 'where': W has 'þat', but although 'þat' agrees in gender with *vatn* 'water', being neuter, sense requires an emendation to *þar* 'where', first proposed by Sveinbjörn Egilsson (*SnE* 1848–87, II 216 and n. 4) and adopted by all subsequent editors.

22,17 heitir...læru '†*lær*†' is named from †*læra*†': No fully convincing explanation of these two nouns has been proposed. Finnur Jónsson (*Skj* B, II 234), Kock (*Skald*, II 121 and *NN* §1445) and *FoGT* 2004, 43 adopt *lær* in the sense 'thigh, upper leg', though Finnur indicates with a question mark that this sense is dubious. *Lær* must be singular, as the verb *heitir* is singular, which rules out Sveinbjörn Egilsson's suggestion (*SnE* 1848–87, II 216–17 nn. 9 and 10) that *lær* stands for *lór*, plural of *ló* 'golden plover'. He further proposed that *læru* could be a variant of *léru* = *leiru* 'mudflat, muddy shore', but this is highly improbable both phonologically and ecologically (cf. *FoGT* 1884, 267–68 n. 4). Another hypothesis is that the form *læru* or *lǫ́ru* may be dative singular of a noun that occurs in *SnE* in a list of pejorative terms for men, viz. *leyra* (*SnE* 1998, I 106, 224–25, II 345, s. v. *leyra* or *lǫra* or *lǫri*; cf. *AEW*: *lǫra* and discussion), which appears in various spellings in the manuscripts and seems to mean 'degenerate person' or 'coward'. The sense of this line might then be 'a thigh is so-called on a degenerate man' (i.e. just as it is on other men), but this interpretation is really clutching at straws. Jón Helgason (1970, 213–14) postulated a **lór* 'sluggishness, inactivity' as the basis for the mutated noun *lǫ́ra*, later *læra* 'degenerate, good-for-nothing'.

22,19 mærr 'land': W has 'mer'. This word is here understood as the poetic noun *mǫ́rr* (later *mærr*) 'land', especially flat land (cf. *LP*: *mǫ́rr*), a term that could sometimes be applied specifically to the Western Norwegian district of that name, Møre (OIcel. Mórr, Mærr). It assumes that the poet understood the semantic relationship between the two terms. To follow the pattern set down in ll. 5–6 (22,17–18), all the ligatures in ll. 7–8 (22,19–20) must be the same, as they would be if the thirteenth-century Old Icelandic change of /ø:/ to /æ:/ is applied. Other editors have understood *mærr* to mean 'a man from Møre'. The problem here is that the name for the inhabitants of Møre only occurs in the plural *Mǿrir, Mærir* (cf. *LP*: 2. *Mǿrir*). Finnur Jónsson (*Skj* B, II 234) understood *mærr* to mean 'swamp, marsh'. Sveinbjörn Egilsson (*SnE* 1848–87, II 218–19) proposed *mær* 'maiden', which is a possible reading, although it does not make a great deal of sense in context. Jón Helgason (1970, 216) suggested that the first word was originally *mór* 'moor, heath' and that the line originally read *kallaz mór á Móri* 'it is called heathland in Møre', which would preserve the non-ligature : ligature graphic correspondence we find in st. 29 and the first *helmingr* of st. 30.

Commentary 101

22,20 mæring 'a prestation': Meaning a lavish gift. Most editors, following Sveinbjörn Egilsson (*SnE* 1848–87, II 218 and n. 3), have emended W's *mæring* to give the nominative singular form of the noun, *mæringr*. Kock (*Skald*, II 121 and *NN* §2356, also Jón Helgason 1970, 216) keeps the manuscript form, which he derives from *mæra* 'praise, honour with gifts' (cf. *LP*: *mæra* 2), interpreting 'it is called a prestation, if a gift is given'.

22,21 Hætta...26 br 'To take risks ... dies when ...': Although st. 31 breaks off before it is complete, the final letters obscured by a hole in W, there is no evidence that the scribe was intending to add two further lines to complete it, as the next line on page 115 of W begins a new chapter of the treatise with a capital letter. As with the second *helmingr* of st. 30, the poet's desire to pair ligature graphs (*límingarstafir*) with non-ligatures in the uneven lines seems to have largely gone by the board, in favour of the maintenance of a particular ligature in both lines of a couplet. In l. 2 (22,22), *hœting* (from *hót* 'threat') and *rœtir* (from *rót* 'root') contain the same vowel phoneme in the root syllable (classical ON /ø:/, younger /æ:/). After the merger of /ø:/ and /æ:/, they would have been represented in writing by the same ligature graph ‹æ›. In ll. 3–4 (22,23–24), there is a historical distinction between *nœra* and *vær*, which originally contained the phoneme /ø:/, and *nær* and *færi*, containing /æ:/, but this distinction would have disappeared around c. 1250. In ll. 5–6 (22,25–26), the root vowels are either of /ø:/ (*œðaz* l. 5 (22,25)) or /æ:/ origin (*œðr* ll. 5 (22,25) and 6 (22,26)).

22,21 Hætta...hættu 'To take risks leads to danger': This statement may well be semi-proverbial and a variation on such adages as *hefir sá er hœttir* 'he who risks, has [wins]'. *Skj* B, II 234 translates as *man må vove faren* 'one must risk danger'. Jón Helgason (1970, 217) proposed an emendation of *hœttu* to *háttu* '[bad] habits', accusative plural of *háttr* 'habits, conduct', to produce the conventional *skothending* rather than *aðalhending* in an odd line.

22,22 hœting 'threatening': Jón Helgason (1970, 217–18) suggested this might rather be *hœtting* 'danger, risk', an alternative form of *hætta* 'danger' (as in l. 1 (22,21)) with the preterite verb *rótti* 'rooted down'.

22,22 rœtir 'plants': A rather strained metaphorical usage of *rœta* (earlier *róta*) 'cause to take root'. Finnur Jónsson (*Skj* B, II 234, *LP*: *rœta*), followed by Longo (*FoGT* 2004, 43), offers a slightly different sense of l. 2, reading *hóting, ef bǫl rótir* 'it is threatening, if misfortune takes root', understanding the verb as impersonal with *bǫl* in the acc. case.

22,23 nær 'better': Normally, *nær* means 'near', but here the comparative degree seems to mean 'better, preferable'; cf. *LP*: *nær* 3.

22,25 skeind 'scratched': Editors have debated whether W reads *skeind* 'scratched' or *skemd* 'hurt, wounded' here. Although the meaning is not appreciably different, this edition takes W's reading to be *skeind*, as did Sveinbjörn Egilsson, Finnur Jónsson (*Skj* A, II 217), Kock, Jón Helgason (1970, 222) and Longo, though Finnur emended to *skemd* in *Skj* B, II 234. Ólsen read *skemd* (cf. *FoGT* 1884, 270 n. 4).

22,25 æðrin 'the vein': W has 'æðr enn', where *enn* could be read as a suffixed definite article, as here and by Ólsen, or as the adverb *enn* 'yet, still' (though, as we do not know the conclusion of l. 6 (22,26), this is hypothetical). Finnur Jónsson emends to *æðr at* and is followed in this by Kock (*Skald*, II 121). The poet is using the noun *æðr* in two senses, 'vein' and 'eider duck', the first sense in l. 5 (22,25), the second in l. 6 (22,26). This homonym was a popular one among Icelandic poets. Two separate riddles, Gestumbl *Heiðr* 35,3[VIII] (*Heiðr* 82) and Anon *Gát* 1,5[III], rely on the same pun on *æðr*.

Chapter 12: Lepos
According to *D*, *lepos* occurs when one uses the plural when speaking to a single person. One example containing speech directed to a prelate is given (ll. 2597–98). *Dg* adds: *Hec figura inuenta est causa honoris* (83r) 'This figure is invented for the sake of honour [i.e. to confer honour on someone]'. *Lepos* is not included among the figures treated in *G*. *Konungs skuggsjá* contains a discussion of the polite use of the plural (ed. Holm-Olsen 1983, 48).

22,28 Arnórr Arnórr jarlaskáld 'Jarls' poet' Þórðarson (born c. 1012), was a son of the farmer and poet Þórðr Kolbeinsson from Hítarnes in western Iceland and Oddný eykyndill 'Island-candle' Þorkelsdóttir. Members of this family appear as characters in *Bjarnar saga Hítdǿlakappa* and in *Gunnlaugs saga ormstungu*. For further details of the full poem from which this couplet is taken and its background, as well as the poet's other compositions, see Whaley (1998, 51–52, 114, 145–48) and Whaley's edition in *SkP* II: 1, 185–86.

Stanza 32
This couplet comprises ll. 3–4 of st. 3 of a *hrynhent* encomium in honour of Magnús inn góði 'the Good' Óláfsson (r. 1035–47), entitled

Hrynhenda, Magnússdrápa. It is the first securely attested skaldic poem in *hrynhent* metre. In the various kings' saga compilations in which the poem appears, principally *Morkinskinna*, *Flateyjarbók* and *Hulda-Hrokkinskinna*, it is said that Arnórr composed the poem shortly after his arrival in Norway from Iceland, when he was summoned by the co-rulers Magnús Óláfsson and Haraldr Sigurðarson to recite eulogies in their honour. Arnórr composed *Hrynhenda* for Magnús and *Blágagladrápa* 'The *drápa* of Dark Geese', which has not survived, for Haraldr. In *TGT* the couplet is cited to demonstrate the use of a plural number in place of a singular (a kind of solecism), while in *FoGT* the same couplet illustrates *lepos*, the courteous use of the plural number when addressing a high-ranking person. The first two lines of the first *helmingr* of this stanza, which precede the couplet quoted here, address Magnús directly and invite him to listen to the poem: *Magnús, hlýð til máttigs óðar*; | *manngi veit ek fremra annan* 'Magnús, hear a mighty poem; I know no other [to be] more outstanding'.

24,1 yðru kappi 'your prowess': The 2nd pers. pl. possessive pronoun *yðru* instead of the singular form is used to compliment the king.

24,2 Jóta gramr 'prince of the Jótar [DANISH KING = Magnús]': Magnús was king of the Danes as well as the Norwegians. In l. 5 of the complete stanza of which this couplet is part he is called *dróttinn Hǫrða* 'lord of the Hǫrðar' [NORWEGIAN KING = Magnús].

24,3 persóna 'person': Grammatical person. The same technical sense of *persóna* is found below (36,7). Elsewhere *skilning* is used in the same sense (34,25 and 36,6).

24,4 soluecismus...5 segir '*solecismus* ... above': This is a cross-reference to the section on solecisms in *TGT* (1884, 16–18). *TGT* presents st. 32 as an example of a solecism and adds the following explanation: *Í talnaskipti verðr soloecismus, sem Arnórr kvað* '[st. 32]'. *Hér er margfallig tala sett fyrir einfaldigri* (*TGT* 1884, 17–18) 'In regard to the change of numbers, solecism occurs, as Arnórr said: "[st. 33]". The plural is here used instead of the singular'.

Chapter 13: Antitosis
FoGT mentions three variants of this figure—the use of one number, one case and finally one tense instead of another—and exemplifies the first two. Concerning the last variant, the treatise refers the reader to *TGT* and states that modern poets should avoid it. *D* (ll. 2599–2603)

describes the same three variants of the figure and gives them in the same order. The relevant section in *G* is: *'Urbem quam statuo uestra est [Aen, I, 573]', antitosis haec est. | Pro numero numerum ponas, exallage fiet | Dicendo 'naues armato milite complent [Aen, II 20]'* (1 40–42) '"The city [accusative], which I found, is yours", this is *antitosis. Exallage* occurs when you use [one] number instead of [another] number by saying "The ships are filled with an armed soldier"'. Both these examples are also found in *Dg*, and *FoGT* imitates them in sts 33 and 34. *G*'s first example is also given in *Dg*: *Antiptosis est accidentis pro accidente positio. Et fit quando ponitur casus pro casu, ut 'Urbem quam statuo, uestra est'* (83r) '*Antitosis* is the use of one grammatical form for another. And it occurs when [one] case is used instead of [another] case, like "The city [accusative] which I found, is yours"'.

24,6 með settu endimarki 'for a definite purpose': It is uncertain what the author means by this. Alternatively, this phrase might be rendered 'with a fixed endpoint' or perhaps 'within certain limits'.

24,7 Um fallaskifti sem hier 'Concerning the change of cases as here': This passage is understood as a defective clause: *Um fallaskifti [verðr antitosis] sem hier*, cf. 24,13. W reads: '… *settu endimarki um fallaskifti sem hier*'. *TGT* treats the use of one case instead of another as a solecistic subtype and provides one example in which it is claimed that the accusative is used instead of the dative: *því hefik heitit mey mætri* 'that I have promised the worthy maiden' (1884, 77). *TGT* evidently considers the form *mey* accusative, but the same form is commonly used in the dative (in addition to *meyju*) (see *FoGT* 1884, 187 n. 2).

Stanza 33

Ólsen is almost certainly correct (*FoGT* 1884, 271 n. 2) when he argues that the grammatical construction of ll. 1–2 (24,8–9) of st. 33 imitates a Latin construction like *urbem quam statuo, uestra est* 'the city which I found, is yours' (*Aen*, I 573) (see introductory commentary to chapter 13 above). The Icelandic example here places *þá mjóva mey* 'that slim girl' in the same position as Latin *urbem* 'city' (accusative) and then in the main clause has the alternative form of the noun *mey*, viz. *mær er þín* 'the girl is yours' in parallel with the Latin nominative *uestra [urbs] est*. Evidently neither Finnur Jónsson (*Skj* B, II 234) nor Kock (*Skald*, II 121) understood how closely the Icelandic imitates the Latin here, because both editors emended W's *þá er* in l. 1

to *þá*. This gives the sense in ll. 1–2 (24,8–9): 'I praise that slim girl for her goodwill; the girl is yours'. However, there is no way that this emended construction can exemplify a change from accusative to nominative case of the noun *mey/mær*.

24,9 fyr vild sína 'for her goodwill': This phrase can either be construed as part of a relative clause, *er eg leyfi fyr vild sína*, as here, or with *mær er þín*, as Ólsen does (*FoGT* 1884, 270, 271 n. 1), understanding it to imply 'of her own free will'. Wellendorf (forthcoming) also supports this interpretation. The imagined scenario may be that of a woman giving a man permission to woo the girl, perhaps her daughter, in marriage.

24,12 rægiligt fall 'the accusative case': *Rægiligt fall* is a calque on Latin *accusativus casus*. *TGT* (1884, 77 and 84) uses the same term, while Modern Icelandic uses *þolfall*, lit. 'suffer case'.

24,12 nefniligu falli 'the nominative case': *Nefniligt fall* is a hap. leg. in Old Norse. Modern Icelandic uses *nefnifall*, lit. 'mention case'.

24,13 Um…17 fylla 'Concerning … "fylla"': Stanza 34 is based on the Latin example *Naues armato milite complent* [*Aen*, II 20] 'The ships are filled with an armed soldier'. *G* uses this line to exemplify the figure *exallage* (I 40–42), while *Gg* makes clear that *exallage* is a subtype of *antitosis*, not a separate figure (p. 58). The author of *Dg* might have had the same example in mind, even though he does not quote it: *Numerus pro numero inquantum resultat improprietas constructibilium, ut 'turba ruunt in me'* [on the origin of this example, see Grondeux 2003], *vel aliter, ut 'multo milite' .i. 'multis militibus'* (83r) '[One] number instead of [another] number so that it results in discord between the elements of the sentence, as in "the crowd are rushing against me", or otherwise, like "many soldier", i.e. "many soldiers"'. The same phenomenon is illustrated by Donatus in *Barbarismus* and classified as a solecism in relation to number (ed. Holtz 1981, 656). In *TGT*'s translation of *Barbarismus* this is reinterpreted as the improper use of the plural when speaking to a single person (discussed above in the section on *lepos*, commentary to 22,27).

Stanza 34
Stanza 34 illustrates a difference in number between the noun subject and its verb. It bears considerable similarities to the figure *G* called *exallage* (see introductory commentary to chapter 13 above). In *G* this example follows immediately upon that used as the basis of st. 33.

24,15 alls framm 'all [the way] forwards': With Ólsen (*FoGT* 1884, 271–72 n. 1) this adverbial phrase is understood to mean that a single detachment of men filled the ships 'all the way forwards to the prow'.

24,16 nafn[1] 'noun': *Nafn* neut. is a direct translation of Latin *nomen*. This technical term is often used in *TGT*, e.g.: *Aristotiles inn spaki kallar tvá parta málsgreinar, nafn ok orð, því at þeir gera meðal sín samtengdir fullkomna málsgrein* (1884, 56) 'Aristotle the Wise says that there are two parts of speech, noun and verb, because in conjunction they make up a complete sentence'.

24,16 orði 'verb': *Orð* neut. is a direct translation of Latin *verbum*. *Orð* is often used in *FoGT*, but this is the only occurrence where it carries the technical meaning 'verb'. It often occurs in a technical sense in *TGT* (an example can be found in commentary to *nafn* in 24,16 above).

24,18 Um...20 verka 'Regarding ... poets': The cross-reference to *TGT* is only partially correct as *TGT* merely provides one example of the change of tense (1884, 77 l. 13–18). *TGT*'s example seems to illustrate the use of the historic present and it is surprising that the writer should think that it was inappropriate for contemporary poets to use this device. The remark that the figure is often found in the works of old poets is paralleled by *D*'s remark that the figure is often found in holy prophecies. To this *Dg* adds: *Et in prophetiis ponitur preteritum perfectum pro futuro, ut in Daniel: 'Affuit ircus ab aquilonibus' etc. ubi 'affuit' ponitur pro 'aderit'* (83r) 'The preterite perfect is also often used in prophecies instead of the future, as in [The Book of] Daniel: "The he-goat had come from the North" etc. where "had come" is used instead of "will come"'. Even though *Dg* explicitly refers to the Book of Daniel, the wording is considerably closer to Walter of Châtillon's *Alexandreis*, V 9 (*Affuit a siccis veniens Aquilonibus hyrcus*, ed. Colker 1978, 119), than to the Book of Daniel VIII.5 (*ecce autem hircus caprarum veniebat ab occidente super faciem totius terrae*, ed. Weber *et al.* 1994, 1360).

Chapter 14: Antitheton

This chapter is the longest in the entire treatise and the writer departs significantly from the treatment of *antitheton* in *D* (ll. 2604–05) and *G* (I 68). Material has been incorporated from the section of *Háttatal* where Snorri describes and illustrates ways in which one may vary the verse-forms of the *dróttkvætt* metre by varying the syntactic structure of the stanzas while retaining the standard metre (*at breyta háttum með máli einu*, SnE 2007, 9–14, at p. 9), i.e. by changing the arrangement of the clauses in a stanza. The writer's terminology in this chapter also betrays his reliance on *Háttatal* (*stælt, langloka, kveðandi* and *orð*). *D*'s definition agrees with the initial definition of *FoGT*, while *G*'s understanding of *antitheton* is more like our 'antithesis': *Uteris antitheta dicens contraria dicta* 'You use *antitheta* when you utter contrary utterances'. *D* gives the example: *est Daniel Noë Job castus rectorque maritus* 'Daniel is chaste, Noah a ruler, Job a husband', and *Dg* explains: *Antitheton prout sumitur in hoc loco est subsequentium ad precedentia reductio, ut cum singula singulis correspondent, ut patet in littera. Est [< Sunt] Daniel etc. castus reducitur ad li Daniel, rector ad Noe, maritus ad Job* (83r) '*Antitheton*, as it is understood here, is the bringing back of the following words to the preceding, so that the individual [items] correspond to the individual [items], as it can be seen in the text: "Daniel is" etc. [l. 2605] "chaste" belongs to Daniel, "ruler" to Noah, "husband" to Job'. A Latin example somewhat similar to *D*'s can be found in the lower margin of f. 27r of AM 671 4to (c.1315–45):

> *Clericus ecclesia laicus Norwegia   leges*
> *exultat   arguitur gaudet confunditur absunt*

'The clergy exults, the church blames, the laity rejoice, Norway is ruined, the laws are absent'. In this example, printed in Kålund 1889–94, II 88, *clericus* is constructed with *exultat*, *ecclesia* with *arguitur* etc. Longo (2006, 1001) presents another Latin example in his detailed treatment of this chapter (2006, 994–1001). The examples of *antitheton* in *FoGT* show that the writer understood the figure to consist of sentences that were split up in one way or another, and the six examples of *antitheton* given in the text show various ways of doing this.

24,21 Antiteton...fyrstum '*Antitheton* occurs ... the first': This definition agrees with the one given in *D* (l. 2604).

24,21 verðr^2...24 langlokum 'it occurs ... long enclosures': This part of the definition and the expressions *stælt* and *langlokum* draw on *Háttatal* (see commentary to 26,22 and 24,24 below and Introduction §5 c for details), but Snorri's theoretical framework has been reconceptualised.

24,22 svá að regla sie haldin undir riettri kveðandi 'while the rules of metrical arrangement are observed': The key words, *regla* and *kveðandi*, are difficult to translate and might partially overlap in meaning. The translation is therefore a paraphrase.

24,22 regla 'arrangement': Old Norse *regla* < Latin *regula* is here understood as '[the correct] arrangement [of elements in a stanza]'. In *Háttatal* the noun *setning* fem. is occasionally used in the same sense, e.g.: *Ǫnnur stafasetning er sú er fylgir setning hljóðs þess er háttr gerir ok kveðandi* (*SnE* 2007, 4) 'Another aspect of spelling is the one that belongs to the arrangement of the sound [i.e. alliteration and assonance] that constitutes a verse-form and metre'. Many of the technical terms of *Háttatal* are notoriously difficult to understand and translate, and a different interpretation is given in Faulkes's translation (1987, 166).

24,23 kveðandi 'metrical arrangement': *Kveðandi* is here understood to mean 'metre, metrical arrangment'. Faulkes lists a number of additional meanings of *kveðandi* in his glossary to *Háttatal* (*SnE* 2007, 128–29).

24,24 langlokum 'with late closures': *Háttatal* also uses the dative of *langloka* without the preposition *með* 'with': *þessi er hinn sjaundi; langlokum* [followed by *Háttatal* 14/*FoGT* st. 35] (ed. Finnur Jónsson 1931, 222) 'this is the seventh [variant], with long enclosures'. The word *langlokum* is found neither in W's text of *Háttatal* nor in the main hands of the manuscripts of *Háttatal* (see *SnE* 2007, 10 l. 31, 42 n. 14,1).

Stanzas 35 and 36

These two stanzas are cited without attribution by the writer of *FoGT*. They are, respectively, sts 14 and 12 of Snorri Sturluson's *Háttatal* 'List of Verse-forms', probably composed c. 1222 with a dual function: as an encomium for King Hákon Hákonarson and his co-regent Jarl Skúli Bárðarson and as a key to Old Norse-Icelandic metres. See further Faulkes's edition of *Háttatal* (*SnE* 2007) and Gade's edition in *SkP* III (forthcoming) for both stanzas. *Háttatal* 14 (st. 35) exemplifies the native phenomenon of *langlokur* 'late closures', a technical term also found as a heading (*langlokum* 'with late closures') in the U manuscript of *Snorra Edda* and as an addition in R; see further *SnE* 2007, 52, 79, 129. The stylistic device exemplified here is also attested in Rǫgnvaldr jarl Kali Kolsson and Hallr Þórarinsson's *Háttalykill* sts 59–60 (RvHbreiðm *Hl* 59–60[III]), and the term *langlokum* is also used there. As the prose text indicates, the late closure here is produced by the syntactic combination of the first and the last line (26,1 and 26,8).

Stanza 12 of *Háttatal* (st. 36 in *FoGT*) has two enclosing clauses in each *helmingr* in ll. 1 (26,14) and 4 (26,17), 5 (26,18) and 8 (26,21), while the inner lines, ll. 2–3 (26,15–16) and 6–7 (26,19–20), of each *helmingr* form independent, intercalated units.

26,9 Hier...10 síðast 'Here these ... *ræðr konungdómi*': This sentence has a parallel in *Háttatal*: *Hér hefr upp mál í inu fyrsta vísuorði ok lýkr ‹í› inu síðasta, ok eru þau sér um mál (SnE* 2007, 11) 'Here the sentence begins in the first line and ends in the last, and they constitute one sentence'.
26,10 regla 'version': The context seems to require that *regla* be translated as 'this arrangement of the words', 'version'. The usual meaning of *regla* is 'rule' (see commentary to 24,22 above).
26,12 Sú...22 háttr 'It ... metre': This description is somewhat similar to the description which accompanies *Háttatal* 12 (= st. 36 of *FoGT*): *Hér er svá: 'Hákon veldr ok hǫldum* [= first line of *helmingr*] | *teitr þjóðkonungs heiti* [= last line of *helmingr*]', *en annat ok it þriðja vísuorð er sér um mál, ok er þat stál kallat* (*SnE* 2007, 10) 'Here it is thus: Happy Hákon commands the name "mighty king" and the freeholders', but the second and the third line constitute one sentence, and that is called *stál* [inlay]'.
26,12 species 'variant': *Species* f. 'kind, type' is a Latin word. It is found three times in this chapter (also in 26,23 and 28,10) and once in chapter 21 (38,1).
26,13 vísuhelmingi 'half-stanza': W's reading *vísuorði* 'line' is semantically at odds with the example given and the text has therefore been emended. This emendation was introduced by *SnE* 1848, 206 and it has been adopted in all subsequent editions.

Stanza 36
See commentary to sts 35 and 36 above. Stanza 12 of *Háttatal* (st. 36 in *FoGT*) has two enclosing clauses in each *helmingr*, in ll. 1 (26,14) and 4 (26,17), 5 (26,18) and 8 (26,21), while the inner lines, ll 2–3 (26,15–16) and 6–7 (26,19–20), of each *helmingr* form independent, intercalated units.

26,22 stælt *Háttatal* 12 (= st. 36) is introduced with the words: *þetta er stælt kallat* (*SnE* 2007, 10) 'this is called *stælt* [equipped with inlay]'.

26,24 orðum 'lines': *Orð*, which usually means 'word', is here understood as *vísuorð* 'line', cf. Ólsen's glossary (1884, s. v.). *Orð* frequently has the same meaning in *Háttatal* (see *SnE* 2007, 48 n. 1, 40–41).

Stanza 37
This anonymous *hrynhent* stanza illustrates a yet more intricate variant of *antitheton*, in which there are five complete clauses, one wrapped inside the next; l. 1 (26,25) is completed by l. 8 (28,6), l. 2 (26,26) by l. 7 (28,5), l. 3 (28,1) by l. 6 (28,4), while ll. 4 (28,2) and 5 (28,3) go together. This ingenious arrangement of clauses appears not to have a precise precedent in earlier Icelandic grammatical treatises. The theme of each complete sentence is the manner of death of one of four kings of Norway, two in battle, the other two from disease.

26,25 Óláfr...28,6 vallar 'Óláfr, who got a famous fall to the ground [death], was able to burn the [heathen] sacrificial buildings' [*Óláfr kunni blóthús brenna—ágætt fall sá hlaut til vallar*]: These lines refer to King Óláfr inn helgi 'the Saint' Haraldsson (r. 1015–30), who died at the battle of Stiklastaðir (Stiklestad) in Verdalen, Trøndelag, on 29 July 1030. He was known for his vigorous opposition to heathendom, characterised here by his burning of *blóthús* 'sacrifical buildings', l. 1 (26,25).

26,26 Magnús Magnús inn góði 'the Good' Óláfsson, son of St Óláfr, r. 1035–47.

28,1 Harald Haraldr harðráði 'Hardrule' Sigurðarson, r. 1046–66.

28,2 hans arfi 'his heir': This phrase, together with *vinr dróttar* 'the friend of the people [RULER = Magnús *or* Óláfr Haraldssynir]' in the following line, may refer to either Magnús Haraldsson or his brother Óláfr kyrri 'the Quiet' Haraldsson. The latter is probably the more likely referent as he was the more prominent of the two brothers and ruled Norway from 1067–93, while Magnús ruled briefly on his own in 1066, during the time Haraldr and Óláfr were in England, and jointly with his brother from 1067–69. Magnús died in 1069 of the illness *reformr* 'ergotism' according to *Morkinskinna* (ÍF 23, 325), brought on by eating fungus-affected grain (Andersson and Gade 2000, 446 n. 2). Óláfr kyrri also died of an unspecified illness at one of his eastern residences in Bohuslän (*Morkinskinna*, ÍF 24, 16; Andersson and Gade 2000, 285; *Ágrip*, ÍF 29, 41; *Fagrskinna*, ÍF 29, 302; *Heimskringla*, ÍF 28, 209).

28,4 riett 'certainly': It is also possible to construe *riett* with *vier frágum* 'we have heard', l. 3 (28,1).

28,4 á enskri sliettu 'on an English field': At the battle of Stamford Bridge, Yorkshire, where Haraldr harðráði was killed on 25 September 1066.

28,5 sóttum píndr 'tormented by illness': Magnús the Good died of an unspecified feverish illness in Jutland on 25 October 1047, according to *Morkinskinna* (ÍF 23, 168–71; Andersson and Gade 2000, 181–84).

28,5 þá er örlög enduz 'when his fortunes came to an end': There is a large hole in W at this point, so the emendations adopted here are conjectural, though supported in the case of *enduz* by *skothending* with *píndr*. The conjecture *örlög* 'fate, fortunes, death' was first suggested by Jón Ólafsson from Grunnavík (cf. *FoGT* 1884, 274 n. 3) and has been accepted by all subsequent editors, as has Ólsen's emendation to *enduz*.

28,7 Hier...9 talt 'Here ... quoted': The writer could have added that the second and the seventh line and the first and the last line also belong together.

28,7 er ið fjórða og ið fimta vísuorð saman um mál 'the fourth line in conjunction with the fifth make up a sentence': W is damaged at this point and has a hole between *vísuorð* and *mál*. *SnE* 1848, 207 and *SnE* 1848–87, II 222 supply *sér um* while *FoGT* 1884, 137 and *FoGT* 2004, 46 supply *saman um*. The emendation *saman um* has been preferred here because it improves the flow of the text and adds lexical variation. A similar construction below (28,24) is also the result of emendation. The main advantage of *SnE* 1848's emendation is that *Háttatal*, upon which the writer drew for this chapter, often uses the construction *vera sér um mál*, e.g.: *en annat ok it þriðja vísuorð er sér um mál* (*SnE* 2007, 10). *SnE* 1818, 345 avoids the problem altogether by jumping from *vísuorð* (28,7) to *vísuorð* (28,8)—probably by mistake.

28,11 en þó eitt efni um alla með inum sömum tveim málum 'yet one subject matter throughout the complete stanza with the same two sentences': An elliptical sentence in which the verb, *er* 'is', and the head noun of the quantifier *allr* 'complete', namely *vísa* 'stanza', have been left out.

Stanzas 38 and 41

Stanzas 38 and 41 are in a variety of the *tøglag* 'journey metre' verse-form that is called *inn nýi háttr* 'the new verse-form' in *Háttatal* (SnSt Ht 73[III]; *SnE* 2007, 31), from where the composer of the *FoGT* stanzas probably borrowed it. Stanza 38 offers a fourth example of *antitheton* in which the first and fourth words of each couplet belong together, in such a way that two clauses are created in a cross-over pattern in each *helmingr*, making four independent clauses in the stanza as a whole, which refer to two legendary subjects, the pirate or sea-king Haki and the Danish king Hrólfr kraki 'Pole-ladder'. Thus words 1, 4, 5 and 8 in the first *helmingr* form one clause, and words 2, 3, 6 and 7 do likewise. In the second *helmingr* words occupying the same numbered positions as in the first *helmingr* (viz. 1, 4, 5 and 8) form another clause referring to the subject of the comparable clause in the first *helmingr*, namely Haki, while the same structure is repeated for words 2, 3, 6 and 7 in the second *helmingr*, and they form a clause about Hrólfr kraki. The two words of each line rhyme internally. The dual rhyming subjects of the stanza, Haki and Kraki, may have been suggested by *Háttatal* 94, where they are also juxtaposed. The theme of the ways in which famous people met their deaths, whether they were legendary or historical, is carried through sts 37, 38 and 41.

28,13 Haki Name of a famous pirate or sea-king. The name can be used generally in poetry for a sea-king, but here there is a specific reference to the brother of the legendary Hagbarðr. Haki is mentioned in *Ynglinga saga* chapters 22–23 (ÍF 26, 43–45) as a fierce and bellicose warrior, who killed Hugleikr, king of the Swedes, at Fyris-vellir 'Plains by the Fyrisån' (Fyris river) near Uppsala, assumed the kingship himself, and was later engaged in a second battle at Fyris-vellir, in which he was mortally wounded and placed at his own request on a pyre on board a burning ship, which was pushed out to sea. Cf. the anonymous couplet quoted in *Skáldskaparmál* (Anon (*SnE*) 16,1[III]; *SnE* 1998, I 97), *Haki var brendr á báli* 'Haki was burned on a pyre'. A rather different account of Haki's death appears in *Saxo* (VII 8, 1–6, ed. Friis-Jensen 2005, I 476–80).

28,13 Kraki 'Pole-ladder': Nickname referring to the tall thin appearance of the legendary Danish king and hero Hrólfr kraki, who was the subject of numerous narratives, including *Hrólfs saga kraka* and the now lost *Skjǫldunga saga*. He was renowned for his generosity and Snorri Sturluson tells an elaborate narrative in *Skáldskaparmál* to account for the gold-kenning 'seed of Kraki' (*SnE* 1998, I 58–59).

Accounts of his and his champions' deaths vary across the sources, but in all cases he dies in battle.

28,23 anatecor '*antitheton*': Corrected to *antitheton* by all editors except *SnE* 1818, 345 who prints 'Ana-*tekor*'.
28,23 er 'in which': *SnE* 1818, 345 emended *en* to *er* and has been followed by all subsequent editors.
28,23 og eru um mál saman 'and constitute one sentence': At this point damage in W has obliterated the characters between *og* and *mál*. The emendation *eru um* was first proposed in *SnE* 1818, 345. It has been adopted in all subsequent editions.

Stanzas 39 and 40
Stanza 39 is the fifth example of *antitheton* in *FoGT*. Here there are four clauses, each of which begins in the first *helmingr* and finishes in the second, following the order abcd : abcd. The following stanza, 40, is a rearrangement of this sequence using almost the same wording, in the order abcd : dcba. Stanzas 39 and 40 are in the metre *runhent*. It is of interest that at least one earlier parallel to the arrangement of st. 39 exists in the skaldic corpus, and this is a *helmingr* attributed to the early eleventh-century skald Þórðr Særeksson or Sjáreksson (ÞSjár Frag 3[III]); it uses exactly the same arrangement of clauses, it is in the same metre, *runhent*, and all its subjects are allusions to Norse myths or legends. This suggests that the *FoGT* example is not just a *tour de force* occasioned by the need to exemplify a Latin rhetorical figure, but part of a native tradition. In the corresponding Latin treatises, examples given are of Old Testament characters, so it seems that the writer of *FoGT* is deliberately implying a parallel of subject-matter between Old Testament examples and figures from Old Norse myth and legend.
28,26 Hákon King Hákon Hákonarson of Norway (r. 1217–63). Born after his supposed father's death, he was regarded as the illegitimate son of King Hákon Sverrisson (d. 1 January 1204) and Inga of Varteig.
28,27 Magnús Magnús lagabøtir 'Law-mender' Hákonarson (r. 1263–80), son of Hákon Hákonarson. As his nickname and l. 6 (28,30) of this stanza indicate, Magnús was celebrated for having modified and unified the laws of Norway. He also promulgated a new law code for Iceland, *Jónsbók* 'Jón's book' (see *NGL*, IV 183–340), which was sent to the island in 1280 and ratified by the *alþingi* (the general legal assembly) in 1281.

28,28 Eiríks 'Eiríkr's': Eiríkr, the elder son of Magnús Hákonarson (r. 1280–99), gained the nickname 'priest-hater' from his poor relations with the Church, but otherwise enjoyed a peaceful rule.
28,29 hans bróðir 'his brother': This was Eiríkr's younger brother, Hákon háleggr 'Long-leg' Magnússon (r. 1299–1319), who succeeded him on the throne of Norway because Eiríkr died childless. Line 8 (30,2) arguably alludes to Hákon's reputation for successfully curbing the power of the Norwegian magnates. Hákon is probably also the subject of st. 10, where he is characterised as *handsterkr* 'strong-handed', perhaps another allusion to his tough domestic policies. On the implications of these references to Hákon's reign, mentioned as having taken place in the past both here and in st. 10, for the dating of *FoGT*, see commentary at 6,13.

30,3 Þessa...háttar 'This stanza ... previous verse-form': This is a paraphrase of the Old Norse text rather than a translation. The prose only mentions one stanza and one verse-form, but two stanzas (sts 40 and 41) are provided. The first can be seen as an addition to st. 39, the second as an addition to st. 38.

Stanza 40
Stanza 40 is a variation, both in wording and verse-form, of st. 39. See comments on that stanza above.
30,10 lögvizku 'of legal learning': W's 'lǫgvizlu' is probably a scribal error caused by the copyist anticipating the following word *lund* 'disposition'.

Stanza 41
Stanza 41 is a variation on st. 38, and both are in *inn nýi háttr* (cf. SnSt *Ht* 73[III]). Minimal word changes allow the poet to rearrange the syntax of the four clauses of st. 41 so that clause 1 reads straight down the left-hand side of ll. 1–4 (30,12–15), clause 2 straight down the right-hand side of ll. 1–4 (30,12–15), clause 3 straight down the left-hand side of ll. 5–8 (30,16–19) and clause 4 straight down the right-hand side of ll. 5–8 (30,16–19).

Chapter 15: Anthypophora
FoGT's definition does not contradict that of *D* (ll. 2606–07), but the setting at an assembly does make it more vivid and concrete than that of *D*. *Dg* paraphrases *D*: *Antipophora est tacite obiectioni prelata*

responsio (83r) '*Anthypophora* is an answer anticipating a tacit objection'. *Dg* also adds two Ovidian examples (*Heroides* 1.37–38 and 1.2). The figure is also defined in *G* (I 79) and in *Gg* (pp. 90–91), but these texts do not add anything of significance for the understanding of *FoGT*.

30,20 Antiposora 'Anthypophora': All earlier editors interpreted the seventh letter of *antiposora* as an *f*. It is difficult to determine whether W has 'antipofora' or 'antipoſora'. However, the scribe normally uses the insular form of *f* ⟨ꝼ⟩ (rather than the carolingian ⟨f⟩), and the character in question has therefore been interpreted as ⟨ſ⟩ and rendered with *s* in the normalised text. Johansson's (2007) transcription of W also interprets the graph in question as ⟨ſ⟩.

Stanza 42
Stanza 42, in *dróttkvætt* metre, illustrates *FoGT*'s definition of *anthypophora* to the extent that both prose explanation and the stanza represent men engaged in legal disputes at an assembly. In the first *helmingr*, the speaker warns another man against bringing a charge against him first, on the ground that he has changed from being compassionate to taking a hard line in such circumstances. In the second *helmingr* he issues a barely veiled threat that if the other man proceeds to lay charges against him, that man will face financial ruin. This is some way from the basic sense of the Latin figure, which involves responding to an anticipated objection.

30,24 kraunk 'distressing': *Krankr* is a late loan word from Middle Low German, used only here in poetry to mean 'hurtful, insulting'; otherwise the sense is 'weak, sick' (cf. Anon *Mey* 36,3[VII] *krankar kvinnur* 'sick women').

Chapter 16: Anticlasis
The definition given in *FoGT* mirrors *D*'s (ll. 2608–09). *D*'s example (*non obsto, sed toto posse resisto* 'I do not stand in the way, I withstand with all my might') also illustrates how the same word/verb, namely *sto*, is used in opposite senses when it occurs twice as the second element of verbal compounds. *Dg* (83r) paraphrases *D* and adds an etymology. *FoGT*'s example looks as if it has been modelled on *D*'s example, but must be considered less successful, because the lexical opposition has been removed, so that only the semantic one remains. It is therefore not correct to state that the same words/verbs are used with opposite meanings.

32,1 gagnstaðliga 'opposing': *Gagnstaðliga* is used adverbially in the text.

Stanza 43

FoGT's representation of the figure *anticlassis* is dependent on the prescription in *D*. The Icelandic examples in the first *helmingr*, *Eg stend eigi að móti* 'I do not stand opposed' and *eg rís við* 'I oppose', are clearly dependent on the similar senses of the verbs *obsto* and *resisto* in the Latin example. In the second *helmingr* the relevance of the examples to the figure is less clear, though both probably indicate that the speaker will fight or oppose his adversary (*þier* 'you' in l. 7 (32,9)); both clauses use forms of the verb *heita* in the sense 'promise' rather than any of its other meanings ('call, be called, invoke').

32,4 mensveigjanda 'the necklace-distributor [GENEROUS MAN]': The emendation *men-* 'necklace' from W's *man-* was first proposed by Ólsen (*FoGT* 1884, 279–80) and has been adopted by all subsequent editors.

Chapter 17: Antimetabola

D (ll. 2610–11) and *FoGT* both describe *antimetabola* as a change in the meaning of an utterance achieved by changing the (order of the) words, but the figure is evidently more mysterious to the writer of *FoGT*, who mentions 'words of obscure signification', than it is to the writer of *D*. *G* (III 81–83) describes a similar figure under the name *commutatio*. Three divergent definitions of *commutatio* are given in Gg. The second of these is: *commutatio est quando uerba commutantur ex quorum commutatione sententia totaliter commutatur* (p. 199) '*Commutatio* is when words are interchanged, from the interchange of words the meaning is changed completely'. The example used in *D* and *FoGT* can be found in many rhetorical treatises (e.g. in *Rhetorica ad Herennium*, IV 39 and Quintilian *Institutiones Oratoriae*, IX 3.85). It is ascribed to Socrates.

32,12 Ansimehisa verðr ef maðr snýr svá sem með orðum myrkrar skilningar '*Antimetabola* occurs when one changes, as it were, [the meaning] with words of obscure signification': This sentence lacks an object and might be corrupt (*snúa* is usually constructed with an object in the dative). The translation follows that in *SnE* 1848–78, II 229 in adding the object 'meaning' and rendering *svá sem* 'as it were'.

Stanza 44

It is obvious from the elaborate prose explanation of the meaning of the *hap. leg. þokumenn* 'fog-men' in l. 2 (32,15, probably a calque on Latin *nebulo* 'a worthless person, wretch') that the writer of *FoGT* considered the use of this word in st. 44 to illustrate the figure he called *antimetabola/ansimehisa*. The use of *þokumenn* does not really illustrate the standard sense of the figure *antimetabola*, which *D*, following earlier authorities like Isidore of Seville, defines as *cum verbis vertit antimetabola sensum*: | *non, ut edas, vivas, sed edas ut vivere possis* (ll. 2611–12) '*antimetabola* changes meaning with words: you should not live so that you may eat, but eat so that you may live'. Thus a rearrangement of the same words in two clauses can bring about a change of meaning. This is not what *FoGT*'s use of *þokumenn* does, but it is notable that the stanza as a whole is influenced by the Latin adage *non ut edas vivas, sed edas ut vivere possis*. This stanza is present in both the X^2 (*LaufE* 1979, 252) and the Y^1 (*LaufE* 1979, 363–64) versions of *LaufE*, together with a version of the prose commentary that follows the stanza, in each case slightly differently worded. The verse text is the same in each, except that in l. 3 (32,16) Y^1 has *klaustrs* (as in *FoGT*), while X^2 has *klaustr*. Neither the stanza nor the prose commentary are in *RE* 1665. In X^2 the extract from *FoGT* about *þokumenn* is included after *Epilogus partis prioris*, possibly as a later addition, while in Y^1 it comes at the end of the section entitled *Upprune nóckurra konga heita*; for a discussion of the significance of these locations, see Faulkes (*LaufE* 1979, 179).

32,16 en 'but': *FoGT* 1884, 280 emends *en* to *etr* 'eats' in order both to supply a main verb in ll. 3–4 (32,16–17) and to bring the Icelandic closer to the Latin source, but it makes sense without emendation, provided the verb is assumed.

32,17 að lífið haldiz 'to stay alive': Literally 'so that life is kept'.

32,18 Þokumenn...22 lifa 'Those ... live': The writer appears much more interested in the exegesis of the example than in the figure itself. The metaphors used in this paragraph—fog, light, darkness—all belong to the standard fare of medieval religious rhetoric, e.g. *strjúk frá augum þér myrkva ok þoku ok hreinsa hjarta þitt ok hugskot af þeiri inni fornu syndaþoku er langliga hefir þar með stórum lýtum legit at þú megir því ǫllu betr á líta ljós guðlegrar miskunnar ok at hann gefi þér birting sinna blezaðra boðorða* (*Barlaams saga*, ed. Rindal 1981, 106) 'Sweep the darkness and fog away from your eyes and cleanse your heart and your thoughts of the old fog of sins which has lain there for long with great errors so that you will be able see the light of divine mercy better and so that He might give you the enlightenment of His blessed commands'. See also *Jóns saga baptista* II (ed. Unger 1874, 866) and the Icelandic Book of Homilies (ed. de Leeuw van Weenen 1993, 97v l. 31–98r l. 4).

32,18 Þokumenn…20 framferðar 'Those … behaviour': These lines are reproduced almost verbatim in the Y-version of *LaufE* (ed. Faulkes 1979, 363) where they form the introduction to st. 44. The same lines are also given in ms. X² of *LaufE*, with some variant readings: *Þokumenn eru þeir kallaðir er öllum peningum sínum sóa með* [W and Y: *alla penninga sína neyta upp í*] *ofáti og ofdrykkju, og bera þeir það nafn sakir snápskapar síns, því* [W: *því að*] *þeir sjá ei* [W: *eigi*, Y: *ekki*] *sátt ljós sinnar* [W and Y: *riettrar*] *framferðar* (*LaufE* 1979, 252 and 363).

32,18 ofáti og ofdrykkju 'indulging in food and drink': The pairing of these two sins is commonplace and can be found already in Rom. XIII.13. One Old Norse example which combines indulging in food and drink with the loss of riches (as in *FoGT*) can be found in the Icelandic Book of Homilies: *Guð seldi þér auðæfi at þú megir vita hversu mikit unað at þeim má vera ef þú hefir ást með auðæfum þínum ok selir þau til tryggrar hirzlu. Ef þú vill þat eigi, þá mun ofát ok ofdrykkju eða lostasemi taka frá þér auðófi þín eða ella mun til koma bráðr dauði ok grípa þau frá þér* (ed. de Leeuw van Weenen 1993, 66v) 'God gave you riches so that you might know what great bliss one might find in them if you love your riches and entrust them to a faithful custodian. If you do not want to do that, then over-eating, over-drinking or lustfulness will take the riches from you or sudden death will come and snatch them away from you'.

32,20 sem í sitjandi myrkvastofuþoku 'as if they sat in the fog of the prison cell': The word division is difficult to determine with certainty. A verbal form is not normally inserted between a preposition and its complement and one might therefore consider whether it would be more appropriate to interpret the text as *sem ísitjandi myrkvastofuþoku* 'as one/those sitting in the fog of the prison cell, as an inmate/inmates in the fog of the prison cell'. The noun *ísitjandi* would then be interpreted as 'one sitting in(side)/inmate'. *Ísitjandi* is not recorded in *ONP* or *LP*, but it is found in *Milska*, a late medieval Icelandic poem, meaning 'possessor' (ed. *ÍM*, I 2 p. 46, st. 37). Morphologically, *sitjandi/ísitjandi* can be analysed as nominative singular as well as nominative plural.

32,21 myrkvastofuþoku 'fog of the prison cell': This compound is not attested elsewhere.

32,22 þykkir…skaðsamlig 'this … detrimental': This judgement is not paralleled by the Latin texts.

Chapter 18: Aposiopasis
The definition agrees with that given in *D* (ll. 2612–15). *Dg*'s example and *Dg*'s exegesis of that example clearly inspired the writer of *FoGT*: *Aposiopesis est sententie per orationem interceptio, et fit quando incipimus fari quicquam et ultro id est uoluntarie desinimus illud quandoque quod cepimus illud tacendo, ut hoc exemplo Terentii: 'Ego ne illam que me que illum que* [< *qua*] *me que me non'* [cf. Terence *Eunuchus* l. 65]. *Hoc est: Ego ne illam digner aduentu meo, que illum preposuit mihi que me spreuit, que non me suscepit heri* (83r) '*Aposiopesis* is the interruption of a sentence in the course of an utterance, and it occurs when we begin to utter something, and on our own initiative, viz. voluntarily, break off whenever we begin by means of leaving it unsaid, as in this example from Terence: "I not her, who me, who him, who me, who me not". That is: I will not deem her worthy of my visit, [she] who preferred him to me, [she] who scorned me, [she] who did not receive me yesterday'. Ólsen quotes a similar gloss in his notes (*FoGT* 1884, 140n.). *Dg*'s explanation of the figure is almost identical to a passage in Priscian's *Institutiones* (*GL*, III 111). *Graecismus* mentions *aposiopesis* (I 15) while *Gg* illustrates the figure with the same example as *Dg* (p. 32). In addition, *Dg* refers to *Graecismus*, III 89–91 where a similar figure is treated under the name *precisio*.

Stanza 45
The figure illustrated by st. 45, in *dróttkvætt* metre, was understood in Antiquity and the Middle Ages as a kind of reticence brought about by strong feelings on the part of the orator resulting in the omission of implicit words. In the case illustrated here the words *eg vil* 'I want' have been supplied to complete l. 4 (32,28) and *kastaði* '[she] rejected' to complete the sense of the relative clause in ll. 5–6 (32,29–34,1). The misogynistic subject-matter of this stanza was probably not the invention of the Icelandic poet, but may have been suggested by an example in a commentary to *D* (cf. *FoGT* 2004, 209–10). Another

influence upon this stanza and on the prose commentary (cf. *reiði-þokka* 34,4, *konu* 34,6) may be a couplet by Einarr Skúlason (ESk Lv 10[III]) quoted and interpreted by Óláfr Þórðarson in *TGT* (1884, 66–67, 174–75); it ostensibly refers to a horse with which the speaker is angry, but has a double meaning, explained in the prose commentary as referring to a married woman whom the speaker of the verse fancies. In the prose commentary the first line of the couplet, *Víst erumk hermð á hesti* 'I truly have anger at the horse', is paraphrased as *legg ek á jó reiðiþokka* 'I place a dislike on the horse', which can be manipulated to give the double sense *legg ek á Jóreiði þokka* 'I place a liking on Jóreiðr' by changing the word boundaries. As the word *reiðiþokki* 'anger, wrath, dislike' is not common in Old Icelandic (there are five citations, but not the one in *FoGT*, in *ONP*, plus one other poetic usage, Anon *Vitn* 12,1[VII]), the possibility of influence from *TGT* is plausible, given also that both stanzas in question refer to men's relationships (or wished-for relationships) with women.

32,29 þá er 'who': Referring back to the woman in question. This emendation of W's *þar er* conforms to the prose gloss and was first proposed in *SnE* 1848–87, II 230. It has been followed by most editors, with the exception of Kock (*Skald*, II 122 and *NN* §2358), who keeps the manuscript reading and introduces several unnecessary and unconvincing emendations in ll. 4–5 (32,28–29).

32,29 frá færumz 'get out of': This emendation of W's 'fra fẹrum' was first proposed by Ólsen (*FoGT* 1884, 281) and has been followed by all subsequent editors except Kock.

34,4 þessur 'these': Neuter nom. pl. of the demonstrative *sjá/þessi*. This form is characteristic of Norwegian and Norwegianising Icelandic manuscripts. Elsewhere, e.g. at 40,1, the writer uses the expected form *þessi*.

34,5 upp taka 'be construed': *Háttatal* (*SnE* 2007, 12) and *TGT* (1884, 92) also use the collocation *taka upp* in this technical sense.

34,9 Þessi…10 borgar 'This … Jerusalem': This allusion refers most likely to Jer. IV.12 (*loquar iudicia mea cum eis* 'I will speak my judgements with them', trans. *Douay-Rheims Bible*) which is a shortened form of Jer. I.16 (*loquar iudicia mea cum eis super omni malitia eorum* 'I will pronounce my judgements against them touching all their wickedness', trans. *Douay-Rheims Bible*). Jer. IV.12 is part of a longer speech 'to this people and Jerusalem' (*populo huic et Hierusalem*, IV.11), and Jer. II.1–XXV.38 comprises the word of God (*verbum domini*, II.1). This biblical passage therefore fits *FoGT*'s reference in all respects. It is furthermore used as an example of the figure *aposiopesis* in Hieronymus's six books of commentary on the book of Jeremiah (*PL* 24 col. 709a). Equally strong arguments cannot be presented in favour of Ólsen's suggestions (*FoGT* 1884, 141n.) that the reference might be to Ezek. XVI or Hos. II.

34,10 Hierusalem borgar 'of the city of Jerusalem': The Old Norse form of the name Jerusalem is *Jórsalaborg*, but the indeclinable Latin form of the name *Hierusalem* was often used as well in Old Norse writings.

Chapter 19: Euphemismos

The definition and the example provided are based on *D* (ll. 2615–16), but the writer's definition is narrower than *D*'s in that *FoGT* speaks of a change of letters in a word rather than a change of words. The writer retains *D*'s Latin example (*exultat* 'exults' vs. *exaltat* 'exalts') in the description of his example, but in the actual example these words have been replaced by Old Norse counterparts (*hlakka* 'cry, exult' vs. *hefja upp* 'raise, exalt'). *Dg* explains and paraphrases *D*: *Euphemismos* [< *Euphonismos*] *est positio uerbi pro uerbo ut in Psalterio: 'Exultabit lingua mea iustitiam tuam'* [Ps L.16 *iuxta lxx*] *.i. 'cum exaltatione decantauit', hoc etiam patet in littera: Exult domini uocem* [< *laudem*] *etc.* (83v) '*Euphemismos* is the replacement of one word by another, as in the Psalter: "My tongue will exult your justice", that is "sang with exaltation". This is also evident in the text: "[My tongue] exults the voice of the Lord etc."'. This figure is not found in *G*.

Stanza 46

The sense and syntactic arrangement of the words in the first *helmingr* of st. 46 have been the subject of some editorial differences. It is assumed here, with Ólsen (*FoGT* 1884, 282 n. 2) and Longo (*FoGT* 2004, 142–43 and 210–11) that the first *helmingr* represents the Biblical king and psalmist David as a penitent sinner, who died and spent time in the grave as a punishment for his sins before being released at the Last Judgement. The second *helmingr* is then represented in direct speech as what he sang from the grave in praise of God's righteousness. For the common medieval representation of David as a type of the penitent sinner, see Canon Gamli's *Harmsól* (Gamlkan *Has* 48–49[VII] and st. 49 Note [All]).

34,13 og í gröf geinginn 'and gone into the grave': *Og* is here construed with *geinginn í gröf* (so *Skj* B, II 181) rather than more awkwardly with other phrases (*ok með sannri iðran*, so *SnE* 1848−87, III 161; *ok enn með sannri iðran FoGT* 1884, 282; *ok huldr grundu FoGT* 2004, 142).

34,14 til stundar 'for a time': Here understood to mean 'for a time, temporarily' (so also *SnE* 1848−87, II 231, III 161, *FoGT* 1884, 282 and 2004, 143) in the sense that David spent time in the grave until the day of Judgement when, as a penitent, he was released from his punishment. Finnur Jónsson (*Skj* B, II 181) takes *til stundar* with the verb *söng* 'sang' and construes *þat sǫng ǫðlingr til stundar*, which he translates as *Dette sang kongen ivrigt (?)* 'The king sang that eagerly (?)', but this sense is hard to match (*LP*: *stund* glosses this usage as *straks* 'straight away').

34,17 hugþekka...20 þína The second *helmingr* of st. 46 is a very clever rendition into Icelandic of the Latin text of Ps. L.16 *Et exultabit lingua mea justitiam tuam* 'And my tongue will exult your righteousness'. After the stanza, the prose text explains that the verb *hlakka* 'cry out, rejoice, exult', l. 5 (34,17) is used here instead of the more common *hefja upp* 'raise, exalt' in order to replace a less prestigious with a more prestigious word.

34,18 hróðrslungin 'eulogy-encircled': This emendation of W's *hróðrslung* as a feminine adjective agreeing with *loftunga* 'tongue of praise', was first proposed by Konráð Gíslason (Konráð Gislason and Eiríkur Jónsson 1875−89, II 205−09) and has been followed by all subsequent editors.

34,19 valdr 'ruler': An emendation of W's *vald* also proposed by Konráð Gíslason (Konráð Gislason and Eiríkur Jónsson 1875−89, II 205−09) to provide a nominative singular masculine noun, which functions as the base-word of a kenning for God.

34,22 hæfi 'exalts': *Hæfi* is 3rd pers. sing. of the preterite subjunctive of the verb *hefja*.

Chapter 20: Synepthesis
Both the writer's definition and his condemnation of this figure agree with *D* (ll. 2617−22). The two examples given in *D* have been combined in *FoGT* into a single stanza.

34,25 skilninga 'persons': See comment to 12,5 above.

Stanza 47

Stanza 47 is in *hrynhent* metre. It is obscure in sense until one realises that it follows *D*'s examples of the figure. The first *helmingr* follows *D*'s example of a change of grammatical number, between singular subject and plural verb, *unica facta fuit mulier, quae sunt modo plures* 'one woman was made, who soon afterwards are many'. *Öl-Giefn, sú er nú eru margar, hafði orðið víngarðr* 'Ale-Giefn < = Freyja> [WOMAN], she who now are many, had become a vineyard' produces a similar example, using a woman-kenning as singular subject, a feminine singular relative construction and a plural verb (*eru*) plus plural adjective (*margar*). In the second *helmingr* there is an abrupt shift from a second to a third person verb, as in *D*'s *nobis parce, deus*; *nobis lavet ille reatus* 'Spare us God! May he wash our guilt away'. The Icelandic example moves from second person *vægðu oss* 'spare us', l. 6 (36,3), to third person *hann þó* 'he washed', l. 7 (36,4). Even the disapproval of the figure expressed very strongly in both the prose and the verse of the Icelandic text finds a more muted parallel in the Latin, *ista sed in nostrum mutatio non venit usum* 'but that change is not part of our usage'. However, the disapproval of obscure language in ll. 5–6 (36,2–3) of the stanza is not paralleled in the Latin, but may be compared with *Lilja* (Anon *Lil* 98[VII]) and other fourteenth-century poetry rejecting elaborate skaldic diction.

34,27 Víngarðr...36,1 eftir 'Ale-Giefn ... chastity': Not only does the first *helmingr* illustrate a change of singular subject to plural verb, but it also provides an instance of obscure language, in this case a woman-kenning *öl-Giefn* 'ale-Giefn' combined with a metaphorical equation between a woman who has lost her virginity and a vineyard that bears fruit. This latter is the *krókr* 'ambiguity' (cf. *LP*: *krókr* 3) referred to in l. 3 (34,29), and this kind of language is deplored in the second *helmingr* as *ósiðr orða* 'a bad habit of words', l. 5 (36,2).

36,5 píslarmerki 'in the sign of his passion': Here understood as a compound of *píslar* 'of suffering, torment' + dat. sg. of *merki* 'mark, sign, banner', referring to Christ's Cross as the symbol of his passion (so *FoGT* 1884, 285 n. 7 and *FoGT* 2004, 145), and taken with *í skíru vatni* 'in pure water', l. 7 (36,4), as representing the two main guarantees of human salvation, the water of baptism and the symbol of Christ's crucifixion. Cf. the more common noun *píslarmark*, which always refers to Christ's Cross. Kock (*NN* §3163) understands *píslar merki* to refer to Christ's blood. Both *FoGT* 1884, 284 and *Skj* B, II 182 construe *ok píslarmerki* with *sekt verka vára*, ll. 7–8 (36,4–5), to give the sense '[he washed] the guilt of our deeds and signs of torment [in pure water]'. This is possible grammatically but less plausible from a doctrinal point of view.

36,7 í vana dragandi 'to be used habitually': On this Latinate passive use of the present participle, see Nygaard (1906 §§238–39).

36,7 persónum 'persons': *persóna* fem. '[grammatical] person' is here used synonymously with *skilning* in 34,25 and 36,6 above. See also commentary to 24,3.

36,7 í Saltara og öðrum heilugum bókum 'in the Psalter and other holy books': A general reference. *Dg* (83v) exemplifies this figure with Ps. III.9 *iuxta lxx* (*Domini est salus et super populum tuum benedictio tua* 'Salvation belongs to the Lord, and your benediction [is] upon your people'), and this may be the passage the writer of *FoGT* had in mind. *Heilugum bókum* 'holy books' is synonymous with 'sacred writings'.

Chapter 21: Oliopomenon

The initial part of *FoGT*'s definition agrees with *D* (ll. 2623–24), while the second part (see commentary on *climax* below at 38,1) has a counterpart in *G* (I 85). *Dg* explains: *Oligopomenon est sub paucis uerbis multorum comprehensio, ut patet in textu auctoris in quo per duos uersiculos historia troiana continetur* (83v) '*Oligopomenon* is the reduction of many words to a few, as can be seen in the text of the writer in which the trojan history is concentrated in two lines'. *G* treats the same figure under the name *brachylogia* (see commentary to 36,27–28 below) and *Gg* explains: *Brachylogia est quando plurima sub uerbis breuibus comprehenduntur* (p. 95) '*Brachylogia* is when many thing are covered in a few words'.

36,9 hefir 'covers': W is damaged at this point and reads 'h[. . .]fr'. Several emendations have been proposed. *SnE* 1818, 348 does not emend and prints 'l . . fir'. *SnE* 1848, 209 emends to *h(leypr y)fir* 'runs through, summarises'. *SnE* 1848–87, II 232–33 emends to *hefir* and translates *exponit* 'puts forth'. *FoGT* 2004, 51 emends to *hefir* and translates *racconta* 'tells' (*FoGT* 2004, 75). *FoGT* 1884, 143 emends to *hefer* [i.e. *hefir*] and suggests that it should be read as 'hęfer (= hœfer)' in the sense '*afpasse* "accommodate", *indskrænke* "reduce"', although *hófa* normally governs dat. rather than acc. *SnE* 1848–87's emendation has been preferred here, and *hefir* is translated 'covers' in the sense 'deals with', cf. the Latin verb *comprehendo* used by *Gg* (see introductory commentary to chapter 21 above). Fritzner gives one example (non-metaphoric) of *hafa* in this sense (*hafa* 13): *hefir einsaman Asía helming heimsbygðarinnar* 'Asia alone covers half the inhabited world'. The quotation is from *Stjórn* I (cf. ed. Astås 2009, 94). Another possibility would be to interpret 'h[. . .]f' as *hefr* from *hefja* 'begin'.

Stanzas 48 and 49
Stanzas 48 and 49 belong together and must be understood as *ávarp theologie* 'a summary of the Bible' conveyed in two *dróttkvætt* stanzas, as the prose commentary characterises them (36,27). Each stanza uses four couplets (*fjórðungalok*) to illustrate four significant events in the life of Christ. In st. 48 the four events relate to Christ's earthly life before his crucifixion, namely his birth from the Virgin Mary, his circumcision (cf. Luke II.21), which was held to prefigure his crucifixion (cf. Anon *Lil* 35,5[VII]), his baptism in the river Jordan by John the Baptist (cf. Anon *Lil* 37[VII]), which foreshadowed the rite of baptism for Christians, and his threefold temptation (cf. Matt. IV.1–11, Luke IV.1–13) by Satan in the wilderness, which anticipated Satan's temptation of mankind (cf. Anon *Lil* 45[VII]). Each couplet contains a kenning for God as Christ.

36,13 umsniðning 'circumcision': The 'in' abbreviation between the second ⟨n⟩ and final ⟨g⟩ has been torn away in W, but the emendation is unproblematical. The only other instance of this noun in poetry is Anon *Lil* 35,5[VII].

36,15 vann... 16 batnað 'gained improvement' [*vann batnað*]: W has *vanr*, an adjective meaning either 'accustomed' or 'lacking', neither of which makes grammatical sense in this context.

36,19 Píndr... 26 hauðri 'Tortured, he rose up ... on the land of life': Stanza 49 enumerates the main events in the life of Christ after the crucifixion in the same manner as in st. 48 (q. v.). These are the Harrowing of Hell and the Resurrection, the Ascension to heaven, the descent of the Holy Spirit at Pentecost, and the Last Judgement. As both Ólsen (*FoGT* 1884, 143n.) and Longo (*FoGT* 2004, 214–15) have pointed out, *FoGT*'s model was almost certainly various commentaries on *D* and *D* itself (ll. 2623–26 and nn.), where *oliopomenon* is said to be a figure in which a series of important events is expressed in few words, and the example is given of a series of short clauses encapsulating the history of the Trojan war.

36,19 með anda angrleystu herfangi 'with the sorrow-liberated booty of souls': As *FoGT* 1884, 287 n. 2 and *FoGT* 2004, 148 have noted, this phrase refers to Christ's Harrowing of Hell after the crucifixion, while the first three words of l. 1 (36,19) *píndr reis upp* 'tortured he rose up', refer to the Resurrection.

36,25 sá...26 hauðri 'he will come to judge the host of the dead on the land of life': This edition follows the interpretation of these lines offered by Kock (*NN* §3164) as the only one that respects the couplet structure of the stanza and also makes theological sense. There is no doubt that these lines allude to the Last Judgement. Finnur Jónsson (*Skj* B, II 182) construed *lífs á hauðri* with *hirðandi alls*, l. 6 (36,24), to produce the sense 'the guardian of all life on earth', but this violates the couplet-based syntax of the stanza and is therefore unlikely to be correct. Ólsen emended the text by adding *ok* between *dauða* and *lífs* in l. 8 (36,26), reading *sá kiemr at dæma drótt dauða ok lífs á hauðri* (*FoGT* 1884, 287–88) 'he will come to judge the host of death [the dead] and life [the living] on earth', but this produces an unmetrical line and rather strained syntax, and must also be rejected.

36,27 ávarp 'a summary': *ONP* has not registered this instance of *ávarp*, written 'au^rp' in W, and glosses the word with 'estimate'. In Modern Icelandic the most common meaning of *ávarp* is 'an address, speech'. Neither 'estimate' nor 'address' make sufficient sense in the present context and *ávarp* has therefore been rendered as 'summary'. *SnE* 1848–87, II 235 and *FoGT* 2004, 76 render *ávarp* in a similar manner (with *summa* and *riassunto* respectively).

36,27 theologie 'of the Bible': *Theologie* is the Latin genitive form of *theologia* fem. *Theologia* has here been rendered as 'the Bible' (see comment to l. 40,23 below).

36,27 Þessi...28 brachilogia 'This ... name': G treats this figure in I 84: *Brachylogia refert quam plurima sub breuitate* 'Brachylogia narrates as much as possible in a brief manner'. *Gg* illustrates this with the example that *Dg* used for *Oliopomenon* (see introductory commentary to chapter 21 above).

36,28 hefir...38,1 fyrri 'this ... previous one': The writer only comments on the etymology of the names of the various figures twice (here and in 46,3–5). *Gg*, which normally gives etymologies, explains *brachylogia* as follows: *Et dicitur a 'brachos' quod est 'breue' et 'logos' quod est 'sermo', quasi 'breuis sermo tamen plura comprehendens'* (p. 95) 'And it is named from *brachos* which means 'brief' and *logos* which means 'utterance', as if meaning 'a brief utterance yet containing much'". Neither *D*, *Dg*, nor the writer of *FoGT* explains the name of the figure *oliopomenon*, but *Gg*'s explanation of the etymology of *brachylogia* agrees with the definition of *oliopomenon* given by *D*, *Dg* and *FoGT*.

36,28 sömu 'same': This word, which is not found in W, was first supplied in *SnE* 1818, 348. All subsequent editors have made the same addition.

38,1 Sumir...2 annarri 'Some ... another': It is uncertain which authorities the writer refers to here. *G* mentions *climax* immediately after *brachylogia*, but does not classify *climax* as a subtype of that figure, writing: *Sitque tibi proprie subscripta gradatio climax* (I 85) 'you shall consider *climax* as properly belonging under [the figure] *gradatio*'. *G* does not illustrate this figure, but two examples are found in *Gg*. This is the second example: *Hic [< Hec] quamcumque uidet cupit et quamcumque cupiuit | Allicit, allectam uitiat, prodit uitiatam* (pp. 96–97) 'The man, whomever he sees, he desires, and he entices whomever he has desired, he depraves the enticed and abandons the depraved'. *Gg*'s example is from *G* (III 50–51) where it is used as an example of the figure *gradatio*. The same example is used by Marbod of Rennes in *De ornamentu uerborum* (ed. Leotta 1998, 14). *Climax* is also described in Isidore of Seville's *Etymologiae* (II 21.4) where the example is: *Ex innocentia nascitur dignitas, ex dignitate honor, ex honore imperium, ex imperio libertas* 'From innocence is born dignity, from dignity honour, from honour rule, from rule freedom'.

38,1 climax W's 'dvnax' is an obvious case of minim confusion and all editors have corrected to *climax* following Árni Magnússon who wrote the corrected form in the right margin of W.

38,1 um jafnar gráður 'by equal steps': *Gráða* 'step' is a loan word from Latin *gradus* 'step'. The image applied here is that of a ladder (Greek κλῖμαξ 'ladder') with steps (*gráður*).

Stanza 50

The metre of the highly didactic if not homiletic st. 50 is *hrynhent*. This stanza is also written on p. 120 of W, on the verso side of the final leaf containing *FoGT*, in a later hand, together with some other text, mainly in Latin. There are two minor variant readings in this version of the stanza. The association between *brachilogia* and *climax* can be found in *G* (I 84–85), and it may be that the writer of *FoGT* was thinking of Eberhard of Béthune when he refers to the opinion of *sumir meistarar* 'some scholars' (38,1). In a different part of *G* (III 49–51), Eberhard describes the figure of *gradatio*, with examples, as follows: *De uoce in uocem descende, gradatio fiet* 'Descend from word to word, it will become *gradatio*'. This is very similar to the strategy of st. 50.

38,10 andar lífs með beisku grandi 'of the life of the soul with bitter injury': All previous editors except Kock (*NN* §2587) have taken *lífs* 'of life' with *með beisku grandi* 'with bitter injury', but, while that is possible, much better sense in a Christian context is produced by taking *lífs* with *andar* '[the whole nature] of the life of the soul'. For the sinner, death destroys the whole nature of the life of the soul if the soul is damned in Hell.

Chapter 22: Homophesis

The initial definition of *homophesis* is based on *D* (ll. 2627–28), but the example (st. 51), and the elaborate exegesis that accompanies the example, have no parallels in *D* or *Dg*. Meissner (1932, 98–101) and D. McDougall (1988, 477–83) traced some of the biblical and patristic sources for this section, but no parallel has been found to the exact combination of sources and imagery found in this chapter. *Homophesis* is not among the figures defined and exemplified by *G* and *Gg*. According to *D homophesis* occurs when something unknown is explained by something that is equally or more unknown. The writer of *FoGT* eclipses *D* and replaces 'unknown' with 'obscure'. *Dg* explains that *homophesis* might occur when a Latin word is explained by a Greek word, *ut interrogando quid sit homo, respondeatur 'antropos'* (83v) 'as by asking what *homo* (a human being) is, the answer given is *anthropos* (a human being)'. The example in *D* is from the realm of astronomy and the named items are all part of an astrolabe. *Dg* gives the following explanation: *Nota quod in astrolabio sunt quedam tabule ad modum ligni uel lapidis* [< *lapis*] *disposite, quarum una dicitur 'alidada' et alia 'ualdagora' que adinuicem coniuncte sunt mediante cauilla que dicitur 'alchitrop'* (83v) 'Note that some flat pieces of wood or stone are placed in an astrolabe. One of these is called "alidada" and the other "valdagora". These are joined to one another by a spike which is called an "alchitrop"'. Kunitzsch provides explanations of the names and functions of these parts of the astrolabe in a glossary of *termini technici* in the Medieval Latin literature on the astrolabe (1982, items number 19 *al-ʿiḍāda*, 3 *basṭ al-kura* and 40 *al-quṭb*). *FoGT*'s example of *homophesis* is drawn from the realm of biblical typology, where events in the Old Testament are understood simultaneously as historical events and prophecies of events that will occur after the birth of Christ.

Stanza 51
Stanza 51, in *dróttkvætt* metre, illustrates the figure the writer of *FoGT* calls *emophasis* (*homophesis*). *FoGT*'s definition is dependent on a similar one in *D* (see introductory commentary to chapter 22 above), where the examples come from the technical language of astrology. Here, however, the lengthy prose commentary that follows the stanza depends upon two excerpts from patristic writings, 'the first a discussion attributed to Augustine of a verse from Habakkuk, and the second an interpretation of Ps. XLI.8, "Abyssus abyssum inuocat in uoce cataractarum tuarum" ascribed to "leo pafi inn málsnialli"' (D. McDougall 1988, 478). The obscurities of the two allusions are connected through the pivotal figure of Christ, whose birth as a human ushered in the new law; the first *helmingr* represents his birth in terms of two Old Testament prophecies, while the allegorical interpretation of the two abysses in the second connects the prophets of the Old Testament and their prophecies with the new law and the words of the apostles and church fathers. David McDougall has suggested (1988, 477–83) that the Fourth Grammarian is likely to have derived his material from a text of the popular medieval homiliary of Paul the Deacon.

38,13 Sæll...16 hingað 'The blessed prince ... into this world [literally hither]': As both Meissner (1932, 98–101) and D. McDougall (1988) have shown, these lines depend upon the Old Latin version of Habakkuk III.2 *In medio duorum animalium cognosceris* ... 'you are recognised between two animals...'. The interpretation of this text offered in *FoGT* is taken from a homiletic tract, *Contra Judaeos, paganos, et Arianos sermo de symbolo*, attributed to Augustine in the Middle Ages, but now included among the writings of Quodvultdeus, Bishop of Carthage 437–53 (D. McDougall 1988, 479). In this tract 'Quodvultdeus seeks to confute the error of the Jews by summoning a series of Old Testament prophets as "witnesses" of the advent of Christ' (D. McDougall 1988, 479). Hab. III.2 is there interpreted, together with Isa. I.3 *Agnouit bos possessorem suum, et asinus praesepium domini sui* 'The ox knoweth his owner, and the ass his master's crib' (trans. *Douay-Rheims Bible*), as a prophecy of the Christ-child in the crib. In the prose of *FoGT* there is a further interpretation of the ox and the ass as representing the Jews and the Gentiles, an 'exegetical commonplace' to be found in a number of patristic commentaries; for the details, see D. McDougall (1988, 480 and nn.).

38,14 kvikvenda 'animals': Most editors (*Skj* B, II 183, *Skald*, II 95) but not Ólsen (cf. *FoGT* 1884, 289 n. 2) restore ‹v› in *kvikvenda* to regularise the metre. The spelling *kvikenda* is also found in the prose text at 38,22; 38,29; 40,9 and 40,12.

38,16 þá er 'when': An emendation from W's *sá er*, first proposed by Ólsen (*FoGT* 1884, 289 n. 3), and adopted by subsequent editors.

38,17 eða...20 vátta 'or when the deep ... phases of the moon': The stanza's second *helmingr* depends upon the second patristic example mentioned above, Ps. XLI.8 *Abyssus abyssum inuocat, in uoce cataractarum tuarum* 'Deep calleth on deep at the noise of thy floodgates' (trans. *Douay-Rheims Bible*). The prose gloss attributes its interpretation of Ps. XLI.8 to *Leo páfi inn málsnjalli* 'Pope Leo the eloquent' (40,1–2), probably Leo the Great. David McDougall (1988, 481) proposed that this might be a reference to the sixtieth tractate of Pope Leo, also available in the homiliary of Paul the Deacon. The prose gloss proposes an allegorical reading of the voice of the two *vatnadjúp* 'abysses' (40,2), the one above the heavens, the other below it, on several levels, including their identification with the old and new laws and the teachings of prophets and apostles. David McDougall (1988, 481) adduces several conventional examples of such parallels. The present interpretation of this *helmingr* follows those of Ólsen (*FoGT* 1884, 289–90) and Kock (*NN* §1410) rather than Finnur Jónsson (*Skj* B, II 183), who construes *borgar niða* 'of the stronghold of the phases of the moon', l. 6 (38,18), with *að djúpi* 'to the deep', l. 5 (38,17), rather than with *um hávar hljóðraufar* 'across the high sound-crevices', l. 7 (38,19), in order to provide one abyss in heaven, the other below it, but his interpretation fails to take account of the prose text's commentary *undirdjúp vatnanna kalla á annað undirdjúp um þær himinborur sem catarakte kallaz* 'the abyss of the waters calls to the other abyss through those openings in the sky which are called cataracts' (38,23–24).

38,20 vátta 'bore witness': Literally 'bear witness'. This verb is both plural and present tense, where one would expect the preterite *váttuðu*; cf. *NN* §1410. The plural usage with a singular subject (*djúp*) can probably be explained, as Ólsen has suggested (*FoGT* 1884, 290 n. 5) because the poet is thinking of two mighty abysses rather than one. Ólsen emended *vátta* to *váttar* (3rd pers. sg. pres.).

38,21 Hier...22 komanda 'Here ... conduct': The reference is to Hab. III.2 in *Vetus latina*: *In medio duorum animalium cognosceris* (ed. Sabbatier 1743–49, II 966) 'You are recognised between two animals' (see Meissner 1932, 98–99). *Cognosceris* is morphologically ambiguous and usually understood as a future passive 'you will be known'. In this commentary, and in accordance with the understanding of the writer of *FoGT* (cf. *sienn*, 38,21), it is rendered as a present passive 'you are recognized'.

38,21 Abbacuch spámanns 'of the prophet Habakkuk': *Abbacuch* is to be interpreted as a genitive. Hebrew names are frequently indeclinable in Latin, and the same is often the case in Old Norse.

38,21 Guð dróttin sienn 'that the Lord God ... is seen': An accusative with infinitive where the infinitive (*vera*) has been left out.

38,23 Dávíð...26 váru 'David ... ark': The first reference here is to Ps. XLI.8. The second reference is to the story of the Flood: *rupti sunt omnes fontes abyssi magnae et cataractae caeli aperta sunt* (Gen. VII.11) 'All the fountains of the great deep were broken up, and the flood gates of heaven were opened' (trans. *Douay-Rheims Bible*).

38,24 cataracte 'cataracts': The declensional form of *cataracte* is Latin, nom. pl. fem. The scribe uses the letter ‹k› rather than ‹c› here ('*katarakte*'), but this has been smoothed out in the normalisation, because the same word is written with ‹c›'s below (at 40,3).

38,27 segir...31 lögmála 'Augustine ... laws': The writer here draws on a passage from Quodvultdeus of Carthage's (d. c. 450) *Contra Judaeos, paganos et Arrianos*: *Quid est 'in medio duum animalium cognosceris', nisi aut in medio duorum testamentorum aut in medio duorum latronum aut in medio Moysi et Heliae cum eo in monte sermocinantium* (ed. Braun 1976, 224) 'What is "you are recognised between two animals", if not in between the two testaments or in between the two robbers or in between Moses and Elijah speaking with him on the mountain [cf. Matt. XVII.3]?'

38,29 Moysi og Helie 'Moses and Elijah': Both names are given in their Latin genitival form.

38,30 myndskiftingu 'the transfiguration': W has 'myndskifting^r', which might be a noun in gen. sg. or nom./acc. pl. The word is the complement of the preposition *í* which usually governs the dative in temporal and locative roles, and it has therefore been deemed advisable to follow *FoGT* 1884, 145 and *FoGT* 2004, 53 and emend *myndskiftingar* to *myndskiftingu* (dat. sg.). *SnE* 1818, 349 left *myndskiftingar* unemended while *SnE* 1848–87, II 236 and *SnE* 1848, 209 conjectured *myndskipting* (acc. sg.).

40,1 þessi...3 cataractarum 'Pope ... cataracts': This might be a reference to Pope Leo's 60th sermon (for Palm Sunday) where he writes: *concurrentibus igitur ad eruditionem nostram et novis testimoniis et antiquis, dum quod prophetica cecinit tuba, evangelica pandit historia, et sicut scriptum est: 'Abyssus abyssum invocat, in voce cataractarum tuarum'; quoniam ad enarrandam gloriam gratie Dei paribus sibi vocibus utriusque Testamenti altitudo respondet* (*De passione domini* IX, *PL* 54, 342–43) 'thus both the new and the old testimonies concur for our instruction, when the evangelic history unfolds what the prophetic trumpet sang, as it is written: "The abyss calls upon the abyss with the voice of your cataracts" because the profundity of each Testament answers the other with equal voices in order to relate the glory of God's mercy' (see Meissner 1932, 101 and D. McDougall 1988, 481).

40,1 Leo páfi inn málsnjalli 'Pope Leo the eloquent': Pope Leo I the Great (r. 440–61).

40,2 tvenn vatnadjúp þau er annað er yfir himnum en annað undir himnum 'two abysses, of which one is above the sky and the other below the sky': For the abyss above the sky, see Gen I.7.

40,2 vatnadjúp 'abysses': *Vatnadjúp* neut. 'abyss' is a *hap. leg.* It is here used synonymously with *undirdjúp* neut. 'abyss'.

40,3 cataractarum 'of the cataracts': This word is given in the genitive plural according to its normal Latin declension.

40,4 himinraufanna 'of the openings in the sky': A brief description of the Flood in *Maríu saga* also combines the rare noun *himinrauf* with the more common *undirdjúp*: *... er undirdjúps brunnar opnuðusk ok þustu í verǫldina, en ofan himinraufarnar* (ed. Unger 1871b, 9–10) '... when the wells of the abyss were opened and gushed out into the world and from above the openings in the sky [were opened]'.

40,5 merkja...predikara 'they symbolise ... and preachers': The interpretation of the voices of the cataracts as the voices of prophets and apostles is a fairly widespread one, but it is not found in Leo's sermon (D. McDougall 1988, 481).

40,5 þá...8 kienningar 'who ... teaching': Although Leo's sermon does not contain this imagery, it is quite common (D. McDougall

1988, 481 and n. 38) and parallels can be found elsewhere in Old Norse literature, e.g. in *Stjórn* I (ed. Astås 2009, 46–47).

40,8 Og...15 lögmáls 'And ... law': An unusually complex sentence. The present translation assumes that a finite verb *er* 'is' has been left out in the subordinate temporal clause *er ið forna lögmál* ... [*er*] *fagrliga fram flutt* ... 'when the old law ... [is] beautifully presented ...'. *SnE* 1848–87, II 239 interprets the words *samþykkjanda nýju lögmáli* as an absolute dative, and sees *fram flutt* and *útskýrt* as appositions to *nýju lögmáli*. This interpretation has not been chosen here because *nýju lögmáli* (which is in the dative) does not agree with *fram flutt* and *útskýrt* (both in the nominative or accusative).

40,9 kvikenda siðvendis 'beings of good conduct': *SnE* 1848–87, II 237 translates *animantia moralitatis* 'beings of morality' and Meissner (1932, 100) uses the term *animalia moralitatis* as if it was in common usage; this is not the case. The ox and the ass are referred to as beings of good conduct, because Isa. I.3 says that these animals know who their master is, in contradistinction to Israel: *cognouit bos possessorem suum et asinus praesepe domini sui. Israhel non cognouit populus meus non intellexit.* 'The ox knoweth his owner, and the ass his master's crib, but Israel hath not known me, and my people hath not understood' (trans. *Douay-Rheims Bible*).

40,13 samþykkjanda 'agreeing': This participle is interpreted as neuter nom. sg. and as modifying *ið forna lögmál* 'the old law' (40,10 above).

40,13 útskýrt 'explained': The context requires a neuter participle here and W's reading *útskýrð* (fem.) has been changed accordingly.

40,14 fyrir predikara nýs lögmáls 'by the preachers of the new law': This use of the preposition *fyrir* is especially prevalent in learned writings (Cleasby and Vigfusson 1957, s. v. *fyrir* with accusative C VIII).

40,18 ástgjöf Heilags Anda 'the gift of grace of the Holy Spirit': *Jóns saga postola* I explains that 'the gift of grace of the Holy Spirit' was given to the apostles when Christ appeared to them after his death and gave them the power to forgive sins (John XX.19–23) and at the feast of Pentecost (Acts II), and also provides an allegorical interpretation of the meaning of this gift (ed. Unger 1874, 414–15).

Chapter 23: Epimone

The basic definition of the figure (the repetition of a single word) is paralleled in *D* (ll. 2630–31). According to *D*, a word is repeated so that one may understand it better. The writer of *FoGT* adds to this that a word may also be repeated for aesthetic reasons, and all four examples provided illustrate this second use of the figure. *G* also defines and illustrates the figure (I 34–37), but *D* is more closely related to *FoGT*. In this chapter the writer of *FoGT* integrates his rhetorical doctrine with more Old Norse poetic terminology and practice than usual.

40,22 til... 23 theologia 'so ... the Bible': This part of the definition is paralleled and exemplified by *D* (ll. 2630–31) and *Dg*. *Dg* explains *D*'s example: '*Expectans expectaui Dominum*' [Ps XXXIX.1]. *Hec figura multum reperitur in sacra pagina* (83v) '"Waiting, I have waited for the Lord". This figure is often found on the sacred page [i.e. in the Bible]'.

40,23 theologia 'the Bible': Given in the ablative case according to the normal Latin declension of the word. Comparison with *D* and *Dg* shows that the writer most likely refers to the Bible.

40,24 í dunhendu 'in *dunhenda*': An indigenous technical term, 'echoing rhyme', sometimes given as *dunhent* 'echoing-rhymed' (cf. *SnE* 2007, 80–81), which was exemplified by Snorri Sturluson in *Háttatal* 24 (SnSt *Ht* 24[III]), and before him in *Háttalykill* 65–66 (RvHbreiðm *Hl* 65–66[III]).

40,24 iðurmæltum hætti 'the *iðurmæltr* verse-form': Like *dunhenda* and *greppaminni*, *iðurmæltr* 'repeatedly spoken' involves the repetition of complete syllables either within a line or from one line to another. *Iðurmæltr* is exemplified in SnSt *Ht* 47[III] and RvHbreiðm *Hl* 57–58[III].

40,25 greppaminni 'poets' reminder' involves repetition of the same or similar words, in this case in a series of questions, posed in the first *helmingr* and answered in the second. Examples are SnSt *Ht* 40[III] and RvHbreiðm *Hl* 45–46[III]. This device may be of some antiquity; cf. Vésteinn Ólason (1969) and Lönnroth (1977). *FoGT* sts 61 and 62 are very similar to *greppaminni*, though here each question and answer occupies a single verse line. See the notes to these stanzas.

40,26 háttaföll *Háttaföll* are metrical faults, and particularly metrical inconsistencies. The writer of *FoGT* seems to be influenced at this point by Snorri Sturluson's use of this term in one place in *Háttatal* to refer to variations of verse-form within a single stanza of a kind that he says are found in ancient poetry (*í fornkvæðum*, *SnE* 2007, 64). He uses the term in the prose commentary to *Háttatal* 58, which is an example of a verse-form he terms *Braga háttr* 'Bragi's verse-form', named after Bragi Boddason (on Bragi, see note to 14,17), though this example does not correspond precisely to any of Bragi's extant stanzas.

40,26 sá má 'he who wants': *SnE* 1848, 202 interpreted W's *sama* as *sá má*. All subsequent editors have accepted this.

Stanzas 52, 53, 54 and 55
The four sts 52–55 give examples of different kinds of repetition of the same word in different positions in the verse line. None of them corresponds exactly to any of the verse-forms *FoGT* names in the preceding prose paragraph, which are in *dróttkvætt* metre (*iðurmælt* would be the closest), although those verse-forms do use repetition as a stylistic characteristic. All four sts 52–55 are in the metre *runhent*, and, although each is free-standing, sts 52 and 55 can be understood to form an outer semantic frame, in which the speaker is Christ, and the addressee mankind. Similarly, sts 53 and 54 belong together and can be understood to refer to the properties of the Christian heaven.

42,2 og 'and': Ólsen (*FoGT* 1884, 291) emends *og* to *ek* (*eg*) in order to have every line of st. 52 begin with the same word.

42,6 Þar...9 þraungt 'There is nothing evil ... nothing constricted': In st. 53 repetition of the word *ekki* 'nothing' occurs in the middle parts of lines.

42,11 Þar...14 vald 'There is unmeasured power ... and eternal power': Stanza 54 has repetition on *vald* 'power' at the ends of lines.

42,16 Eg...19 þig 'I bless you ... I save you': In this stanza, 55, there is repetition of words both at the beginnings (*eg* 'I') and ends (*þig* 'you') of lines.

Chapter 24: Homopathion
The writer has reversed the order of presentation of the two figures *anthropospathos* (*D* ll. 2634–35) and *homopathion* (*D* ll. 2636–39), so that *homopathion* is followed by *anthropospathos*. The writer's initial definition of the figure and the example with the heart and the tongue agree with *D*, but nothing in *D* or *Dg* parallels st. 56 or the explanation of st. 56 in 44,3–8.

42,20 Antopazia 'Homopathion': The name of the figure given in *FoGT* is quite far from the form in which it appears in *D*. But the definition and the initial example show that 'antopazia' must indeed be considered a (corrupted) form of 'homopathion'.

42,20 ef 'in which': See commentary to *ef* above (12,4).

42,22 samþykk 'to agree with': *samþykk* is interpreted as an adjective modifying *tunga* fem. 'tongue'.

Stanza 56

This *dróttkvætt* stanza is cited in *FoGT* as an example of the figure *antopazia* (*homopathion*), in which an attribute of one entity enables an attribute of another. It is also recorded in *LaufE* (mss GKS 2368 4°ˣ and AM 743 4°ˣ) and in Resen's *Edda* of 1665 (Kk 1v) (Faulkes 1977). In *FoGT* the stanza is not attributed to a named poet, while Resen's *Edda* attributes it in a footnote to an 'Einar Skess'. Mss 2368ˣ and 743ˣ of the longer (Y) version of *LaufE* attribute it to the twelfth-century Icelandic priest Einarr Skúlason (born c. 1090); for a biography of this prolific poet, see *SkP* II: 2, 537. In *SkP* this stanza has the siglum ESk Lv 13ᴵᴵᴵ. In *LaufE* the stanza appears in the section on kennings for the sun under the heading *figura*. The prose context is very similar to that of *FoGT* and was probably influenced by it. No context for the stanza outside these pedagogical works is known.

42,23 af mæni 'from the roof-ridge': *Mæni* is an emendation from all manuscripts' *mæðu* (fem. dat. sg.) 'weariness', which makes little sense in context and does not produce internal rhyme. The kenning *mænir hofs moldar* 'the roof-ridge of the temple of the ground' [SKY > ZENITH] is unique in skaldic poetry and may suggest the poet's acquaintance with the concept of the zenith, introduced to Western Europe from Arabic sources, probably during the twelfth century (cf. *AÍ*, II xxxvii). In the treatise *Rím* II, the word *cenit* (i.e. 'zenith') is used in a discussion of the pole star (*AÍ*, II 110).

42,27 Veit... 44,2 dauða 'I know ... nor death': The interpretation of the stanza's second *helmingr* is uncertain. That offered here, and explained in greater detail in Clunies Ross and Gade (2012), is in accordance with *FoGT*'s prose gloss, which discusses how the moon takes its office, to shine upon the earth, from the sun, and has no light of its own. In accordance with that view, the kenning *prýði fróns* 'the adorner of the earth', l. 6 (42,28), is understood to refer to the sun and *fljótum fielaga* 'its swift companion', l. 5 (42,27), to the moon. The service the sun performs for its companion is to illuminate it. Lines 7–8 (44,1–2) must refer to the fact that the moon gives off no light of its own but takes its light from the sun. Other interpretations of the *helmingr* are possible, however. The most likely alternative interpretation is that *prýði fróns* refers to the moon and *fljótum fielaga* to the sun, whether *prýði* is understood from *prýðir* masc. 'adorner' or from *prýði* fem. 'adornment', but this is inconsistent with the prose gloss and with the stanza's classification by *LaufE* under kennings for the sun. Many medieval cosmological sources state that the moon is swifter in its course than the sun (cf. *Konungs skuggsjá*, ed. Holm-Olsen 1983, 10; Clunies Ross and Gade 2012), but an alternative view, that the sun is the faster of the two, occurs in some texts, for example, in *Rím* I (*AÍ*, II 58 and 78).

44,4 það...8 vestri 'it ... west': Cf. *Rím* I (*AÍ*, II 59–60). *Rím* I does not speak about the four points of the compass as *FoGT* does, but the doctrine appears to be the same: *sér lítit fyrst af, en annan dag ǫðru meira. Er þat þá fullt er þat er gagnvart sólunni. Þá teksk enn af smám þeim af tunglinu, svá sem þat nálgask sólina* (*AÍ*, II 59) 'One can see a little [part of the moon] to begin with, but more each day. It is full when it is directly opposite the sun. Then it wanes again bit by bit as it approaches the sun'.

Chapter 25: Anthropospathos
The initial part of the definition agrees well with *D* (ll. 2634–35), but the writer of *FoGT* develops *D*'s example (the anger of God) in st. 57 and adds an interpretation with homiletic qualities. The figure is also exemplified in *G* (II 10).

Stanza 57
Stanza 57 is in the metre *hrynhent*. It is close in sentiment to *D*.
44,12 þann 'that one who': Demonstrates loss of the relative particle *er* in the combination demonstrative + relative particle (Nygaard 1906 §261). Ólsen (*FoGT* 1884, 293 n. 1) suggested adding the relative particle *er* to W's *þann* here on the ground that the scribe of *FoGT* does not elsewhere demonstrate loss of the particle before a demonstrative. He has been followed by *Skj* B, II 184, *Skald*, II 96 and *FoGT* 2004, 55. However, in a fourteenth-century text this loss would not be unexpected. The referent of *þann* is God and the allusion is to Gen. III.8, in which Adam and Eve are said to hear the voice of God as he walked in the garden of Eden in the cool of the day. The allusion is also to the first humans' sinful condition, having eaten the forbidden fruit and having hidden themselves because they were afraid to come face to face with God.
44,14 þenna...15 sitja 'greatly wise Stephen recognised him standing [lit. to stand]': The reference is to Acts VI, in which a certain deacon

named Stephen, a man of wisdom and faith (VI.6), rails against persecutors of the infant Church and has a vision of heaven in which he sees Jesus standing at God's right hand (Acts VI.55–56). Finnur Jónsson (*Skj* B, II 184) gives the name in the form *Stéfánús*, Kock (*Skald*, II 96) as *Stefánús*, but there is no reason to depart from W's spelling with 'ph'. Length has been judged here to be on the penultimate syllable (cf. Modern Icelandic *Stefán*) in a Type A line, position 5–6, treated as disyllabic with resolution in position 1.

44,15 og spámenn sitja 'and prophets [saw him] sit': The verb must be understood from the previous clause. The allusion is to the common image, in written texts and the visual arts, of God seated on a throne with his heavenly retinue around him; cf., among others, 1 Kings XXII.19, 2 Chr. XVIII.18, Isa. XXXVII.16.

44,21 með sannleik 'literally': Literally 'in truth'.

44,21 Og...46,2 miskunn 'And it is ... because of his grace': This elegant homiletic section has no parallel in the known sources of *FoGT*.

44,28 sjálfa '-selves': Sveinbjörn Egilsson's emendation (*SnE* 1848, 211) has been adopted by all subsequent editors.

46,3 Hefir...5 hluti 'This ... things': Ólsen (*FoGT* 1881, 148) quotes a parallel to the first part of this etymology culled from Thurot (1868, 476). A similar etymology is found in *Gg*: *Et dicitur ab 'anthropos' quod est 'homo' et 'pasis' 'passio', quasi 'humana passio' attributa Deo et e conuerso* (p. 157) 'And [the figure] is named from *anthropos* [man] which means *homo* [man] and *pasis* [> *pathos* "suffering"] *passio* [suffering], something like "human suffering" attributed to God and the other way around'. The writer of *FoGT* equates Gr *pasis* with *setning* 'placement' which is not too far from the meaning of the (rare) Greek word πᾶσις 'acquisition, possession' (see Liddell and Scott 1940, s. v.). The second half of his etymological explanation (from *setning* to *hluti*) appears to have been based on an equation between Greek *pasis* and Old Norse *setning* 'placement'. On the etymology of *anthropos* in Norse texts, see also Nordal 2001, 304.

46,5 mannliga reglu 'human constraints': *Mannliga reglu* is in the accusative singular.

46,5 þeir...9 saman 'those ... omnipotence': The anthropomorphites are often mentioned in patristic literature. The writer's wording recalls that found in Isidore of Seville's listing of heresies in his *Etymologiae*: *Anthropomorphitae dicti pro eo, quod simplicitate rustica Deum* *habere humana membra, quae in divinis libris scripta sunt, arbitrantur; ἄνθρωπος enim Graece, Latine homo interpretatur: ignorantes vocem Domini, qui ait: 'Spiritus est Deus'. Incorporeus est enim, nec membris distinguitur, nec corporis mole censetur* (VIII 5.32) 'The Anthropomorphites are called so because out of rustic simplicity they believe that God has the human limbs that are described in the Holy Writings; for the Greek word *Anthropos* [man] means *homo* [man] in Latin'. They are ignorant of the word of God which said: "God is spirit" [John IV.24]. Indeed, he is incorporeal, does not have limbs, and should not be thought of as having bodily weight'.

46,8 óbrugðligr 'unvarying': *óbrugðligr* is a *hap. leg.* in Old Norse. The positive form of the adjective (without the privative prefix) *brugðligr* 'inconstant' is a *hap. leg.* as well.

Chapter 26: Synacrismos

This figure is found in *G* where it is defined as follows: *Crimina uel laudes oratio colligat una | Multa simul, sic fit et habet fieri synacrismos* (I 63–64) 'When one sentence collects many crimes or praises at the same time, thus *synacrismos* occurs and is held to occur'. *Synacrismos* is not found in *D*. *Gg* provides a few examples (pp. 79–80), but they all differ from the examples of *FoGT* in that they praise or castigate one single character (rather than many characters as do those in *FoGT*).

46,10 Simatrismos 'Synacrismos': Comparison with the Latin text shows that *synacrismos* is the correct form.

46,10 í einum capitulo og klausu eða versi í látínu 'in one chapter, [one] clause or [one] line in Latin': *G* confines the use of the figure to a single sentence.

46,10 í einum capitulo 'in one chapter': *Capitulo* is here declined in accordance with its normal Latin declension (in the ablative). As a loan word in Old Norse, it took the form *kapítuli* masc. The prefixed *einum* probably indicates that the writer regarded Latin *capitulum* neut. as a masculine noun like Old Norse *kapítuli*.

Stanzas 58, 59 and 60

The three sts 58, 59 and 60 are said to illustrate the figure of *synacrismos*, which the prose text defines as the collection of praise or vices in one or more stanzas of Old Norse poetry. The manner in which this is carried out in these three stanzas is very ingenious. As far as the subject-matter is concerned, all the examples presented are of praise, and the individual subjects are characters from the Old Testament, except for the last example, which refers to God. However, all these stanzas contain a number of stereotyped metrical faults, which stand out because all other stanzas in *FoGT* are metrically regular. Stanzas 58,1, 5 (46,13 and 46,17) and 59,1, 5, 7 (46,21, 46,25 and 46,27) all have metrically illicit *hendingar* on weakly stressed *lofar* 'praises' and fully stressed *ævi* 'life' (voiced intervocalic [f] and [v]). In st. 60,1 (48,1), *lofar* alliterates (but does not rhyme) and there is suspended resolution. This line does not correspond to any metrical type attested in Germanic alliterative poetry. Hence it appears that all of these stanzas illustrate the rhetorical figure *synacrismos* on two different levels: they unite 'praise' on the textual level and 'faults' at the metrical level.

46,13 Ábiels...20 aldir 'Innocence extols ... Shem forever': Stanza 58 divides neatly into couplets (*fjórðungar*), devoting one couplet to the virtues of each of four characters from the Biblical Book of Genesis: Abel, son of Adam and Eve, the victim of the first murder by his brother Cain; Enoch, son of Jared and great-grandfather of Noah (Gen V.18); Noah himself and his son Shem (Gen V–IX).

46,15 öld...16 einkiend 'specific to mankind': Most editors regard *öld* as dative singular 'to mankind', though Kock (*NN* §2588) argues that it is an adverbial accusative meaning 'for ever'. *SnE* 1848–87, II 247 proposed that *einkiend* means 'well known to [all men]', translating *omnibus hominibus nota* (cf. *Skj* B, II 184 *kendte for menneskene* 'known to mankind'), but it is more likely that *einkiendr* means 'specific to, belonging to'; cf. *ONP*: ²*einkenna* A 2) pret. part. *einkenndr* and 3) 'specify as belonging to', i.e. indicating that human beings alone of living creatures have understanding of morality. Cf. *LP*: *einkendr*.

46,15 Ienóch mildan 'gentle Enoch': This Enoch is the figure mentioned in Gen. V, the son of Jared and great-grandfather of Noah, who lived for three hundred and sixty-five years, walked with God and was eventually taken by him into heaven.

46,16 siðavendni 'integrity of morals': *Hap. leg.*; cf. the similar compound *siðvendis* 'of uprightness' in stanza 51,2 (38,14).

46,17 Nóe 'of Noah': The latinate genitive singular of *Nói* (see *LP*: *Nói*), treated as a monosyllable, with resolution under full stress; *Skald*, II 96 has bisyllabic *Nóé*, which would be metrically irregular. For Noah's purity, see Gen. VI.9.

Commentary 141

46,19 Siem...20 aldir 'The observance ... forever': The association of Noah's son Shem with religious observance alludes to a tradition, originally midrashic, that Shem was the same person as Melchisedech, and that there was a direct line of priesthood from Noah to Aaron, transmitted by primogeniture. Cf. Honorius Augustodunensis, *Summa gloria de apostolico et augusto sive de praecellentia sacerdotii prae regno liber*, chapter II (*PL* 172, col. 1260C). The idea goes back at least to Jerome. So far, no direct source in Old Norse has been identified.

46,21 Trúa...28 þjónan 'Faith extols ... life of Aaron': Stanza 59 continues the theme of st. 58, praise for the virtues of Old Testament characters. Whereas those celebrated in st. 58 all come from the earlier chapters of Genesis, the first four mentioned in st. 59 come from this book's later chapters: Abraham, his son Isaac, Jacob, son of Isaac and Joseph, son of Jacob. The story of Aaron, brother of Moses, comes in Exod., and looks forward to st. 60. Abraham is associated with faith because of his obedience to God, who required him to sacrifice his son Isaac; the latter symbolises hope, as the physical sacrifice was averted. Lines 3–4 (46,23–24) may refer to Gen. XXVIII.15–30, where Jacob is said to have worked for fourteen years for Rachel's father, before being allowed to marry her. The reference to Joseph is clearly to his exile in Egypt and his ability to interpret prophetic dreams, principally those of the Egyptian Pharaoh, while the lines on Aaron allude to his role as the first high priest of the Hebrews, nicely balancing the reference to Shem in st. 58,7–8 (46,19–20).

46,23 Jácób 'Jacob': W places a stop after *vísan*, l. 2 (46,22) and reads *ván ... Jácóbs* in l. 3. Finnur Jónsson (*Skj* B, II 184) deleted the final ‹s› (genitive singular) of *Jácóbs* to give an accusative singular object of *lofar* 'praises' and brought this clause into line with others in the stanza, as has been done in this edition. Ólsen kept the manuscript reading *Jácóbs*, on the model of the construction in 58,5 (46,17), but emended *lofar* to *lofaz* 'is praised' (*FoGT* 1884, 294 and n. 2), reading *Ástsemð Jakobs lofast einum hugar fremðum*, which he paraphrased as *På grund af Jakobs udmærkede sjælelige egenskaber priser man hans kærlighed* 'on the basis of Jacob's remarkable spiritual qualities one praises his love'.

48,1 Moysen 'Moses': The spelling of the manuscript. Also possible are *Móisen*, *Moísen*, and length on the last syllable (*-én*, so *Skald*, II 96). Moses the lawgiver is well represented in skaldic verse; cf. Anon *Leið* 18,2[VII] *lagavísum Móisi* 'law-wise Moses' and especially Anon

Law 1,5^(VII) *Móyses kunni lögmáls list* 'Moses was skilled in the art of law-giving'.

48,2 brennfagra 'burning fair': The epithet is *hap. leg.* and probably alludes to Exod. XIX.16–20, which describes how God appeared before Moses on Mount Sinai in fire and smoke when he gave him the Ten Commandments.

48,3 þig…4 beima 'Everything … men': Some emendation of these two lines is necessary to achieve grammatical sense. *SnE* 1848–87, II 246–47 n. 2 first suggested emending W's *allr*, l. 3 (48,3) to *allt*, but collocated it as *allt beima* 'everything of men', i.e. all men, which is unidiomatic. Ólsen also adopted the minimal emendation of W's *allr* to *allt* (*FoGT* 1884, 295), and his construal 'everything of all the world' is followed in this edition. Finnur Jónsson in *Skj* B, II 185 emends *þik* to *herr*, l. 3 (48,3), and *jǫfurr* (nominative) to *jǫfur*, l. 4 (48,4), reading *allr herr beima lofar með ǫllu jǫfur alls heims*, which Finnur translates as *hele menneskenes skare lovpriser fuldkomment hele verdens konge* 'the whole troop of humans praises completely the king of the whole world'. Kock (*NN* §3165, *Skald*, II 96) emends *þik* to *þing* and *allr* to *allt*, l. 3 (48,3), as well as *jǫfurr* to *jǫfur*, l. 4 (48,4), collocating *allt þing beima* 'all the assembly of men' and *jǫfur alls heims* 'the lord of all the world', l. 4 (48,4). *FoGT* 2004, 57 follows Kock's emendations.

Chapter 27: Teretema

G defines this figure as follows: *Cum quis multotiens interrogat est teretema, | Quod bene rhetoricum datur aspiciendo colorem* (I 86–87) 'When one often asks, it is *teretema*, which gives a good rhetorical colour [ornament] for the one who will consider it'. Stanzas 61 and 62 are clearly inspired by the examples given in *Gg*. *Gg*'s first example is: *Quis moritur? presul. Cur? pro grege. Qualiter? ense. Quando? natali. Quis locus? ara Dei* (p. 97). 'Who dies? The bishop. Why? For the flock. How? By the sword. When? At Christmas. At what place? The altar of God'. These lines come from a poem on the murder of Thomas Becket (d. 29 Dec. 1170) (ed. Harbert 1975, 17). In sts 61 and 62 Christ and St Óláfr have replaced St Thomas.

Stanza 61

Stanzas 61 and 62, the last in *FoGT*, are both in a form of *dróttkvætt* called in *Háttatal sextánmælt* 'sixteen times spoken' (cf. SnSt *Ht* 9^(III); *SnE* 2007, 9). In the two *FoGT* stanzas eight questions are matched by eight replies, each pair given in a single line of poetry. *Sextánmælt* is very similar to the verse-form called *greppaminni* 'poets' reminder', which is mentioned in *FoGT* in connection with the figure of *epimone* (see commentary to 40,25). Whereas the subject of st. 61 is the death of Christ and its significance for mankind, st. 62, in strikingly similar wording, refers to the death of the Norwegian king Óláfr Haraldsson at the Battle of Stiklestad (Stiklastaðir) on 29 July 1030 and the implications of the saint's death for mankind. The parallel emphasises the sanctity of the king.

48,10 Hvessu 'how': W has *hversu*, but all editors have followed Ólsen (*FoGT* 1884, 295–96) in normalising to assimilated *hvessu* in view of the *skothending* with *krossu*.

48,11 Lassarus 'Lazarus': Lazarus of Bethany, brother of Martha and Mary, whose death and resurrection by Christ is described in John XI. His revival from the dead was regarded as a foreshadowing of the resurrection of Christ and the gospel narrative was often interpreted as an illustration of the two natures of Christ as man and deity. The idea that his burial place was also the place where Christ was crucified has not been traced to a source.

48,12 Helzt 'about': Taken here (so also *SnE* 1848–87, II 248 and Kock, *Skald*, II 96 and *NN* §2494) with *að nóni* (there is a stop in the manuscript before 'helldz'). Ólsen (*FoGT* 1884, 295 and 296 n. 3), following Konráð Gíslason (1849, 304), proposes the manuscript punctuation is a mistake and that *helzt* should be understood with *hvienær* in the same line, as do Finnur Jónsson (*Skj* B, II 185), translating *når omtrent* 'about when', and Longo (*FoGT* 2004, 57). The same editors construe the very close verbal parallel in st. 62,3 (48,20) in the same way.

48,12 að nóni 'at the ninth hour': At nones, c. 3 p.m. The same hour is given in st. 62 (48,20) as the time that St Óláfr fell. Cf. commentary to 6,7.

48,17 með minnr þraungdum spurningum 'with less compressed questions': The verb *þraungva* usually means 'squeeze, compress, make narrow, rush'. It is uncertain what the writer refers to here. The questions of st. 62 are not substantially different from those of st. 61. *Gg* also gives two variants of the figure. In the first variant (quoted above in the commentary to 48,6), every question deals with the same subject (namely the murder of Thomas Becket). In the second the questions deal with various subjects but that does not seem to be the case with st. 62.

Stanza 62
Stanzas 61 and 62 are closely parallel in structure and wording, thus emphasising the sanctity of St Óláfr Haraldsson, the subject of st. 62. His death at the battle of Stiklestad is implicity compared to Christ's crucifixion, and his opponents to the Jews. The effect of Óláfr's death, the stanza claims, is to restore mankind to health and to curb the spread of sin.

48,21 Öfund vöknuð 'awakened ill-will': Probably a reference to the various personal scores that the magnates who opposed Óláfr at Stiklestad wished to settle, possibly directed especially at the motivation of Kálfr Árnason (see below), whose stepsons had been killed by Óláfr (cf. ÍF 27, 300−03).

48,22 Kálfr It is generally assumed that this is a reference to Kálfr Árnason, a Norwegian magnate who dealt Óláfr one of his fatal wounds at Stiklestad, although there is some doubt about whether this assailant was Kálfr Árnason or Kálfr Arnfinnsson (cf. ÍF 27, 385 and n. 2).

48,23 bændu 'requested': From *bæna* (earlier *bǿna*) 'to request, entreat'. W reads *bendu* 'intended [by means of a sign]', from *benda* (cf. *LP*: 2. *benda*).

48,25 Hvað sýtir Fira lýti 'What laments? Men's sin': Finnur Jónsson is surely right in his gloss to this line in *Skj* B, II 236, that it refers to the expectation that Óláfr's death and sainthood will make it more difficult for sin to flourish.

DOCTRINALE

(ll. 2560–2639)

DOCTRINALE

2560 Est et HOMOZEUXIS, quando rem notificabis
ex alia, cui rem possis conferre priorem,
quae sit nota minus, per eam, quae notior exstat.
Tres species: icon, paradigma, parabola, subsunt.
In simili genere qui comparat, efficit ICON;
2565 haec solet ex usu quandoque PARABOLA dici.
Sed dici poterit de iure parabola, si quis
inter dissimiles res comparat, utputa: 'Semen
est evangelium, quod nutrivit bona terra,
quod petra suscepit, quod spinae detinuerunt'.
2570 Hic PARADIGMA facit, qui primum comparat et post
assignat simile: 'Domini sunt semina verbum,
spinae divitae, mens arida petra vocatur'.
   Alterius vox una tenens vim praepositiva,
ut 'supra' pro 'de', fit PROTHESEOS PARALANGE.
2575 Cum plus significas, dicis minus, haec tibi fiat
LIPTOTA; fit sub ea firmando negatio bina.
Describendo locum TOPOGRAPHIAM faciemus.
CHRONOGRAPHIA solet certum describere tempus.
Si dicatur agens patiens res vel vice versa,
2580 sive modo simili tibi sit conversio facta,
fiet HYPALLAGIUM: 'Perflavit fistula buccas'.
Personamque novam formans das PROSOPOPOEIAM.
Absenti sermo directus APOSTROPHA fiet;
sic loquor absenti, scriptam dum mitto salutem.
2585 Est adiectivum substantivo resolutum
aut e converso; sic HENDIADIM tibi formo:
'Armatum'que 'virum' designo per 'arma virumque';
'armato'que 'viro' decet 'arma virumque' notare.
Extra materiam describens vana vagatur
2590 auctor, et hanc EBASIM plures dixere figuram.
EMPHASIS efficitur, si fixum proprietatem
significans ponis, ubi debet mobile poni.
Sic loquor expresse dicens: 'Davus scelus ipsum'.
Est EFFLEXEGESIS exponens dicta priora.
2595 Dum retices, quod turpe sonat, dic EUPHONIAM:
'Circuit' haec et 'relliquiae' dant 'relligio'que.

DOCTRINALE

HOMOZEUXIS is when you will denote one thing by a second with which you might compare the first thing, that which is less known by that which is more known. Three subtypes exist: *icon, paradigma, parabola*. He who makes comparisons between things of a similar kind, brings about ICON; in practice, this is usually called PARABOLA. But it can rightfully be called *parabola* if one makes comparisons between different things, for example: 'The seed is the gospel that the good soil nourished, which the rock received, which the thorns held back'. He brings about PARADIGMA who first compares and then specifies the likeness: the seeds are the word of the Lord, the thorns riches; the arid mind is called a rock.

One preposition which carries the meaning of another, like 'above' instead of 'of', gives PROTHESEOS PARALANGE.

When you signify more, but say less, this gives you LIPTOTA. In this figure, a double negation becomes a confirmation.

We will bring about TOPOGRAPHIA by describing a place.

CHRONOGRAPHIA usually describes a certain time.

If the active thing is called passive or the other way around, or you make a similar transposition, it will become HYPALLAGIUM: 'The pipe blew through the jaws'.

You make PROSOPOPOEIA by fashioning a new character.

Speech directed to someone absent will become APOSTROPHA. In this way, I speak to someone absent when I send a written greeting.

An adjective is transformed into a noun or the opposite—in this way I create HENDIADYS for you. And I denote 'an armed man' by 'arms and a man', and it is fitting that 'arms and a man' designates 'an armed man'.

The author wanders away from the material and describes insignificant matters, and many called this figure EBASIS.

EMPHASIS is brought about if you mention a fixed quality where a changable one should be mentioned. I speak emphatically when I say: 'Davus [is] crime incarnate'.

EFFLEXEGESIS explains what has been said earlier.

When you refrain from saying something because it sounds disagreeable, say a EUPHONIA: *circuit, relliquiae* and *relligio* produce this.

Dicitur esse LEPOS sermo directus ad unum
utens plurali, velut hic: 'Nostis, bone praesul'.
Pro numero numerum, pro casu ponere casum
te facit ANTITOSIS inter se dissona iungens.
Saepius audivi tempus pro tempore poni:
'Ludere' = 'ludebat ad ludendumque vocabat';
inque prophetiis mutantur tempora sacris.
Verba per ANTITHETON respondent ultima primis:
'Est Daniel Noë Job castus rectorque maritus'.
Respondens ad ea, tibi quae sunt obicienda.
Das ANTHYPOPHORAM, cum nil tamen obiciatur.
Sensus oppositos notat ANTICLASIS eodem
verbo: 'Non obsto, sed toto posse resisto'.
Cum verbis vertit ANTIMETABOLA sensum:
'Non, ut edas, vivas; sed edas, ut vivere possis'.
Incipimus fari quicquam quandoque, sed illud
ultro desinimus intercipimusque, tacendo;
vult APOSIOPASIS dici defectio talis.
Est EUPHEMISMOS pro verbo ponere verbum:
'Exsultat domini vocem mea lingua superni'.
Contingens verbi mutat SYNEPTHESIS: 'Ecce
unica facta fuit mulier, quae sunt modo plures'.
Ista sed in nostrum mutatio non venit usum.
Dicuntur binae species synepthesis esse,
scilicet haec et ea, qua personam variamus:
'Nobis parce, deus; nobis lavet ille reatus'.
Vult OLIOPOMENON ex dictis plura notare;
moto sermone sic plura licet memorare:
'Urit amor Paridem; nuptam rapit; armat Atriden
ultio; pugnatur; fit machina; Troia crematur'.
Exponens HOMOPHESIS est non nota per aeque
vel magis ignota: Dic 'alchitrop' esse 'cavillam',
quae tenet 'allidadam' cum 'valdagora' sociatam.
Saepe prius dicta geminat tibi theologia
EPIMONENque vocat, haec si repetitio fiat,
ut, quod dicetur, sic certius esse probetur:
'Expectando' David 'expectans' sic geminavit.
Si, quae sunt hominis, assignentur deitati,
ANTHROPOSPATHOS est: Sic saepe 'Dei' legis 'iram'.
Si sint res aliquae concordi foedere iunctae,

Speech directed at one person using the plural is called LEPOS, like this: 'Ye know, good prelate'.

ANTITOSIS, connecting discordancies, makes you use one number instead of another, one case instead of another. I have often heard one tense used instead of another: 'to play' for 'he played' and 'he called to play'; tenses are often changed in holy prophecies.

The last words agree with the first through ANTITHETON: 'Daniel, Noah, Job is chaste, a helmsman and married'.

When you respond to possible objections even though none are raised, you make an ANTHYPOPHORA.

ANTICLASIS signifies conflicting meanings with the same word: 'I do not stand in the way, I withstand with all my might'.

ANTIMETABOLA inverts the meaning along with the words: 'You should not live so that you may eat, but eat so that you may live'.

Whenever we begin to say something but break off voluntarily and stop by being silent . . . such ellipsis should be called APOSIOPASIS.

EUPHEMISMOS is to use one word instead of another: 'My tongue exults the voice of the Lord above'.

SYNEPTHESIS changes the contingency of a word: 'See, one woman was made, who soon afterwards are many'. But that change is not part of our usage. There is said to be two kinds of *synepthesis*; namely this one, and the one in which we change the person: 'Spare us God! May he wash our guilt away'.

OLIOPOMENON wants to denote many things by what is said. In this way, it is possible to make mention of many things quickly: 'Love burns Paris, he steals the bride, revenge arms the son of Atreus, the battle rages, the scheme is carried out, Troy is burned'.

HOMOPHESIS explains something unknown by something equally or more unknown: say that an *alchitrop* is the *cavilla*, which holds the *allida*, which is connected with the *valdagora*.

The Bible often repeats things which have been said earlier and summons EPIMONE. This repetition occurs, so that that which is said is shown with greater certainty. David, waiting by waiting, made such a repetition.

ANTHROPOSPATHOS is if some human traits are assigned to the deity: thus you often read 'the anger of God'.

id, quod inest uni, reliquam dices operari:
Sic linguam cordi concordem dic meditari
ac HOMOPATHION talem dic esse figuram.

(text from D = Reichling 1893, 172–78)

If there are some matters brought together by a joint tie, then you might say that that which belongs to one causes the other. Say in this way that the tongue is considered united with the heart and call such a figure HOMOPATHION.

TECHNICAL TERMS USED IN *FoGT*

For words of non-Norse origin and obvious calques and loan translations, Latin or Greek equivalents have been given in addition to translations. The writer presumably did not have first-hand knowledge of Greek so terms of Greek origin have therefore found their way into the text via Latin. In addition to *ONP*, Fritzner and Cleasby and Vigfusson (1957), the list mainly draws upon the work of Thurot (1868), Ólsen (1884), Lausberg (1990) and Liddell and Scott (1996).

aclacassis < *anticlasis* < Gr. ἀντανάκλασις 'bending back, use of a word in an altered sense': 32,1.
afganga *fem.* 'digression', cf. Lat. *evagatio* 'wandering': 14,17.
anatecor *see* **antiteton**.
ansimehisa < *antimetabola* < Gr. ἀντιμεταβολή 'transposition': 32,12.
antiposora < *anthypophora* < Gr. ἀνθυποφορά 'reply': 30,20.
antiteton < *antitheton* < Gr. ἀντίθετον 'antithesis': 24,21; 26,11; 28,23 (*anatecor*).
antitosis < Gr. ἀντίπτωσις 'resistance, opposition', gramm. 'interchange of cases': 24,6; 24,13.
antopazia < *homopathion* < Gr. ὁμοιοπάθεια? 'similarity of affection, sympathetic emotion': 42,20.
antropuspatos < *anthropospathos* < Gr. ἀνθρωποπαθῶς? 'with human feelings': 44,9.
aposiopesis < *aposiopasis* < Gr. ἀποσιώπησις 'becoming silent': 32,23.
apostropha < Gr. ἀποστροφή 'turning away': 12,4.
atkvæði *neut.* 'pronunciation': 20,27.
ávarp *neut.* 'summary', not recorded in this sense in the standard dictionaries: 36,27.
bethgraphia compound of Hebrew *beth* 'house' and Gr. γραφία 'writing', apparently unparalleled: 4,21.
brachilogia < Gr. βραχυλογία 'brevity in speech/writing': 36,28.
capitulum *neut.* (*masc.*?) 'chapter': 46,11.
catenphaton < *cacenphaton* < Gr. κακέμφατον 'ill-sounding': 20,25; 20,26.
climax < Gr. κλῖμαξ 'ladder, climax': 38,1.
cosmographia < Gr. κοσμογραφία 'description of the world': 6,1.

Technical terms

cronographia < *chronographia* < Gr. χρονογραφία 'chronological record': 6,5.
drápa *fem.* 'a long poem with refrain(s)': 14,18.
dreifa (*fð*) 'derive', cf. Lat. *derivare*: 22,1.
dróttkvæðr *adj.* 'composed in the court metre': 36,27.
dunhenda *fem.* 'echoing rhyme': 40,24.
dynax *see* **climax**.
dæmi *neut.* 'example', cf. Lat. *exemplum*: 14,16; 16,9; 16,11; 16,19; 16,25; 20,20; 24,18.
ebasis < Gr. ἔκβασις 'going out of, digression': 14,17; 16,3; 16,9; 16,21.
efni *neut.* 'subject matter', cf. Lat. *materia*: 14,17; 16,3; 20,17; 28,11.
efnisafganga *fem.* 'digression from the subject-matter': 18,1.
eiginligr *adj.* 'proper, specific': 20,21; 46,7.
emophasis < *homophesis* < Gr. ὁμοιόφησις? 'saying similarly'?: 38,11.
emphasis < Gr. ἔμφασις 'setting forth, exposition, narration': 18,3; 18,17.
endiadis < *hendiadys* < Gr. ἓν διὰ δυοῖν 'one through two': 12,27; 14,13; 14,14.
epimenon < *epimone* < Gr. ἐπιμονή 'dwelling, tarrying': 40,21.
eptirkomandi *pres. ptc.* 'following, future', cf. Lat. *futurus*: 20,23.
euphemismos < Gr. εὐφημισμός 'euphemism': 34,11.
euphonia < Gr. εὐφωνία 'euphony': 20,25; 20,27; 20,29.
exflexigesis < *efflexigesis* < Gr. ἐπεξήγησις 'detailed account, explanation': 20,4; 20,15; 20,22.
fall *neut.* 'case', cf. Lat. *casus*: 24,6; 24,12 (twice).
fallaskifti *neut.* 'change of cases', *hap. leg.*: 24,7.
figúra *fem.* < Lat. *figura* 'figure (of speech)': 2,7; 6,11; 8,4; 8,13; 8,25; 12,4; 12,17; 12,24; 12,27; 16,18; 18,6; 20,14; 20,15; 20,21; 20,28; 26,10; 28,10; 32,11; 32,22; 34,9; 34,10; 36,6; 36,28; 40,21; 42,15; 42,20; 44,9; 44,20; 46,3; 46,10; 48,5; 48,6; 48,17.
finngalknað *pret. ptc.* 'made similar to a *finngalkn* (a kind of monster)', used of incongruous metaphors: 20,1.
fjórðungr *masc.* 'quarter stanza, couplet': 28,21.
flytja (*flutti*) 'move', *flytja (fram)* 'pronounce': 40,13; 40,22.
fornskáld *neut.* 'poet of old': 24,20.
framburðr *masc.* 'publication, reading aloud': 12,26.
frásögn *fem.* 'statement, story': 16,10; 20,15.
fyrirsetning *fem.* 'preposition', cf. Lat. *prepositio*: 2,9.

giegna (*nd*) 'meet', *giegna saman* 'belong together, agree', cf. Lat. *convenire* 'come together, agree': 26,9.
gierandi *masc.* 'agent', cf. Lat. *agens* lit. '(an) acting (one)': 6,22 (twice).
glósa (*að*) 'explain': 20,15; 38,11.
glósa *fem.* 'gloss' < Lat. *glo(s)sa* 'a foreign word requiring explanation' < Gr. γλῶσσα 'tongue': 20,14; 38,23.
gráða *fem.* 'step', cf. Lat. *gradus*: 38,2.
grein *fem.* 'explanation, distinction': 20,14; 20,27.
greining *fem.* 'explanation, exposition': 20,4.
greppaminni *neut.* 'poets' reminder': 40,25.
háttafall *neut.* 'fall (fault) of metre': 40,26.
háttr *masc.* 'mode, metre', cf. Lat. *modus*: 16,21; 20,2; 20,3; 24,24; 26,12; 26,22; 28,25; 30,3; 40,24; 48,7.
helmingr *masc.* 'half, half-stanza': 28,11; 28,22; 28,24.
hljóða (*að*) 'sound', cf. Lat. *sonare*: 20,30.
hlutr *masc.* 'thing, part', cf. Lat. *res* 'thing': 8,16 (twice); 8,27; 10,13 (twice); 12,27; 12,28 (twice); 14,1 (twice); 14,2; 14,5; 14,6; 14,14 (twice); 14,15 (twice); 16,9; 16,21; 18,3 (twice); 20,1; 20,4; 20,17; 20,18; 20,23 (twice); 24,19; 30,20; 38,11 (twice); 42,20; 46,5; 48,6.
hræriligr *adj.* 'moveable', cf. Lat. *mobile*: 18,3.
icona < *icon* < Gr. εἰκών 'image, similitude, comparison': 20,17.
iðurmæltr *adj.* 'repeatedly said': 40,24.
ísetning *fem.* 'insertion': 8,15.
jarteignakvæði *neut.* 'poem about miracles': 16,23.
játan *fem.* 'affirmation': 4,8.
kienna (*nd*) 'attribute': 18,29.
kienning *fem.* 'teaching': 12,2; 22,18; 40,8; 40,14.
klausa *fem.* 'clause', cf. Lat. *clausula*: 46,11.
kveða (*kvað, kváðu, kveðit*) 'compose, say, sing, recite': 2,2; 2,11; 10,16; 10,17; 10,25; 12,7; 12,18; 18,18; 20,5; 22,28; 24,24; 26,24; 32,24; 34,26; 44,11.
kveðandi *neut.* 'metre': 24,23.
kvæði *neut.* 'poem': 16,3; 16,11; 24,2.
kynkvísl *fem.* 'lineage, branch': 20,22.
langloka *fem.* 'long closure/ending': 24,24.
lepos Lat. 'pleasantry': 22,27.
liðinn *pret. ptc.* 'past', cf. Lat. *praeteritus*: 20,23.
líking *fem.* 'likeness, comparison, simile': 20,19.
líkja (*kt*) 'make like', *líkja eftir* (*e-m*) 'imitate (sth.)': 24,19; 40,27.

límingarstafr *masc.* 'conjoined character (digraph)': 20,29.
liptota < Gr. λιτότης 'plainness, simplicity, understatement': 2,10; 2,20.
mál *neut.* 'speech, utterance, sentence': 22,1; 26,12; 26,14; 26,23; 26,24; 28,7; 28,8 (twice); 28,10; 28,11; 28,12; 28,22; 28,23; 28,24; 32,23; 42,4; 48,16.
málsgrein *fem.* 'sentence': 38,2.
margfalda (*að*) 'make manifold, pluralize': 24,3.
margfaldr *adj.* 'manifold, plural': 22,27; 24,16 (twice).
meistari *masc.* 'master, teacher, grammarian': 38,1.
merkja (*kt*) 'signify': 2,10; 2,20; 4,2; 12,1; 12,2; 18,4; 18,29; 20,16; 22,27; 38, 29; 40,5; *vera merkt fyrir e-t* 'being signified by sth.': 14,5; 'signify sth.': 7,27.
nafn *neut.* 'noun, name', cf. Lat. *nomen*: 12,5 (pronoun?); 20,30; 24,16 (twice); 32,19; 34,10; 38,28 (twice); 46,3 (twice).
nauðsyn *fem.* 'necessity', cf. Lat. *necessitas*: 8,14; 16,26; 38,7; 38,8; 44,24.
nefniligr *adj.* 'nominative', cf. Lat. *nominativus*: 24,12.
neiting *fem.* 'negation', cf. Lat. *negatio*: 4,8.
norrönuskáldskap *neut.* 'norse poetry': 20,24.
onopomenon < *oliopomenon* < Gr. compund of ὀλίγος 'little, small' and ?: 36,9.
orð *neut.* 'word': 2,11; 2,20; 22,1; 22,2; 24,21; 24,22; 26,9; 26,24; 28,21; 30,24; 32,2; 32,12; 34,4; 34,9; 34,11; 34,22; 34,23; 36,9; 38,21; 40,21; 40,23; 44,13; 'verb', cf. Lat. *verbum*: 24,16.
óskiftiligr *adj.* 'indivisible': 12,28 (twice); 14,5; 46,7.
parabola < Gr. παραβολή 'juxtaposition': 20,18.
paradigma < Gr. παράδειγμα 'pattern, model, example': 20,20.
persóna *fem.* 'person', cf. Lat. *persona*: 8,15; 22,27; 24,3; 36,7.
prepositio Lat. 'preposition': 2,1.
prologus Lat. 'prologue': 12,25.
prosopophia < *prosopopoeia* < Gr. προσωποποιία 'dramatisation': 8,15; 10,13.
protheseos paraloge < *protheseos paralange* < Gr. πρόθεσεως παραλλαγή 'interchange of prepositions': 2,1.
regla *fem.* 'rule, metre', cf. Lat. *regula*: 24,22; 26,10; 'constraint': 46,5.
rægiligr *adj.* 'accusative', cf. Lat. *accusativus*: 24,12.
samfastr *adj.* 'bound, conjoined': 14,15.

setja (*setti*) 'place, put': 2,7; 4,7; 8,8; 8,13; 12,25; 14,18; 16,23; 20,28; 24,6; 38,22; 38,23; 40,21; 40,23; 46,4; *setja fram* 'present', *setja fyrir e-u* 'place/use instead of sth.': 12,28; 14,11; 24,12; 24,19; 34,11; *setja í stað e-s* 'place/use instead of sth.' 14,14; 14,15; 34,23.
simatrismos < *synacrismos* < Gr. συναθροισμός 'collection, union': 46,10.
sineptesis < *synepthesis* < Gr. συνέμπτωσις 'formal coincidence, similarity of form': 34,25.
skáld *neut.* 'poet': 4,13; 4,15; 4,26; 6,1; 6,11; 8,16; 8,25; 12,12; 12,16; 14,17; 14,18; 16,3; 16,9; 15,17; 24,19.
skáldskapr *masc.* 'poetry': 8,13.
skáldskaparháttr *masc.* 'metre of poetry': 40,26.
skifta (*ft*) 'change, swap': 2,9; 20,1; 20,29; 24,22; 36,6; 36,7.
skiftiligr *adj.* 'divisible': 14,1.
skilning *fem.* '(grammatical) person': 12,5; 34,25; 36,6; 'signification': 2,10; 32,1; 32,13; 46,7.
skraut *neut.* 'ornamentation': 10,21; 16,26.
skrúð *neut.* 'ornament', cf. Lat. *ornatus*: 8,13.
skýra (*rð*) 'explain': 20,15; 20,20; 20,22.
skýring *fem.* 'explanation': 20,4.
soluecismus < *soloecismus* < Gr. σολοικισμός 'soloecism': 24,4; 24,18.
species Lat. 'kind, type': 26,12; 26,23; 28,10; 38,1.
stafr *masc.* 'letter, character': 20,2; 34,11.
standa (*stóð, stóðu, staðit*) 'stand (written)': 2,1; 4,8; 14,16; 22,2 (twice); 24,16; 29,27; 24,18; 24,24; 26,10; 34,9; 34,12; *standa til* 'warrant': 2,11.
stef *neut.* 'refrain': 16,3; 16,4; 16,23.
stórkvæði *neut.* 'grand poem': 20,3.
stæla (*lt*) 'equip with *stál* (intercalary clause)': 24,24; 26,26.
sundrlauss *adj* 'disjoined, separate': 12,27; 14,14.
svara (*að*) 'answer, correspond with': 24,21; 30,20; 48,16.
taka (*tók, tóku, tekit*) 'take', *taka upp* 'construct': 34,5.
tal *neut.* 'number': 22,27; 24,6; 34,25; 36,6.
tala (*að*) 'speak': 8,25; 12,4; 12,6; 12,17; 22,28; 24,3; 44,21; *tala af e-u* 'speak about sth': 4,26; *tala með/fyrir figúru* 'speak figuratively': 20,21; 34,9.
talnaskifti *neut.* 'change of numbers', *hap. leg.*: 24,13.
theologia *fem.* Lat. 'theology, The Bible': 36,27; 40,23.

therethema < *teretema* < Gr. ἐρώτημα 'that which is asked, question': 48,6.
tilfelli *neut.* 'contingency, accidental quality', cf. Lat. *accidens*: 18,4; 18,29; 44,20.
tímaskifti *neut.* 'change of tense': 24,18.
tími *masc.* 'tense', cf. Lat. *tempus*: 6,5; 24,6.
tophographia < *topographia* < Gr. τοπογραφία 'description of place': 4,15.
umskifti *neut.* 'exchange': 24,6; 34,11; 34,23; 34,25.
undirstaða *fem.* 'foundation, essence, nature': 20,21.
undirstaðligr *adj.* 'substantive', cf. Lat. *substantivus*: 18,3.
útþanning *fem.* 'extension' *hap. leg.*: 2,20.
verk *neut.* '(literary) work', cf. Lat. *opus*: 24,20.
vers *neut.* 'verse, poetry', cf. Lat. *versus*: 46,11.
vísa *fem.* 'stanza': 14,19; 14,21; 16,12; 18,6; 18,30; 20,1; 20,2; 20,3; 24,22; 26,23; 28,8; 28,11; 28,23 (twice); 30,3; 34,4; 34,12; 36,27; 46,11; 48,16.
vísuhelmingr *masc.* 'half-stanza': 26,12; 26,13; 32,11; 38,23.
vísuorð *neut.* 'line of poetry': 28,7; 28,8; 28,24; 48,16.
ypallage < *hypallage* < Gr. ὑπαλλαγή 'interchange, exchange': 6,21.
yrkja (*orti, ort*) 'compose': 14,18.
þolandi *masc.* 'passive' *hap. leg.*, cf. Lat. *patiens* lit. 'suffering (one)': 6,21; 6,22.

BIBLIOGRAPHY

Achard, Guy, ed. 1989. *Rhétorique à Herennius*. Paris: Les Belles Lettres.
Aen = Virgil's *Aeneid* in Mynors 1969.
AEW = Vries, Jan de 1962. *Altnordisches etymologisches Wörterbuch*. 2nd rev. edn. Rpt. 1977. Leiden: Brill.
AÍ I = Kristian Kålund, ed. 1908. *Alfræði íslenzk. Islandsk encyklopædisk litteratur I. Cod. mbr. AM. 194, 8vo*. Samfund til udgivelse af gammel nordisk litteratur 37. Copenhagen: Møller.
AÍ II = Natanael Beckman and Kristian Kålund, eds 1914–16. *Alfræði íslenzk. Islandsk encyklopædisk litteratur II. Rímtǫl*. Samfund til udgivelse af gammel nordisk litteratur 41. Copenhagen: Møller.
Almqvist, Bo 1965–74. *Norrön niddiktning. Traditionshistoriska studier i versmagi*. Two Parts. I. *Nid mot furstar*. II. *Nid mot missionärer. Senmedeltida nidtraditioner*. Stockholm: Almqvist & Wiksell.
Andersson, Theodore M. and Kari Ellen Gade, trans. 2000. *Morkinskinna. The earliest Icelandic chronicle of the Norwegian kings (1030–1157)*. Islandica 51. Ithaca and London: Cornell University Press.
ANG = Noreen, Adolf 1923. *Altnordische Grammatik I. Altisländische und altnorwegische Grammatik (Laut- und Flexionslehre) unter Berücksichtigung des Urnordischen*. 4th edn. Halle: Niemeyer.
Asmussen, Georg et al. 2002. *Archiv der Bergenfahrerkompanie zu Lübeck und des Hansischen Kontors zu Bergen in Norwegen von (1278) bzw. 1314 bis 1853*. Findbücher 9. Lübeck: Archiv der Hansestadt Lübeck.
Astås, Reidar, ed. 2009. *Stjórn*. 2 vols. Norrøne tekster 8. Oslo: Riksarkivet.
Bekken, Otto B. and Marit Christoffersen 1985. *Algorismus i Hauksbók i europeisk perspektiv*. Fagseksjon for matematikk/ Fagseksjon for norsk. Skrifter 1985: 1. Kristiansand: Agder distriktshøgskole.
Bekken, Otto B. 1986. *On the Cubus Perfectus of the Algorismus in Hauksbók*. Fagseksjon for matematikk. Skrifter 1986: 2. Kristiansand: Agder distriktshøgskole.

Beowulf 2008 = Robert D. Fulk, Robert E. Bjork and John D. Niles, eds 2008. *Klaeber's Beowulf and the Fight at Finnsburg*, ed. Fr. Klaeber. Toronto, Buffalo and London: Toronto University Press.

Björn K. Þórólfsson 1925. *Um íslenskar orðmyndir á 14. og 15. öld og breytingar þeirra úr fornmálinu*. Reykjavík: Fjelagsprentsmiðjan. Rpt. 1987. Rit um íslenska málfræði 2. Reykjavík: Málvísindastofnun Háskóla Íslands.

Blöndal, Sigfús. 1949. 'St. Nikulás og dýrkun hans, sérstaklega á Íslandi'. *Skírnir* 123, 69–97.

Braun, R., ed. 1976. *Opera Quodvultdeo carthaginiensi episcopo tributa*. Corpus Christianorum, Series Latina 60. Turnhout: Brepols.

Broberg, Sven Grén, ed. 1909–12. *Rémundar saga keisarasonar*. Samfund til udgivelse af gammel nordisk litteratur 38. Copenhagen: Møller.

Cahill, Peter, ed. 1983. *Duggals leiðsla*. Stofnun Árna Magnússonar á Íslandi, Rit 25. Reykjavík: Stofnun Árna Magnússonar á Íslandi.

Calboli, Gualtiero, ed. 1969. *Cornifici Rhetorica ad C. Herennium*. Bologna: Casa Editrice Pàtron Soc.

Camargo, Martin 2006. 'Latin composition textbooks and *Ad Herennium* glossing. The missing link?' In *The rhetoric of Cicero in its medieval and early Renaissance commentary tradition*. Ed. Virginia Cox and John O. Ward. Brill's Companions to the Christian Tradition 2. Leiden: Brill, 267–88.

Cecchini, Enzo *et al*., ed. 2004. *Derivationes*. Edizione nazionale dei testi mediolatini 11, serie 1/6. Florence: SISMEL.

Chase, Martin, ed. 2007. '*Lilja*'. In *SkP* VII: 2, 554–677.

Cizek, Alexandru N., ed. 2009. *Konrad von Mure: Novus Grecismus auf der Grundlage aller vorhanden Handschriften erstmals herausgegeben*. Münstersche Mittelalter-Schriften 81. Munich: Fink.

Cleasby, Richard and Gudbrand Vigfusson 1957. *An Icelandic-English Dictionary*. Oxford: Clarendon. 2nd edn with a supplement by Sir William A. Craigie.

Clunies Ross, Margaret 1987. *Skáldskaparmál. Snorri Sturluson's* ars poetica *and medieval theories of language*. The Viking Collection 4. Odense: Odense University Press.

Clunies Ross, Margaret 1993. 'Bragi Boddason', in *Medieval Scandinavia. An encyclopedia*. Ed. Philip Pulsiano and Kirsten Wolf. New York: Garland Publishing, 55–56.

Clunies Ross, Margaret 2005. *A history of Old Norse poetry and poetics*. Cambridge: D. S. Brewer.

Clunies Ross, Margaret. Forthcoming. 'The *Fourth Grammatical Treatise* as medial poetics'. In *Mediality in Late Medieval Iceland*. Ed. Jürg Glauser and Kate Heslop. Zurich: Chronos.

Clunies Ross, Margaret and Kari Ellen Gade 2012. 'Cosmology and skaldic poetry'. *Journal of English and Germanic Philology* 111, 199–207.

Colker Marvin L. 1974. 'New evidence that John of Garland revised the *Doctrinale* of Alexander de Villa Dei'. *Scriptorium* 28, 68–71.

Colker, Marvin L., ed. 1978. *Galteri de Castellione Alexandreis*. Padova: Editrice Antenore.

Collings, Lucy Grace 1967. 'The "Málskrúðsfræði" and the Latin tradition in Iceland'. Unpublished MA Thesis. Cornell University.

Cook, Robert and Tveitane, Mattias, eds 1979. *Strengleikar. An Old Norse translation of twenty-one Old French lais*. Norrøne tekster 3. Oslo: Norsk historisk kjeldeskrift-institutt.

Copeland, Rita 1991. *Rhetoric, hermeneutics and translation in the Middle Ages. Academic traditions and vernacular texts*. Cambridge: Cambridge University Press.

Copeland, Rita and Inike Sluiter 2009. *Medieval grammar and rhetoric. Language arts and literary theory, AD 300–1475*. Oxford: Oxford University Press.

Cormack, Margaret 1994. *The saints in Iceland. Their veneration from the conversion to 1400*. Subsidia Hagiographica 78. Brussels: Société des Bollandistes.

D = Dietrich Reichling, ed. 1893. *Das Doctrinale des Alexander de Villa-Dei. Kritisch-Exegetische Ausgabe*. Monumenta Germaniae paedagogica 12. Berlin: A. Hofmann.

Daly, Lloyd W. and Bernadine A. Daly, eds 1975. *Summa Britonis sive Guillelmi Britonis Expositiones vocabulorum Biblie*. Padova: Antenore.

De Leeuw van Weenen, Andrea, ed. 1993. *The Icelandic homily book. Perg. 15 4° in the Royal Library, Stockholm*. Reykjavík: Stofnun Árna Magnússonar á Íslandi.

Dg = *Doctrinale cum comento* [Ludovici de Guaschis] 1494. Venice: M. de Suffreno de Bonellis de Monteferato <http://gallica.bnf.fr/ark:/12148/bpt6k58377b, accessed 1 July 2013>

DI = *Diplomatarium Islandicum. Íslenzk fornbrefasafn, sem hefir inni að halda bref og gjörninga, dóma og máldaga, og aðrar skrár, er snerta Ísland eða íslenzka menn*. 1857–1972. 16 vols. Copenhagen: Møller.

Douay-Rheims Bible = Swift Edgar, ed. 2010–13. *The Vulgate Bible. Douay-Rheims Translation.* 6 vols. Cambridge, Mass.: Harvard University Press.

Dronke, Ursula, ed. and trans. 1969. *The Poetic Edda* I. *Heroic Poems.* Oxford: Clarendon Press.

Duggan, A. J. 2004. 'Cricklade, Robert of (d. in or after 1174)'. *Oxford Dictionary of National Biography.* Oxford: Oxford University Press. <http://www.oxforddnb.com/view/article/23730, accessed 5 July 2013>

Eiríkur Jónsson and Finnur Jónsson, eds 1892–96. *Hauksbók udgiven efter de arnamagnæanske håndskrifter no. 371, 544 og 675, 4° samt forskellige papirshåndskrifter.* Copenhagen: Thieles bogtrykkeri.

Faral, Edmond, ed. 1924. *Les arts poétiques du XIIe et du XIIIe siècle.* Recherches et documents sur la technique littéraire de moyen age. Paris: Librairie Honoré Champion.

Faulkes, Anthony, ed. 1977. *Edda Islandorum. Völuspá. Hávamál.* Stofnun Árna Magnússonar á Íslandi, Rit 14. Vol. II of *Two Versions of Snorra Edda from the 17th Century.* Reykjavík: Stofnun Árna Magnússonar.

Faulkes, Anthony, ed. 1979. *Edda Magnúsar Ólafssonar* (*Laufás Edda*). Stofnun Árna Magnússonar á Íslandi, Rit 13. Vol. I of *Two versions of Snorra Edda from the 17th century.* Reykjavík: Stofnun Árna Magnússonar.

Faulkes, Anthony, trans. 1987. *Snorri Sturluson Edda.* London: Dent.

Faulkes, Anthony 2008. 'Snorri Sturluson. His life and work'. In *The Viking world*, ed. Stefan Brink with Neil Price. Routledge: London and New York, 311–14.

Finch, R. G. 1993. 'Vǫlsung-Niflung cycle'. In *Medieval Scandinavia. An encyclopedia*, ed. Phillip Pulsiano and Kirsten Wolf. New York and London: Garland Publishing Inc, 707–10.

Finnur Jónsson. 1926–28. *Ordbog til de af samfund til udg. af gml. nord. litteratur udgivne Rímur samt til de af Dr. O. Jiriczek udgivne Bósarímur.* Samfund til udgivelse af gammel nordisk litteratur 51. Copenhagen: Jørgensen.

FoGT 1884 = Björn Magnússon Ólsen, ed. 1884, 120–51, 238–96.

FoGT 2004 = Longo, Michele. n. d. [2004]. 'Il Quarto Trattato Grammaticale Islandese. Testo, traduzione e commento'. Dottorato di Ricerca in 'Linguistica Sincronica e Diacronica' (XV Ciclo). Università degli Studi di Palermo: Facoltà di Lettere e Filosofia.

Foote, Peter 1959. *The Pseudo-Turpin chronicle in Iceland: A contribution to the study of the Karlamagnús saga*. London Mediæval Studies, Monograph 4. London: University College.

Foote, Peter 1984. 'Latin Rhetoric and Icelandic Poetry. Some Contacts'. In *Aurvandilstá. Norse Studies*. Ed. Michael Barnes et al. The Viking Collection 2. Odense: Odense University Press, 249–70. First published in *Saga och sed* (1982), 107–27.

Friis-Jensen, Karsten, ed. 2005. *Saxo Grammaticus. Gesta Danorum – Danmarkshistorien*. 2 vols. Dansk oversættelse ved Peter Zeeberg. Copenhagen: Det Danske Sprog- og Litteraturselskab & Gads Forlag.

Fritzner = Johan Fritzner 1883–96. *Ordbog over det gamle norske sprog*. 3 vols. Kristiania: Den norske Forlagsforening. Vol. 4: *Rettelser og tillegg* v. Finn Hødnebø, 1972.

G = Ioh. Wrobel, ed. 1887. *Eberhardi Bethuniensis Graecismus*. Corpus grammaticorum medii aeui I. Bratislava: G. Koebner.

Gade, Kari Ellen 1985. 'Hanging in Northern law and literature'. *Maal og minne*, 159–83.

Gade, Kari Ellen 2007a. 'Introduction. 9. Normalisation of fourteenth-century poetry'. In *SkP* VII. Ed. Margaret Clunies Ross. Turnhout: Brepols, lxv–lxvii.

Gade, Kari Ellen 2007b. 'Ælfric in Iceland'. In *Learning and understanding in the Old Norse world. Essays in honour of Margaret Clunies Ross*. Ed. Judy Quinn, Kate Heslop and Tarrin Wills. Medieval Texts and Cultures of Northern Europe 18. Brepols: Turnhout, 321–39.

Gade, Kari Ellen. Forthcoming. 'Introduction' to *Háttalykill*, in *SkP* III.

Gg = Anne Grondeux, ed. 2010. *Glosa super* Graecismum *Eberhardi Bethuniensis capitula I–III de figuris coloribusque rhetoricis*. Corpus Christianorum, Continuatio Mediaeualis 225. Turnhout: Brepols.

Gísli Sigurðsson 2000. 'Óláfr Þórðarson hvítaskáld and oral poetry in the West of Iceland c. 1250. The evidence of references to poetry in *The Third Grammatical Treatise*'. In *Old Icelandic literature and society*. Ed. Margaret Clunies Ross. Cambridge Studies in Medieval Literature 42. Cambridge: Cambridge University Press, 96–115. First published as 'Ólafur Þórðarson hvítaskáld og munnleg kvæðahefð á Vesturlandi um miðja 13. öld. Vitnisburður vísnadæmanna í 3. Málfræðaritgerðinni', in *Samtíðarsögur. The contemporary sagas. Forprent. The ninth international saga conference*. Ed. Sverrir Tómasson *et al.* 2 vols. Akureyri 1994, I 220–32.

GL = Heinrich Keil, ed. 1855–80. *Grammatici Latini*. 8 vols. Leipzig: Teubner.

Glei, Reinhold F. 2005. 'Alexander de Villa Dei (ca. 1170–1250), Doctrinale'. In *Lateinische Lehrer Europas. Fünfzehn Portraits von Varro bis Erasmus von Rotterdam*. Ed. Wolfram Ax. Cologne: Böhlau, 291–312.

Grondeux, Anne 1999. 'La révision du *Graecismus* d'Evrard de Béthune par Jean de Garlande'. *Revue d'histoire des textes* 29, 317–25.

Grondeux, Anne 2000. *Le* Graecismus *d'Evrard de Béthune à travers ses gloses. Entre grammaire positive et grammaire spéculative du XIIIe au XVe siècle*. Studia Artistarum 8. Turnhout: Brepols.

Grondeux, Anne 2001. 'Terminologie des figures dans le *Doctrinale* d'Alexandre de Villedieu et le *Graecismus* d'Évrard de Béthune'. In *Métalangage et terminologie linguistique. Actes du colloque international de Grenoble*. Ed. Bernard Colombat and Marie Savelli. Orbis Supplementa 18. Leuven: Peeters, 315–30.

Grondeux, Anne 2003. '*Turba ruunt* (Ov. Her. 1,88?). Histoire d'un exemple grammatical'. *Archivum latinitatis medii aevi* 61, 175–222.

Grondeux, Anne 2009. 'Teaching and learning lists of figures in the Middle Ages'. *New medieval literatures* 11, 133–58.

Gutiérrez Galindo, Marco A. 1993. *Alejandro de Villadei – El Doctrinal. Una gramática latina del Renacimiento del siglo XII*. Clásicos latinos medievales 2. Madrid: Ediciones Akal.

Halldór Halldórsson 1975. *Old Icelandic heiti in Modern Icelandic*. University of Iceland Publications in Linguistics 3. Reykjavík: Institute of Nordic Linguistics.

Halliwell, James Orchard, ed. 1839. *Rara mathematica or A collection of treatises on the mathematics and subjects connected with them*. Cambridge: John William Parker.

Haraldur Bernharðsson 2002. 'Skrifandi bændur og íslensk málsaga. Vangaveltur um málþróun og málheimildir'. *Gripla* 13, 175–95.

Harbert, Bruce, ed. 1975. *A thirteenth-century anthology of rhetorical poems. Glasgow ms. Hunterian V.8.14*. Toronto: Pontifical Institute of Mediaeval Studies.

Haugen, Einar, ed. and trans. 1972. *The first grammatical treatise. The earliest Germanic phonology. An edition, translation and commentary*. 2nd edn. London: Longman.

Haye, Thomas, ed. 1995. *Johannes de Garlandia – Compendium Gramatice. Auf der Grundlage aller bekannten Handschriften erstmals herausgegeben und eingeleitet*. Cologne: Böhlau.

Heizmann, Wilhelm 1993. *Wörterbuch der Pflanzennamen im Altwestnordischen*. Ergänzungsbände zum RGA 7. Berlin: De Gruyter.

Holm-Olsen, Ludvig, ed. 1983. *Konungs skuggsiá*. 2nd edn. Norrøne tekster nr. 1. Oslo: Norsk Historisk Kjeldeskrift-Institutt.

Holtsmark, Anne. 1960. 'Grammatisk litteratur om modersmålet'. In *Kulturhistorisk leksikon for nordisk middelalder* V. Ed. Finn Hødnebø et al. Oslo: Gyldendal, cols 414–19.

Holtz, Louis, ed. 1981. *Donat et la tradition de l'enseignement grammatical. Étude sur l'Ars Donati et sa diffusion (ive–ixe siècle) et édition critique*. Paris: Centre National de la recherche scientifique.

Horace = D. R. Shackleton Bailey, ed. 2001. *Q. Horatius Flaccus: Opera*. Bibliotheca Teubneriana. Leipzig: Saur.

Hreinn Benediktsson 1959. 'The vowel system of Icelandic'. *Word* 15, 282–312.

Hreinn Benediktsson 1965. *Early Icelandic script. As illustrated in vernacular texts from the twelfth and thirteenth centuries*. Íslenzk Handrit, Series in folio II. Reykjavík: The Manuscript Institute of Iceland.

Hreinn Benediktsson, ed. and trans. 1972. *The first grammatical treatise*. University of Iceland Publications in Linguistics 1. Reykjavík: Institute of Nordic Linguistics.

ÍF = Íslenzk fornrit. Reykjavík: Hið íslenzka fornritafélag.

ÍF 1 (parts 1 and 2) = Jakob Benediktsson, ed. 1968. *Íslendingabók. Landnámabók*. Rpt. as one volume 1986.

ÍF 2 = Sigurður Nordal, ed. 1933. *Egils saga Skalla-Grímssonar*.

ÍF 3 = Sigurður Nordal and Guðni Jónsson, eds 1938. *Borgfirðinga sǫgur*.

ÍF 4 = Einar Ól. Sveinsson and Matthías Þórðarson, eds 1935. *Eyrbyggja saga*.

ÍF 9 = Jónas Kristjánsson, ed. 1956. *Eyfirðinga sǫgur*.

ÍF 14 = Jóhannes Halldórsson, ed. 1959. *Kjalnesinga saga*.

ÍF 17 = Guðrún Ása Grímsdóttir, ed. 1998. *Biskupa sögur* III.

ÍF 23–24 = Ármann Jakobsson and Þórður Ingi Guðjónsson, eds 2011. *Morkinskinna* I–II.

ÍF 25 = Ólafur Halldórsson, ed. 2006. *Færeyinga saga. Óláfs saga Tryggvasonar eptir Odd munk Snorrason.*
ÍF 26–28 = Bjarni Aðalbjarnarson, ed. 1941–51. *Heimskringla* I–III.
ÍF 29 = Bjarni Einarsson, ed. 1985. *Ágrip af Nóregs-konunga sǫgum.*
ÍF 34 = Finnbogi Guðmundsson, ed. 1965. *Orkneyinga saga.*
ÍM = Jón Helgason, ed. 1936–38. *Íslenzk miðaldakvæði. Islandske digte fra senmiddelalderen.* 2 vols. Copenhagen: Munksgaard.
Indrebø, Gustav, ed. 1931. *Gamal norsk homiliebok.* Oslo: Kjeldeskriftfondet.
Irvine, Martin 1994. *The making of textual culture. 'Grammatica' and literary theory 350–1100.* Cambridge: Cambridge University Press.
Isidore of Seville's *Etymologiae* = W. M. Lindsay, ed. 1911. *Isidori Hispalensis episcopi Etymologiarum siue originum libri XX.* 2 vols. Oxford: Clarendon.
Iversen, Ragnvald, ed. 1963. *Absalon Pedersen: Dagbok og Oration om Mester Geble.* Oslo: Universitetsforlaget.
Jakob Benediktsson, ed. 1980. *Catilina and Jugurtha by Sallust and Pharsalia by Lucan in Old Norse: Rómverjasaga, AM 595 a–b 4to.* Early Icelandic manuscripts in facsimile 13. Copenhagen: Rosenkilde & Bagger.
Jakobsen, Alfred 1993. 'Thómas saga erkibiskups'. In *Medieval Scandinavia. An encyclopedia.* Ed. Phillip Pulsiano and Kirsten Wolf. New York and London: Garland Publishing Inc, 643–44.
Johansson, Karl G. 1997. *Studier i Codex Wormianus. Skrifttradition och avskriftsverksamhet vid ett isländskt skriptorium under 1300-talet.* Nordistica Gothoburgensia 20. Gothenburg: Acta Universitatis Gothoburgensis.
Johansson, Karl G., ed. 2007. *AM 242 fol (Codex Wormianus). Snorra-Edda, the four grammatical treatises, Rígsþula, Maríukvæði, and ókennd heiti. An electronic edition.* Available at www.menota. org/tekstarkiv.xml. <accessed 28 June 2013>
Jón Helgason 1970. 'Þriðji íhaldskarl'. *Fróðskaparrit* 18, 206–26.
Jón Helgason and Anne Holtsmark, eds 1941. *Háttalykill enn forni.* Bibliotheca Arnamagnæana 1. Copenhagen: Munksgaard.
Jón Jóhannesson 1940. 'Björn at Haugi'. In *Afmælisrit helgað Einari Arnórssyni.* Reykjavík: Ísafoldarprentsmiðja, 135–40. Rpt. in English translation by G. Turville-Petre, *Saga-Book* 17 (1969), 293–301.

Jón Ólafsson 1786. *Om Nordens gamle Digtekonst, dens Grundregler, Versarter, Sprog og Foredragsmaade. Et Priiskrift*. Copenhagen: August Friderich Stein.

Jón Þorkelsson 1888. *Om digtningen på Island i det 15. og 16. århundrede*. Copenhagen: Høst & søns forlag.

Kålund, Kristian 1889–94. *Katalog over den arnamagnæanske håndskriftsamling*. 2 vols. Copenhagen: Gyldendalske boghandel.

Kendall, Calvin B., ed. and trans. 1991. *Bede. Libri II De arte metrica et De schematibus et tropis – The art of poetry and rhetoric*. Bibliotheca Germanica, Series nova, vol. 2. Saarbrücken: AQ-Verlag.

Kirby, Ian J., ed. 1976–80. *Biblical quotation in Old Icelandic-Norwegian religious literature*. Stofnun Árna Magnússonar á Íslandi, Rit 9–10. Reykjavík: Stofnun Árna Magnússonar.

Knappe, Gabriele 1998. 'Classical rhetoric in Anglo-Saxon England'. *Anglo-Saxon England* 27, 5–29.

Kolsrud, Oluf, ed. 1952. *Messuskýringar. Liturgisk symbolik frå den norsk-islandske kyrkja i millomalderen*. Oslo: Jakob Dybwad.

Kommentar = Klaus von See et al. 1997– . *Kommentar zu den Liedern der Edda*. 7 vols. (in progress). Heidelberg: Winter.

Konráð Gíslason 1849. 'Nogle Bemærkninger om Skjaldedigtenes Beskaffenhed i formel Henseende'. *Det Kongelige Danske Videnskabernes Selskabs Skrifter*. Femte Række. Historisk-philosophisk Afdeling. 4, 283–315.

Konráð Gíslason and Eiríkur Jónsson, eds 1875–89. *Njála. Udgivet efter gamle håndskrifter af Det kongelige nordiske oldskrift-selskab* 4. 2 vols. Copenhagen: Thiele.

Kopp, Jane Baltzell 1971. 'Geoffrey of Vinsauf. The new poetics'. In *Three medieval rhetorical arts*. Ed. James J. Murphy. Berkeley: University of California Press, 27–108.

Kuhn, Hans 1929. 'Das Füllwort of-um im Altwestnordischen. Eine Untersuchung zur Geschichte der germanischen Präfixe. Ein Beitrag zur altgermanischen Metrik'. Ergänzungsheft zur *Zeitschrift für vergleichende Sprachforschung auf dem Gebiet der indogermanischen Sprachen* 8. Göttingen: Vandenhoeck & Ruprecht.

Kunitzsch, Paul 1982. *Glossar der arabischen Fachausdrücke in der mittelalterlichen europäischen Astrolabliteratur*. Nachrichten der Akademie der Wissenschaften in Göttingen I. Philologisch-historische Klasse 1982: 11. Göttingen: Vandenhoeck & Ruprecht.

LaufE 1979 = Faulkes, Anthony, ed. 1979.

Lausberg, Heinrich 1990. *Handbuch der literarischen Rhetorik: Eine Grundlegung der Literaturwissenschaft*. 3. Auflage, mit einem Vorwort von Arnold Arens. Stuttgart: Franz Steiner.
Leotta, Rosario, ed. 1998. *Marbodo di Rennes: De ornamentis verborum – Liber decem capitulorum. Retorica, mitologia e moralità di un vescovo poeta (secc. XI–XII)*. Florence: SISMEL.
Liddell, Henry George and Robert Scott 1996. *A Greek-English lexicon with a revised supplement*. Revised and augmented throughout by Sir Henry Stuart Jones, with the assistance of Roderick McKenzie, and with the cooperation of many scholars. Ninth edition. Oxford: Clarendon.
Lind, Erik Henrik 1920–21. *Norsk-isländska personbinamn från medeltiden*. Uppsala: A.-B. Lundequistska Bokhandeln.
Longo, Michele 2006. 'Un esempio di contaminazione di tradizioni nel Quarto Trattato Grammaticale Islandese'. In *Studio linguistici in onore di Roberto Gusmani* II. Ed. Raffaella Bombi *et al.* Alessandria: Edizioni dell'Orso, 989–1003.
Loth, Agnete, ed. 1969–70. *Reykjahólabók. Islandske helgenlegender.* Editiones Arnamagnæanæ, Ser. A, 15–16. Copenhagen: Munkgaard.
Louis-Jensen, Jonna 1981. 'Vǫndr er María mynduð'. In *Speculum Norroenum. Norse studies in memory of Gabriel Turville-Petre*. Ed. Ursula Dronke *et al.* Odense: Odense University Press, 328–36. Rpt. in *Con Amore. En artikelsamling udgivet på 70-årsdagen den 21. oktober 2006*. Ed. Michael Chesnutt and Florian Grammel. Copenhagen: C.A. Reitzels forlag, 59–69.
LP = Finnur Jónsson, ed. 1931. *Lexicon poeticum antiquæ linguæ septentrionalis. Ordbog over det norsk-islandske skjaldesprog oprindelig forfattet af Sveinbjörn Egilsson*. 2nd edn. Copenhagen: Møller.
LP (1860) = Sveinbjörn Egilsson, ed. 1860. *Lexicon poëticum antiquæ linguæ septentrionalis*. Copenhagen: Societas Regia antiquariorum septentrionalium.
Lönnroth, Lars 1977. 'The riddles of the Rök stone. A structural approach'. *Arkiv för nordisk filologi* 92, 1–57. Rpt. with Postscript in *The Academy of Odin. Selected papers on Old Norse literature*. The Viking Collection 19 (2011). Odense: University Press of Southern Denmark, 279–355.
Malm, Mats 2009. 'Varför heter det kenning?'. In *Snorres Edda i europeisk og islandsk kultur.* Ed. Jon Gunnar Jørgensen. Reykholt: Snorrastofa, 73–90.

Mankin, David, ed. 2011. *Cicero – De Oratore Book III*. Cambridge: Cambridge University Press.

Marenbon, John 2003. *Boethius*. Great medieval thinkers. Oxford: Oxford University Press.

Marold, Edith 2012. General introduction, § 5.1.1.B. 'The terminology of *Snorra Edda*'. In *SkP* I: 1, 61–63.

McDougall, David 1988. '"Pseudo-Augustinian" passages in *Jóns saga baptista* 2 and the *Fourth grammatical treatise*'. *Traditio* 44, 463–83.

McDougall, Ian 1986–89. 'Foreigners and foreign languages in medieval Iceland'. *Saga-Book* 22, 180–233.

Meissner, Rudolf 1921. *Die Kenningar der Skalden. Ein Beitrag zur skaldischen Poetik*. Rheinische Beiträge und Hilfsbücher zur germanischen Philologie und Volkskunde 1. Bonn and Leipzig: Schroeder. Rpt. 1984. Hildesheim etc.: Olms.

Meissner, Rudolf 1932. 'Zwei Prophetenzitate in der 4. Gramm. Abhandlung der Snorra Edda'. *Zeitschrift für deutsches Altertum und deutsche Literatur* 69, 97–106.

Mommsen, Theodore, ed. 1882. *Iordanis Romana et Getica*. Monumenta Germaniae historica, Auctores antiquissimi, 5.1. Berlin: Weidmann. Rpt. 1961.

Mosetti Casaretto, Francesco, ed. 1997. *Teodulo: Ecloga. Il canto della verità e della menzogna*. Florence: SISMEL.

Murphy, James, J. 1974. *Rhetoric in the Middle Ages. A history of rhetorical theory from Saint Augustine to the Renaissance*. Berkeley: University of California Press.

Mynors, R. A. B., ed. 1969. *Opera P. Vergili Maronis*. Oxford: Clarendon.

NGL = Rudolf Keyser *et al.*, ed. 1846–96. *Norges gamle Love indtil 1387*. 5 vols. Christiania: Chr. Gröndahl.

NN = Ernst Albin Kock. 1923–44. *Notationes Norrœnæ. Anteckningar till Edda och skaldediktning*. Lunds Universitets årsskrift. Lund: Gleerup.

Nordal, Guðrún 2001. *Tools of literacy. The role of skaldic verse in Icelandic textual culture of the twelfth and thirteenth centuries*. Toronto, Buffalo and London: Toronto University Press.

Nordal, Sigurður, ed. 1931. *Codex Wormianus (The younger Edda) MS. No. 242 fol. in The Arnemagnean Collection in the University Library of Copenhagen*. CCI 2. Copenhagen: Levin & Munksgaard.

NRSV = Wayne A. Meeks, gen. ed. 1993. *The HarperCollins study Bible. New revised standard version with the apocryphal/ deuterocanonical books*. New York: HarperCollins Publishers.

Nygaard, Marius 1906. *Norrøn syntax*. Kristiania: Aschehoug. Rpt. 1966.

Ólafur Halldórsson, ed. 1904. *Jónsbók. Kong Magnus Hakonssons Lovbog for Island vedtaget paa Altinget 1281 og Réttarbœtr. De for Island givne Retterbøder af 1294, 1305 og 1314*. Copenhagen: Møller.

Olmer, Emil 1902. *Boksamlingar på Island 1179–1490 enligt diplom*. Gothenburg: Wald. Zachrissons boktryckeri.

Ólsen, Björn Magnússon, ed. 1884. *Den tredje og fjœrde grammatiske afhandling i Snorres Edda tilligemed de grammatiske afhandlingers prolog og to andre tillæg*. Samfund til udgivelse af gammel nordisk litteratur 12. Copenhagen: Fr. G. Knudtzons Bogtrykkeri.

Olsen, Magnus, ed. 1906–08. *Vǫlsunga saga ok Ragnars saga loðbrókar*. Samfund til udgivelse af gammel nordisk litteratur 36. Copenhagen: Møller.

ONP = Helle Degnbol *et al.*, ed. 1989– . *A Dictionary of Old Norse Prose. Ordbog over det norrøne prosasprog*. Indices + Vol. 1– . Copenhagen: The Arnamagnæan Commission. The dictionary's word-list and other materials are available online at http://onp.ku.dk

Ovid's *Heroides* = A. Ramírez de Verger, ed. 2003. *Ouidius. Carmina amatoria*. Leipzig: Teubner.

Paasche, Frederik 1928. 'Esras aabenbaring og Pseudo-Cyprianus i norrön litteratur'. In *Festskrift til Finnur Jónsson, 29. maj 1928*. Ed. Johs. Brøndum Nielsen *et al*. Copenhagen: Levin & Munksgaard, 199–205.

Petersens, Carl af, ed. 1879. *Jómsvíkinga saga (efter Cod. AM 510, 4: to) samt Jómsvíkinga drápa*. Lund: Gleerup.

Physiologus = Verner Dahlerup 1889. '*Physiologus* i to islandske bearbejdelser'. *Aarbøger for nordisk Oldkyndighed og Historie*, 14–290.

PL = J.-P. Migne, ed. 1844–55. *Patrologia latina*. 217 vols. *Patrologiae cursus completus* [accessed through http://pld.chadwyck.com/].

Poole, Russell 1991. *Viking poems on war and peace. A study in skaldic narrative*. Toronto, Buffalo and London: Toronto University Press.

Porter, Pamela 2006. 'Preserving the past. England, Iceland and the movement of manuscripts'. In *Care and conservation of manuscripts* 9. Ed. Gillian Fellows-Jensen and Peter Springborg. Copenhagen: Museum Tusculanum Press, 173–90.

Quintilian's *Institutiones Oratoriae* = Jean Cousin, ed. 1975. *Quintilien: Institution oratoire*. 6 vols. Paris: Les belles lettres.

Raschellà, Fabrizio D., ed. and trans. 1982. *The so-called second grammatical treatise. An orthographic pattern of late thirteenth-century Icelandic*. Florence: Felice Le Monnier.

Raschellà, Fabrizio D. 2000. 'Vowel change in thirteenth-century Icelandic. A first-hand witness'. In *International Scandinavian and Medieval studies in memory of Gerd Wolfgang Weber.* Ed. Michael Dallapiazza *et al*. Hesperides 12. Trieste: Parnaso, 383–89.

Reichling, Dietrich, ed. 1893. *Das Doctrinale des Alexander de Villa-Dei. Kritisch-Exegetische Ausgabe*. Monumenta Germaniae paedagogica 12. Berlin: A. Hofmann.

RE 1665 = Faulkes, Anthony, ed. 1977.

Rhetorica ad Herennium in Achard 1981.

Rindal, Magnus, ed. 1981. *Barlaams ok Josaphats saga*. Norrøne tekster 4. Oslo: Norsk historisk kjeldeskrift-institutt.

Rolfe, John C., ed. and trans. 1948–52. *Ammianus Marcellinus, Rerum gestarum libri*. 3 vols. rev. and rpt. Loeb Classical Library 300, 315 and 331. Cambridge, Mass.: Harvard University Press.

Rosier-Catach, Irène 2009. 'Alexander de Villa Dei'. In *Lexicon Grammaticorum. A bio-bibliographical companion to the history of linguistics*. Gen. ed. Harro Stammerjohann. Second edition, revised and enlarged. Tübingen: Max Niemeyer Verlag, 30–31.

Sabbatier, Pierre, ed. 1743–49. *Bibliorum sacrorum latinæ versiones antiquæ, seu vetus italica, et cæteræ quæcunque in codicibus mss. & antiquorum libris reperiri potuerunt: quæ cum Vulgata latina, & cum textu græco comparantur. Accedunt præfationes, observationes, ac notæ, indexque novus ad Vulgatam è regione editam, idemque locupletissimus*. Reims: Apud Reginaldum Florentain.

Schindel, Ulrich 2001. *Die Rezeption der hellenistischen Theorie der rhetorischen Figuren bei den Römern*. Göttingen: Vandenhoeck & Ruprecht.

Schulman, Jana 2010. *Jónsbók. The laws of later Iceland – The Icelandic text according to MS AM 351 fol. Skálholtsbók eldri*. Bibliotheca Germanica, Series nova 4. Saarbrücken: AQ Verlag.

Skald = E. A. Kock, ed. 1946–50. *Den norsk-isländska skaldediktningen*. 2 vols. Lund: Gleerup.

Skj = Finnur Jónsson, ed. 1912–15. *Den norsk-islandske skjaldedigtning*. A 1–2. *Tekst efter håndskrifterne*. B 1–2. *Rettet tekst*. 4 vols. Copenhagen: Gyldendal. Rpt. 1967 (A) and 1973 (B). Copenhagen: Rosenkilde & Bagger.

SkP = Margaret Clunies Ross, Kari Ellen Gade, Edith Marold, Guðrún Nordal, Diana Whaley and Tarrin Wills, eds 2007– . *Skaldic Poetry of the Scandinavian Middle Ages*. 9 vols. Turnhout: Brepols. See also the edition's database at abdn.ac.uk/skaldic/db.php

SkP I = Diana Whaley, ed. 2012. *Skaldic Poetry of the Scandinavian Middle Ages*. Vol. I. *Poetry from the kings' sagas 1: From mythical times to c. 1035*. Parts 1–2. Turnhout: Brepols.

SkP II = Kari Ellen Gade, ed. 2009. *Skaldic Poetry of the Scandinavian Middle Ages*. Vol. II. *Poetry from the kings' sagas 2: From c. 1036 to c. 1300*. Parts 1–2. Turnhout: Brepols.

SkP III = Kari Ellen Gade and Edith Marold, eds. Forthcoming. *Skaldic Poetry of the Scandinavian Middle Ages*. Vol. III. *Poetry from treatises on poetics*. Turnhout: Brepols.

SkP VII = Margaret Clunies Ross, ed. 2007. *Skaldic Poetry of the Scandinavian Middle Ages*. Vol. VII. *Poetry on Christian Subjects*. Parts 1–2. Turnhout: Brepols.

SnE 1818 = Rasmus Rask, ed. 1818. *Snorra Edda ásamt Skáldu og þarmeð fylgjandi ritgjörðum*. Stockholm: Hin Elménska prentsmiðja.

SnE 1848 = Sveinbjörn Egilsson, ed. 1848. *Edda Snorra Sturlusonar, eða Gylfaginning, Skáldskaparmál og Háttatal*. Reykjavík: Prentsmiðja Helga Helgasonar.

SnE 1848–87 = Jón Sigurðsson *et al.*, ed. 1848–87. *Edda Snorra Sturlusonar. Edda Snorronis Sturlæi*. 3 vols. Copenhagen: Legatum Arnamagnæanum. Rpt. Osnabrück: Zeller, 1966. *FoGT* is in Vol. II (1852), pp. 190–249, with Latin translation by Sveinbjörn Egilsson. Commentary is in Vol. III (1880–87), pp. 153–63.

SnE 1924 = Finnur Jónsson, ed. for Det Arnamagnæanske Legat. 1924. *Edda Snorra Sturlusonar. Codex Wormianus AM 242, fol.* Copenhagen and Kristiania: Gyldendal and Nordisk forlag.

SnE 1931 = Finnur Jónsson, ed. 1931. *Edda Snorra Sturlusonar udgivet efter håndskrifterne*. Copenhagen: Gyldendal.

SnE 1998 = Faulkes, Anthony, ed. 1998. *Snorri Sturluson, Edda. Skáldskaparmál.* Parts I and II. University College London: Viking Society for Northern Research.
SnE 2005 = Faulkes, Anthony, ed. 2005. *Snorri Sturluson, Edda. Prologue and Gylfaginning.* 2nd edn. University College London: Viking Society for Northern Research.
SnE 2007 = Faulkes, Anthony, ed. 2007. *Snorri Sturluson, Edda. Háttatal.* 2nd edn. University College London: Viking Society for Northern Research.
Stefán Karlsson 1973. 'Icelandic lives of Thomas à Becket. Questions of authorship'. In *Proceedings of the first international saga conference, University of Edinburgh, 1971.* Ed. Peter Foote, Hermann Pálsson and Desmond Slay. University College London: Viking Society for Northern Research, 212–43. Rpt. with Afterword in Stefán Karlsson 2000, 135–52.
Stefán Karlsson 1979. 'Islandsk bogeksport til Norge i middelalderen'. *Maal og minne*, 1–17. Rpt. with Afterword in Stefán Karlsson 2000, 188–205.
Stefán Karlsson 2000. *Stafkrókar: Ritgerðir eftir Stefán Karlsson gefnu út í tilefni af sjötugsafmæli hans 2. desember 1998.* Ed. Guðvarður Már Gunnlaugsson. Stofnun Árna Magnússonar á Íslandi, Rit 49. Reykjavík: Stofnun Árna Magnússonar.
Stefán Karlsson 2004. Trans. Rory McTurk. *The Icelandic Language.* University College London: Viking Society for Northern Research.
Storm, Gustav, ed. 1888. *Islandske annaler indtil 1578.* Christiania: Det norske historiske kildeskriftfond. Rpt. 1977. Oslo: Norskhistorisk kjeldeskrift-institutt.
Stotz, Peter 1996. *Handbuch zur lateinischen Sprache des Mittelalters.* Dritter Band. *Lautlehre.* Munich: Beck.
Sverrir Tómasson. 1982. 'Icelandic Lives of St Nicholas'. In *Helgastaðabók. Nikulás saga Perg. 4to nr. 16 Konungsbókhlöðu í Stokkhólmi.* Ed. Selma Jónsdóttir, Stefán Karlsson and Sverrir Tómasson. *Íslensk Miðaldahandrit – Manuscripta Islandica Medii Aevi II.* Reykjavík: Sverrir Kristinsson, 147–76.
Sverrir Tómasson 1993. 'Formáli málfræðiritgerðanna fjögurra í Wormsbók'. *Íslenskt mál* 15, 221–40. Rpt. in Sverrir Tómasson 2011, 199–217.
Sverrir Tómasson 2011. *Tækileg vitni: Greinar um bókmenntir gefnar út í tilefni sjötugsafmælis hans 5. apríl 2011.* Reykjavík: Stofnun Árna Magnússonar í íslenskum fræðum.

Taylor-Briggs, Ruth 2006. 'Reading between the lines. The textual history and manuscript transmission of Cicero's rhetorical works'. In *The rhetoric of Cicero in its medieval and early Renaissance commentary tradition*. Ed. Virginia Cox and John O. Ward. Brill's Companions to the Christian Tradition 2. Leiden: Brill, 77–108.
Terence's *Andria* and *Eunuchus*. In Robert Kauer and Wallace M. Lindsay, ed. 1926. *P. Terenti Afri Comoediae*. Oxford: Clarendon.
TGT 1884 = Ólsen, Björn Magnússon, ed. 1884, 1–119, 161–237.
Thilo, Georg and Hermann Hagen, eds 1881–1902. *Servii grammatici qui feruntur in Vergilii carmina commentarii*. 3 vols. Leipzig: Teubner.
Thurot, Charles 1868. 'Notices et extraits de divers manuscrits latins pour servir à l'histoire de doctrines grammaticales au moyen âge'. *Notices et extraits des manuscrits de la Bibliothèque impériale et autres bibliothèques* 22, 1–540.
Unger, C. R., ed. 1871a. *Codex Frisianus. En Samling af norske Konge-Sagaer*. Christiania: P. T. Malling.
Unger, C. R., ed. 1871b. *Mariu saga. Legender om Jomfru Maria og hendes Jertegn*. Christiania: Brögger & Christie.
Unger, C. R., ed. 1874. *Postola sögur. Legendariske fortællinger om Apostlernes liv, deres kamp for kristendommens udbredelse samt deres martyrdød*. Christiania: B. M. Bentzen.
Vésteinn Ólason 1969. 'Greppaminni'. In *Afmælisrit Jóns Helgasonar 30. júní 1969*. Ed. Jakob Benediktsson *et al*. Reykjavík: Heimskringla, 198–205.
Vogt, Walther Heinrich 1930. 'Bragis Schild. Maler und Skalde'. *Acta Philologica Scandinavica* 5, 1–28.
Weber, Robert *et al*., ed. 1994. *Biblia sacra iuxta vulgatam versionem*. Fourth improved edition. Stuttgart: Deutsche Bibelgesellschaft.
Wellendorf, Jonas. Forthcoming. 'Virtues and Vices. The Fourth Grammatical Treatise'. In *Mediality in Late Medieval Iceland*. Ed. Jürg Glauser and Kate Heslop. Zürich: Chronos.
Whaley, Diana, ed. and trans. 1998. *The poetry of Arnórr jarlaskáld: An edition and study*. Westfield Publications in Medieval Studies 8. Turnhout: Brepols.
Widding, Ole 1961. 'Kilderne til den norrøne Nicolaus saga'. *Opuscula* II, 1. Bibliotheca Arnamagnæana 25, 1. Copenhagen: The Arnamagnæan Commission, 17–26.

Widding, Ole, Hans Bekker-Nielsen and L. K. Shook 1963. 'The lives of the saints in Old Norse prose. A handlist'. *Mediaeval studies* 25, 294–337.

Wills, Tarrin, ed. 2001. 'The foundation of grammar. An edition of the first section of Óláfr Þórðarson's grammatical treatise'. PhD thesis: The University of Sydney.

Wood, Cecil 1960. 'Skaldic notes'. *Scandinavian Studies* 32, 155–58.

Þorvaldur Bjarnarson, ed. 1878. *Leifar fornra kristinna frœða íslenzkra: Codex Arna-Magnæanus 677 4to auk annara enna elztu brota af ízlenskum guðfrœðisritum*. Copenhagen: Hagerup.

INDEX

Aaron (Árón) 46–47, 141.
Abel (Ábiel) liv, 46–47, 140.
Abraham (Ábrám) liv, 46–47, 141.
Adam (Ádám) li, liv, lvii, lix, 44–45, 137, 140.
Alcuin *Dialogus de rhetorica et de uirtutibus* xxx
Alexander de Villa-Dei *Carmen de algorismos* xxxiii, *Doctrinale* xxxii–xxxvi *et pass.*
Ammianus Marcellinus *Rerum gestarum libri qui supersunt XXXI* 78.
Arinbjǫrn hersir 76.
Arngrímr Brandsson xii, 72, *Guðmundardrápa* l.
Árni Lárentíusson xii.
Arnórr jarlaskáld Þórðarson xliv, xlviii, 22–23, 102–03, *Þorfinnsdrápa* ix, *Hrynhenda, Magnúsdrápa* 103, *Blágagladrápa* 103.
Áslaug 16–17, 76, 82.
Atlamál 56.
Auðunn illskælda xlv.
Augustine 38–39, 129, 131.
Barði Guðmundarson 2–3, 52–53.
Barlaams saga 93, 117.
Bede *De schematibus et tropis* xxx, 94.
Beowulf 78.
Bergr Gunsteinsson 72.

Bergr Sokkason xii, xlv, *Nikulás saga erkibiskups* xii, 57.
Bible Gen. 131, 137, 140–41, *Exod.* 141–42, *1 Kings* 138, *2 Chr.* 138, *Ps.* 122, 124, 129–31, *Sir.* 67, *Isa.* 129, 133, 138, *Jer.* 120, *Baruch* (Barruk) lv, 10–11, 67–68 *Daniel* 106–07, 148–49. *Habakkuk* (Abbacuch) 38–39, 129, 131, *Matt.* 61, 93, 125, 131, *Mark* 61, 93, *Luke* 61, 80–81, 93, 125, *John* 67, 133, 139, 143, *Acts* 55, 133, 137–38, *Rom.* 118, *2 Esdras* 67–69, Syrian apocalypse of *Baruch* 67.
Bjarnar saga Hítdœlakappa 102.
Bjarni Kolbeinsson *Jómsvíkingadrápa* 53.
Bjǫrn at Haugi 77.
Boethius (Boetius) 20–21, 94 *Commentary on Aristotle's On interpretation* 94, *The consolation of Philosophy* 94.
Bragi Boddason xlvi, xlviii, xlix, 14–17, 67, 76–79, 81, 134–35, *Ragnarsdrápa* xlvi, xlix, lv, 16–17, 76–77.
Brynhildr 82.
Búi digri Vésetason 18–19, 87.
Cain 140.
Carmen de figuris xxix–xxxi.

Cassiodorus *Commentary on the psalms* xxxv.
Christ (Kristr) xlvi, li, lv, lxi, 7, 10–11, 17, 21, 37, 39, 55, 61, 67, 81, 89–90, 123, 125–26, 129, 133, 135, 142–44.
Clárus saga xii.
Codex Frisianus 97.
David (Dávíð) 34–35, 38–41, 121–22, 131, 148, 149.
Davus 83–84, 146–47.
Diomedes 95.
Donatus xxi–xxii, xxv–xxx, xxxv, xxxix, xli, 91, 96, 105, *Barbarismus* xix, xxii, xxv–xxix, xxxiv–xxxvi, xxxix, xli–xliii, xliv, 64, 91, 92, 105.
Duggals leizla 60.
Eberhard of Béthune xix, xxxv, 127–28, *Graecismus* xxxv *et pass.*
Egill Skallagrímsson xlviii.
Egils saga 76.
Eilífr xlviii, 20–21, 89.
Eilífr Goðrúnarson xlvi, 89.
Eilífr kúlnasveinn xlvi, 89. *Kristdrápa* 89.
Eilífr Snorrason 89.
Einarr skálaglammr *Vellekla* 53.
Einarr Skúlason xlv–xlvi, xlviii, lvi, 120, 136.
Eiríkr jarl Hákonarson 86.
Eiríkr Magnússon 28–31.
Eiríkr viðsjá xlv, xlvii, xlviii, 2–3, 52.
Elijah (Helias) 38–39, 131.
Elizabeth (mother of John the Baptist) 80–81.

Enoch (Ienóch) 46–47, 140.
Ermanaric (Erminrekr, Jǫrmunrekr) 14–15, 76–79, 82.
Erpr 15–17, 77, 79.
Eyjólfr Brúnason xlvi–xlvii, 12–13, 71.
Eysteinn beli 77.
Fagrskinna xlvii, 86–87, 110.
Finnboga saga ramma 99.
First Grammatical Treatise xiv, 62.
Flateyjarbók 50, 103.
Fourth Grammatical Treatise i *et pass.*
Gamli kanóki *Harmsól* 121.
Gátur 102.
Gátur Gestumblinda 102.
Geoffrey of Vinsauf *Poetria nova* xiv, xxxii, l, 66.
Gerhard III of Holstein 63.
Gestr Þórhallsson xlvii.
Gísli Þorsteinsson 52–53.
God (Guð) lvi, lxi, 4–7, 11–13, 16–17, 21, 26–27, 34–41, 44–47, 49, 53, 55, 57, 60–61, 67, 73, 79, 92, 118, 120–23, 125, 131–32, 137–42, 149.
Grettis saga 85.
Grímnismál 56, 64, 77.
Gríms saga loðinkinna 85.
Guðmundar saga biskups D xii.
Guðmundr Arason 72.
Guðrún Gjúkadóttir 14–15, 53, 78.
Guðrúnarhvǫt 117.
Gunnlaugs saga ormstunga 102.
Habakkuk (Abbacuch) 38–39, 129, 131.
Hagbarðr 112.

Haki (sea king) 28–31, 112.
Hákon Hákonarson xvi, 26–27, 28–31, 70, 108–09, 113.
Hákon jarl Sigurðarson 2–3, 18–19, 50–51, 86–87.
Hákon Sverrisson 113.
Hákon V háleggr Magnússon xiii, liv, 6–7, 61, 114.
Haldanus Biargrammus 86–87.
Halldórr skvaldri xlv.
Halldórr ókristni *Eiríksflokkr* 88.
Hallfreðr vandræðaskáld *Erfidrápa Óláfs Tryggvasonar* 88.
Hallur prestr *Nikulásdrápa* 57, 80, *Hrynhent Nikulásdrápa* 57.
Hamðir xlix, 14–15, 17, 76–79, 82.
Hamðismál 77–79.
Haraldr Sigurðarson 28–29, 103, 110–11.
Háttalykill by Rǫgnvaldr Kali Kollsson and Hallr Þórarinsson xv, lvi, 108, 134.
Haukr Valdísarson *Íslendingadrápa* 50.
Hávamál 85.
Heiðarvíga saga xii, xlvii, 52.
Heilagra manna drápa 72.
Heilagra meyja drápa 115.
Heilags anda drápa 55.
Heimir 82.
Heimskringla 70, 97, 110.
Hieronymus *Commentary on the book of Jeremiah* 121.
Honorius Augustodunensis *Summa gloria de apostolico et augusto sive de praecellentia sacerdotii prae regni liber* 141.
Horace *Sermones* 83, *Ars poetica* 83.
Hrabanus Maurus (?) *Veni creator spiritus* 55.
Hrafn Sveinbjarnarson 72.
Hrólfr kraki 28–31, 112.
Hrólfs saga kraka 112.
Hugh of Pisa *Derivationes* xl.
Hugleikr 112.
Hulda-Hrokkinskinna 103.
Hymiskviða 88.
Icelandic book of homilies 70, 118.
Inga of Varteig 113.
Isaac (Ísách) 46–47, 141.
Isidore of Seville *Etymologiae* 62, 117, 127, 138.
Isocrates xxx.
Jacob (Jácób) 46–47, 141.
Jared 140.
Jesus Christ (Kristr) xlvi, li, lv, lxi, 7, 10–11, 17, 21, 37, 39, 55, 61, 67, 80–81, 89–90, 123, 125–26, 129, 133, 135, 138, 142–44.
Job 107, 148–149.
John of Garland xxxvii.
John the Apostle (Jón) 73.
John the Baptist (Jón, Johannes baptisti) liv, 16–17, 80–81, 125.
Jómsvíkingasaga xlvii, 86–87.
Jónakr 14–15, 78–79.
Jóns saga baptista II 182.
Jóns saga postola 133.
Jónsbók lv, 63, 65, 113.
Jordanes *Getica* 78.
Joseph (Jóséph) 46–47, 141.

Kálfr Árnason 48–49, 144.
Kálfr Arnfinnsson 144.
Konrad of Mure *Novus grecismus* xxxvii.
Konungs skuggsjá 102, 137.
Landnámabók 50, 76.
Lausavísa on Lawgiving 141–42.
Lazarus (Lassarus) 48–49, 143.
Leiðarvísan 90, 141.
Leo the Great (Leo inn málsnjalli) 40–41, 129–30, 132.
Líknarbraut 99.
Lilja 1, 123.
Litla Skálda xvi.
Lokasenna 77.
Magnús Hákonarson 114.
Magnús Haraldsson 29, 110.
Magnús inn góði Óláfsson 25–27, 102–03, 110–11, 113.
Magnús lagabœtir Hákonarson 28–31.
Magnús Óláfsson *Laufás Edda* xi–xii, xiv–xlvii, 59, 61, 71, 77, 87, 117–18, 136–37.
Máni skáld 64.
Manuscripts
  Archiv der Hansestadt, Bergenfahrer, Lübeck
    AHL 1409 xlvi.
  The Arnamagnæan manuscript collection, Copenhagen and Reykajvík
    AM 66 fol (Hulda) lxiv, 24.
    AM 242 fol (Codex Wormianus) xi *et pass.*
    AM 291 4° lxiv, 18.
    AM 303 4^{ox} lxiv, 18.
    AM 510 4° lxiv, 18.
    AM 645 4° 95.
    AM 671 4° 58, 107.
    AM 672 4° 93.
    AM 713 4° 72.
    AM 732 b 4° 58.
    AM 743 4^{ox} lxiv, 42, 44, 136.
    AM 748 I b 4° xli, xliv, lxiv, 2, 50, 95.
    AM 748 II 4° xliv, 14, 16, 24, 76–77.
    AM 761 a 4^{ox} 71, 89.
    AM 761 b 4^{ox} 53, 70.
    AM 921 III 4° 70.
  British Library, London
    BLAdd 11250 item no. 422 xli.
  Bibliothèque nationale de France, Paris
    BNF lat. 14746 lxii.
  Uppsala University Library
    DG 11 xliv, lvi, 98, 108.
  The Royal Library, Copenhagen
    GKS 1005 fol (Reykjavík) (Flateyjarbók) lxiv, 18, 24, 51, 103.
    GKS 1009 fol (Morkinskinna) lxiv, 24, 103, 110–11.
    GKS 1010 fol (Hrokkinskinna) lxiv, 24.
    GKS 2367 4° (Codex Regius) (Reykjavík), lvi, lxiv, 14, 16, 26, 76–77.
    GKS 2368 4^{ox} (Reykjavík), lxiv, 42, 44, 136.
  National Library of Sweden, Stockholm
    Holm Perg 7 4° lxiv, 18.

Holm Perg 18 4°, lxiv, 2, 52–53.
University of Oslo Library OsloUB 371 fol[x] lxiv, 18.
Utrecht University Library Traj 1374[x] xlix, lxiv, 14, 16, 76–72, 98.
Marbod of Rennes *De ornamentis uerborum* xxxi, xxxv–xxxvi, 127.
Markús Skeggjason xlviii.
Martha 73, 143.
Mary 73, 80–81, 125, 143.
Matthew of Vendôme *Ars versificatoria* 83.
Melchisedech 141.
Messuskýringar 67.
Milska 118.
Morkinskinna 103, 110–11.
Moses (Moyses) liv, 38–39, 48–49, 131, 141–42.
Niels Ebbesen 63.
Nikulásdrápa xlv–xlvi, xlix, lv, 16–17, 57, 79–80.
Nikulás Bergsson *Leiðarvísir* 57.
Njǫrðr 53.
Noah (Nói) 38–41, 46–47, 107, 140–41, 149–50.
Norwegian book of homilies 58, 93.
Oddný eykyndill Þorkellsdóttir 102.
Oddr Snorrason *Life of Óláfr Tryggvason* 50.
Óðinn xviii, 85.
Óláfr Haraldsson, St liv, 26–27, 49, 110, 142–44.
Óláfr hvítaskáld Þórðarson vii, xiii, xli–xlii, xliv–xlix, lii, lv, lvi, 12–13, 18–21, 71, 87–88, 96, 98, 120. *Third Grammatical Treatise* vii, ix, xi, xiii–xiv, xvi–xix, xxi–xxii, xxv–xxviii, xxxvi, xl, xlii–xxlviii, l, lii–liv, lxiii, 50–51, 62, 64, 71, 82, 86–88, 91–93, 95–98, 103–06, 120, *Málfrœðinnar grundvǫllr* xiv, xv, 96, *Málskrúðsfrœði* xiii, xvi, xviii–xxii, xxvi–xxviii, xxxvi, xli–xliv, lxiii, 96.
Óláfr kyrri Haraldsson 29, 110.
Óláfr svartaskáld Leggsson xlvii, 72.
Orkneyinga saga xv.
Paul the Deacon *Homiliary* lvi, 129–30.
Peter of Riga *Aurora* xl.
Pétrs saga postola 69, 73.
Petrus Croccus vii.
Physiologus 88.
Placitusdrápa 53.
Priscian *Institutiones grammaticae* xv, xxv, 119.
Prologue to the Grammatical Treatises in W xii, xx.
Quintilian xix, 75, 116.
Quodvultdeus 129, 131.
Ragnarr loðbrók xlix, 14–15, 17, 76–78, 82.
Randvér 14–15, 77–78.
Rhetorica ad Herennium xxii–xxv, xxviii–xxix, xxxi–xxxii, xxxv, 116.
Robert of Cricklade 72.
Rúnólfr Ketilsson 59.
Satan 125.
Second Grammatical Treatise xiv–xv, 97.

Servius *Commentaries on the works of Virgil* xxvi, 61–62, 75.
Shem (Siem) 46–47, 140–41.
Sigvatr Þórðarson xlviii.
Sigrdrífumál 76.
Sigurðr Fáfnisbani 81.
Sigvaldi jarl Strút-Haraldsson 18–19, 86.
Sivaldus (king of Sweden) 86.
Skáldatal 50, 76.
Skjǫldunga saga 112.
Skúli Bárðarson xvi, 70, 108.
Sneglu-Halla þáttr 50.
Snorra Edda see Snorri Sturluson.
Snorri goði Þorsteinsson 2–3, 52.
Snorri Sturluson vii, xii–xiii, xv–xvii, xlv–l, lii, lv–lvi, lx, 12–13, 61–62, 69–71, 76, 81, 87, 106–08, 112, 134, *Snorra Edda* xii, xlv–xlix, lii, liv, lvi, lxii, 76–77, 97, 108, *Gylfaginning* xv, 56, 63, *Skáldskaparmál* xv–xvi, xlv–xlvii, xlix, 76–79, 81, 87, 89, 95, 112, *Háttatal* xii, xv–xvi,xlv–xlvi, l, lii–liii, lv–lvi, 61–62, 70, 87, 97, 106–09, 111–12, 120, 134, 142.
Solomon (Salomon) 20–21, 58, 91.
Sǫrli xlix, 14–15, 17, 75–79, 81.
Nicholas, St xii, xlv, liv, 16–17, 57–58, 80–81.
Starkaðr gamli xlviii.

Stephen (Stephánus) 44–45, 137–38.
Stjǫrnu-Odda draumr 53.
Stjǫrnu-Oddi *Geirviðarflokkr* 53.
Summa Britonis xl.
Svanhildr 77.
Terence *Andria* 83, *Eunuchus* 119.
Theoderic the Great 94.
Theodulus *Ecloga* 64.
Theophrastus xxix.
Third Grammatical Treatise see Óláfr Þórðarson.
Thomas (Thómas) Becket xlvii, xlix, liv, 12–13, 71–72, 142–43.
Thómas diktur erkibyskups 71.
Thómas saga I 71.
Thómas saga erkibiskups II xii, 71.
Tydeus 95.
Þjóðólfr Arnórsson xlviii.
Þórðr Kolbeinsson 102.
Þórðr Særeksson/Sjáreksson 113.
Þorkell inn auðgi 86.
Þorleifr jarlsskáld Rauðfeldarson xlv–xlviii, 2–3, 50–51, *Jarlsníð* 50.
Þorleifr skúma xlvi–xlviii, lv, 18–19, 86.
Þorleifs þáttr jarlsskálds 50.
Þulur *Á* 56, *Bjarna* 59, *Orma* 63.
Valdimar IV 62.
Víga-Styrr 2–3, 52.
Vígfúss Víga-Glúmsson 150.

Virgil xxix, *Aeneid* xxii, 50–51, 61, 63, 69, 74–75, 92, 104, *Georgics* 75.
Vitnisvísur af Maríu 120.

Vǫlsunga saga 81.
Walter of Châtillon *Alexandreis* 106.
Ynglinga saga 112.